PRA...

THE LOST AIRMAN

"*The Lost Airman* tells the suspenseful story of a truly remarkable American shot down over enemy-occupied territory in World War II who amazingly managed to stay a step ahead of the Nazis for over six months and get back home. A terrific, thrilling tale you won't want to miss."

—Alex Kershaw, *New York Times* bestselling author of *Avenue of Spies* and *The Liberator*

"*The Lost Airman* is a deeply researched, finely wrought gem. The story of Staff Sergeant Arthur Meyerowitz's harrowing struggle to escape from Nazi-infested France across the snowbound Pyrénées to Spain will haunt you long after you've put this riveting book down. The courage, quick wits, and sheer guts displayed by Meyerowitz and the men and women of the French Resistance who gambled their lives to help him are simply extraordinary."

—Jack Cheevers, author of *Act of War*, winner of the Samuel Eliot Morison Award for Naval Literature

THE
LOST
AIRMAN

A TRUE STORY OF ESCAPE
FROM NAZI-OCCUPIED FRANCE

SETH MEYEROWITZ
WITH PETER F. STEVENS

CALIBER

Dutton Caliber
An imprint of Penguin Random House LLC
375 Hudson Street
New York, New York 10014

The Library of Congress has catalogued the hardcover edition as follows:

Meyerowitz, Seth, author.
The lost airman: a true story of escape from Nazi-occupied France / by Seth Meyerowitz;
with Peter F. Stevens.—First edition.
pages. cm.
ISBN 978-1-59240-929-7
1. Meyerowitz, Arthur, 1918–1971.   2. World War, 1939–1945—Underground
movements—France—Biography.   3. United States. Army Air Forces. Bombardment
Squadron, 715th—Biography.   4. Airmen—United States—Biography.
5. Escapes—France—History—20th century.   6. Taillandier, Marcel,
1911–1944.   7. France—History—German occupation, 1940–1945—Biography.
I. Stevens, Peter F., date, author.   II. Title.   III. Title: True story of escape from
Nazi-occupied France.
D802.F8M47 2016
940.54'4973092—dc23
[B]
2015025114

Publishing History
Berkley Caliber hardcover edition / January 2016
Caliber trade paperback edition / November 2016
First Dutton Caliber trade paperback edition: 2017
Dutton Caliber trade paperback ISBN: 9781592409723

Printed in the United States of America
10   9   8   7   6   5

For my grandfather Arthur . . .
and the men and women of France who saved his life.

CONTENTS

|||||||||||||||||||||||||||||||||||||||||||

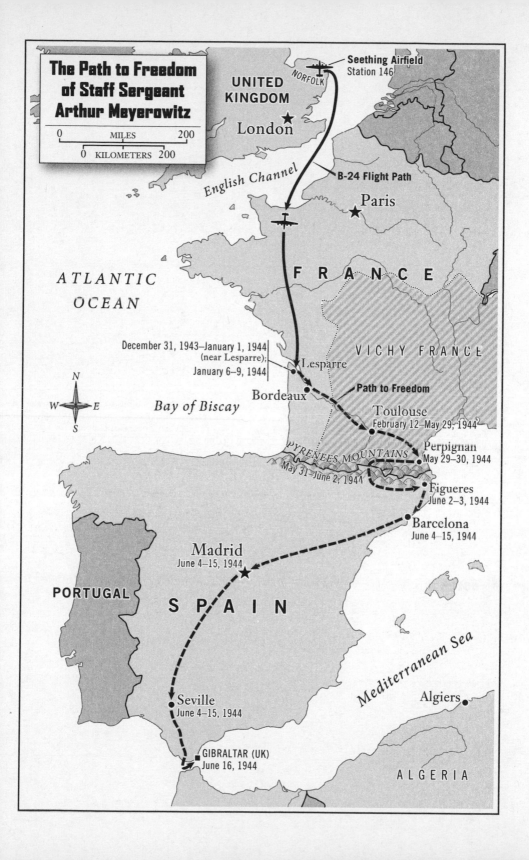

The Path to Freedom
of Staff Sergeant
Arthur Meyerowitz

0 MILES 200
0 KILOMETERS 200

Seething Airfield
Station 146

NORFOLK

UNITED
KINGDOM

London

B-24 Flight Path

English Channel

Paris

F R A N C E

ATLANTIC
OCEAN

VICHY FRANCE

December 31, 1943–January 1, 1944
(near Lesparre);
January 6–9, 1944

Lesparre

Path to Freedom

Bordeaux

Toulouse
February 12–May 29, 1944

Bay of Biscay

Perpignan
May 29–30, 1944

N
W E
S

PYRENEES MOUNTAINS
May 31–June 2, 1944

Figueres
June 2–3, 1944

Barcelona
June 4–15, 1944

Madrid
June 4–15, 1944

PORTUGAL

S P A I N

Mediterranean Sea

Algiers

Seville
June 4–15, 1944

GIBRALTAR (UK)
June 16, 1944

ALGERIA

FOREWORD

||||||||||||||||||||||||||||||||||||||||||||||||||

January 2012

So, here I am, sitting on a plane on my way to Europe. It is the middle of January 2012, and this will be my first time in Europe. I am headed on an adventure, a personal pilgrimage of sorts, some sixty-eight years in the making. I am hoping to pay tribute to Arthur Meyerowitz and a valiant band of French men and women who saved his life in 1944. I'm filled with excitement and unable to sleep. I have no idea what awaits me in France, what vestiges remain of Arthur and what or who I will find when I arrive. The thought that I might talk with people who actually *knew* the airman Arthur Meyerowitz conjures emotions I could not have imagined a month ago.

Less than a month ago I didn't know Arthur Meyerowitz, at least not in the way that you can really "know" someone. I knew he was born in the Bronx. I knew he had a brother, Seymour, and his parents were David and Rose. I knew that he went to war to fight for his country at twenty-five (a few years younger than I am now) and when he took HIS flight to France aboard a B-24 bomber named *Harmful*

Lil Armful he too didn't know what to expect or what awaited him. What he did know was, more likely than not, he wouldn't be coming home. Staff Sergeant Arthur Meyerowitz was a top-turret gunner in the U.S. Army's 8th Air Force and he was going to war.

I knew that Arthur hadn't made more than two flights before he was shot down by the Luftwaffe and that his family desperately hoped for news from the War Department. It was months before any news would come. He was considered MIA, an American Jew in Nazi-occupied France, and he was in trouble. No one knew if he was alive or dead until he stumbled into Gibraltar more than six months later. And, lastly, I knew that people in France had saved his life. I could remember that the French national anthem was played at my bar mitzvah and other big family events but never understood the magnitude or the true significance of what it had meant.

This is what I knew for my whole life about my grandfather Arthur. Then, in December 2011, all of that would change.

How it all started:

It started with an invitation to Spain. I had met some people while vacationing in Mexico and they invited me to visit them in Madrid. I looked at the logistics and realized I could make it work, in under a month no less. I asked my father, Arthur's son, where Arthur had been in France. I wanted to see if perhaps I could visit those places and look around. There was no information to pass on; my father simply didn't have insight for me. Arthur died more than ten years before I was born, and a box of letters and a couple of vague stories were the only things that remained of Arthur's wartime experiences.

"A challenge," I thought to myself. I was pretty computer savvy, having grown up fascinated by computers and the Internet. I learned to build websites at the age of twelve and had transitioned that into a career in the online marketing world. In some ways, I had been training most of my life to crack this case. I could not have imagined, however, just how remarkable a story awaited me.

First I looked through a forgotten box of letters written in French to my grandfather from the French men and women who had saved him. Once I got online, it took me only about twenty-four hours to make my first major discovery: Arthur's recently declassified government file and debrief from when he turned up in Gibraltar some six months after the Germans blasted *Harmful Lil Armful* out of the skies above France.

Within thirty-six hours I found a book about the Resistance by a scholar name Bernard Boyer, whose pages included some of the French men and women who had written to Arthur after the war. By the end of the first week, I was on the phone with Patrick, the son of Gisèle Chauvin, a brave and amazing Resistance operative who took Arthur in at one of the most perilous points of his journey and surely saved his life.

So, here I am, flying to meet Patrick and his family. Going to meet Bernard, whose father was the head of a Resistance group who saved Arthur as well. I have appointments to meet museum directors and local historians who could help me unravel my grandfather's harrowing odyssey in Occupied France all those years ago. I even persuaded my father to accompany me on this search, this once-in-a-lifetime journey. All of this has happened in about three weeks.

January 3, 2015

It is just over seventy-one years since Arthur's journey into France and just about two years from my first trip there. I was lucky enough to make two more trips to France in November of 2013 and then in August of 2014 with some of my family. There were eight of us and it was truly incredible to be able to bring my family and the Chauvins together. We spent several wonderful days with Patrick and his family, and three generations of Meyerowitzes got to experience what it was like to be in France, in the towns and places our father, grandfather, and great-grandfather survived in. We went back to the Chauvins' home in Lesparre, went to the maquis outside that town, visited Toulouse and the landmarks there and made some amazing memories that I'm sure Arthur could never have imagined.

We are just days away from submitting our first draft of this manuscript and I can't believe how far the story has come and how much more we have uncovered. With the help of countless experts, archive visits, solid research by our writer, Peter Stevens, and some lucky finds, we have been able to piece together this incredible story, one that is so much more in-depth than I ever could have imagined.

I have taken the time to put the story I've discovered down on paper and hope I have done it justice. I hope it pays respect to the French families and individuals who risked and, in many cases, gave up their lives for Arthur. A single man in a massive war.

So now I think I know Arthur. At least more than I had when this all started. He was an incredible man and fought through so much to make it back home to his family. He was brave and heroic but knew he could never repay those people who had saved him more than seventy years ago. This is my attempt to repay the favor, to expose this adventure and shed light on the French Resistance groups and the war that was being fought on the ground in France. Not the war fought by the Allied and Axis armies. Instead the war fought by the people of France who wanted their freedom and gave all they had to secure it but still found it in their hearts to make the ultimate sacrifice for a man they never knew who just dropped from the sky one day.

Here is Arthur's story, and the story of countless people whom he crossed paths with. I hope you enjoy reading it as much as I've enjoyed putting it together.

THE
LOST
AIRMAN

||||||||||||||||||||||||||||||||||||||||||||||

A NEEDLE IN A HAYSTACK

On June 26, 1944, a young man lurched across the searing sand of Rockaway Beach, New York. As he picked his way through a maze of blankets, beach chairs, and umbrellas, throngs of beachgoers stared at him. He looked out of place in long pants hiked up to his ankles and a sweat-dampened, white button-down shirt embroidered with his name. Among the crowd in bathing suits and trunks, it was not his attire that caught people's attention. It was the cardboard sign he held aloft. He was looking for the proverbial needle in a haystack.

The young man had received a frantic telephone call an hour earlier at the beachfront candy store where he worked. An urgent voice had launched him out into the sweltering heat with a message he had hastily scrawled on the cardboard. He was hoping to find someone, a husband and wife whom he had never met, had never even seen.

Scores of men and women were watching the candy clerk as they enjoyed the hot summer day, some casting brief glances, others staring intently. They instinctively understood the sign's message. America had now been at war with Nazi Germany and Imperial Japan for some two and a half years, and most people on the beach knew someone in uniform. Many had lost a loved one in action. As more and more beachgoers realized what the young man was doing, they stepped aside to let him pass. A handful of the more curious ones trailed him down the shoreline.

Frequently wiping his brow, squinting from the sunlight, he wandered up and down the beach for more than an hour, his face flushed from the heat and visibly sunburned. As the minutes dragged on, he could not help but think that he had been dispatched on a well-intentioned but futile errand. He wondered what the chances were that his message would find the two total strangers in the dense crowds. Still, he kept walking, with the sign over his head, through the forest of umbrellas.

He stopped to take a few long breaths, his arms aching from holding up the sign. Several yards behind him, a middle-aged couple and a pretty, black-haired young woman stumbled through the thick white sand toward him. Tears streamed down their sun-darkened faces. They had spotted the words hastily scrawled on the cardboard sign.

CHAPTER 1

||||||||||||||||||||||||||||||||||||||||||

"JUST A MILK RUN"

December 31, Early Morning of New Year's Eve, 1943
Seething Airfield, Norfolk, England

An icy gust slapped against Staff Sergeant Arthur Meyerowitz as he stepped outside from the 448th Bomb Group's aluminum-walled mess hall just after 5 a.m. Wincing, he turned up the fleece collar of his leather bomber jacket and tugged his cap and earmuffs tightly. He peered for a few moments at the neat rows of cylindrical barracks arrayed on frost-cloaked farmland along the southern flank of Seething Airfield, home to his unit, the 715th Squadron, in Norfolk, England. He lingered on the mess hall's stoop as other airmen and pilots brushed past him.

A hell of a way to spend the last day of the year, he thought, but he had to do the premission checks for *Harmful Lil Armful*, a B-24 Liberator in the 448th Bomb Group. He had been up since 2:30 a.m., when he had been rousted from sleep by an officer's flashlight and ordered to go out with *Harmful Lil Armful*, whose flight engineer and top-turret gunner, Sergeant George Glevanick, had just been rushed to the base hospital. Now, after the premission briefing and breakfast, Arthur steeled himself for his second mission.

His maiden mission had come on December 24 aboard a B-24 named *Consolidated Mess*. The target was a Nazi V-1 missile site at Labroye, a relatively short hop across the English Channel in the Pas-de-Calais, in northern France. With luck, Arthur might be back at Seething in time for the New Year's Eve parties that he had planned to attend on base and in Norwich, some ten miles away on the east coast.

Lucky bastard, he mused about Glevanick, shivering. At least Glevanick was guaranteed to make it into 1944. Then Arthur lowered his shoulder against the raw wind and stepped off the stoop onto a muddy path that wound toward three concrete airstrips.

A few yards from the mess hall, Arthur spotted a group of young Englishwomen, slowed down, and removed his cap and earmuffs as he passed them. Despite the early hour, they were waiting to pick up their 8th Air Force boyfriends who had two-day passes for New Year's Eve and Day. Usually, the girlfriends had to stand outside the main gate, but they had been allowed on the base for the holidays after a security check.

As they waited for their airmen to emerge from the building, the women were chatting amid a swirl of cigarette smoke. Running his hand through his dense, dark hair, Arthur shot them a grin. Several smiled back at the handsome twenty-five-year-old airman.

A pretty blonde spotted Arthur's shoulder patch, which was emblazoned with the image of a grinning, muscular rabbit clad in a superhero's costume and cape who was perched atop a light blue bomb.

"The 715th, is it? Where are the Rabbits off to, then, in such a rush so close to New Year's?" she called out.

"We've got a date with some Germans," he replied.

"Good luck—and give the bastards our regards," another woman chimed in as Arthur picked up his pace and waved.[1]

Attention from women was something Arthur was used to. The five-foot ten-inch, 160-pound staff sergeant possessed the street smarts and swagger of his Bronx neighborhood, and he exuded a confidence to which women were drawn. Before enlisting in the Army, Arthur had loved dressing stylishly, heading to the Garment District and stretching part of his paychecks into good deals on fashionable clothes. His family was accustomed to seeing beautiful young women on his well-tailored sleeves.

At Norfolk, Arthur enjoyed chatting with attractive Englishwomen, but it never went beyond a few pints and dances in town or on base. Tucked in the breast pocket of his flight suit, his wallet held a snapshot of Esther Loew, his dark-haired, dark-eyed girlfriend back in the Bronx. An aunt had introduced him to the pretty twenty-one-year-old Esther before he had shipped out to England, and he was quickly smitten, so much so that he had considered marriage. He had decided, however, that with the casualty rate of bomber crews in the European and Pacific theaters of operation reaching the highest of any service branch—even more than the submarine fleet—he could not justify making her another in the sadly burgeoning ranks of young war widows. Still, she intended to wait for him, and he could not talk her out of it.

Arthur carried another memento of home besides Esther's photo. Around his neck was a thin gold chain with a *chai*, the Hebrew symbol for "life." His mother had given it to him before he had left for England.

As the rows of B-24s lining the airstrip materialized through the mist and freezing rain, Arthur had no time to think of Esther and of his parents and brother back in New York. *Harmful Lil Armful* had to be inspected, and his crewmates depended on Arthur, the flight engineer, to make sure that the plane was fit to fly. Everyone knew that the Allied invasion of Fortress Europe loomed. The waves of American and British bombers pounding German targets in France around the clock were "preparing the ground" for Operation Overlord, the largest amphibious assault in history. What no one except the top brass knew yet was where and when the Allies would strike across the English Channel.

||||||||||||||||||||||||||

A few hours earlier at the mission briefing, the 448th's charismatic commander, thirty-seven-year-old Colonel James M. Thompson, had unveiled a huge map of Europe and thrust a pointer at three red-circled spots. Silence enveloped the crowded room as the pilots and crews waited to hear Thompson, whose neatly parted salt-and-pepper hair and trim Clark Gable mustache made him the very picture of a tough pilot and leader, speak in his no-nonsense Texan drawl. From airfields across eastern and central England, 250 B-17s and B-24s, including *Harmful Lil Armful*, would be escorted by hundreds of P-47 Thunderbolt and P-51 Mustang fighter planes as they unleashed a daylight strike against the Nazi airfield at La Rochelle/Laleu, south-west of the Brest Peninsula. If the clouds over the site proved too dense, the secondary target was another Nazi airstrip, at Château-bernard.

Thompson, a nerveless pilot who had racked up fifty-five missions over Europe and had earned a reputation for never sugarcoating danger for his men, told the assembled airmen that German flak and fighter attacks all the way into and out of the target run would be intense.

Arthur knew they would soon be "in the soup" over France.

Arthur could never have envisioned that he would see France or England, let alone go to war. Still, the eldest son of David and Rose Meyerowitz had always thirsted for adventure.

Arthur was born on August 15, 1918, in the Bronx, in a tough neighborhood largely composed of Jewish, Irish, and Italian families crowded into old, yellow-brick, flat-roofed apartment buildings that clotted Findlay Avenue. At 1205 Findlay Avenue, built in 1915, the Meyerowitz family lived in a third-floor, one-bedroom apartment.

David and Rose had a second child, Seymour, on August 11, 1927. When Seymour was old enough, he and Arthur shared a Murphy bed in the living room.

Forty-three-year-old David Meyerowitz had emigrated from Romania to New York as a boy and had been compelled to leave school at eighth grade to help the family survive. He went on to work as a driver and salesman in the wholesale bakery business and to marry Rose Blumenthal, a vivacious, dark-haired woman born and raised in the Bronx. With the onset of the Great Depression in 1929, times turned increasingly tight for the Meyerowitz family and their Findlay Avenue neighbors. David always managed to keep his family fed, housed, and clothed, but money was always short. He and Rose were constantly juggling the bills, unable to think about moving out of their apartment.

To survive on Findlay Avenue, Arthur learned how to use both his instincts and his fists. He had to because on the corners of Findlay and adjoining streets, Russian and Eastern European Jews, Irish, and Italian kids claimed patches of local asphalt as their personal turf. In Arthur's building people watched out for each other, and when a job was lost or an illness struck families, neighbors helped out as best they could.

Raised to respect women and imbued with a strong sense of right and wrong, Arthur was never afraid to stand up to bullies. Once, when the din of a man beating his wife echoed down the third-floor hallway of the apartment complex, Arthur rushed toward the noise and started banging on the neighbors' apartment door. The husband opened it, red-faced and sweating. In the small living room, his wife was sobbing, her clothes disheveled, bruises rising on her face.

Arthur, clenching his fists at his side, glared at the older man, who backed away a step as Arthur stood in the doorway, saying nothing, his eyes still fixed on the neighbor. Then Arthur leaned forward, jabbed a finger just under the man's chin, and nodded in the direction of the cringing woman. Arthur turned around and waited for the door to close. He lingered in the hall, listening as the man and the woman talked in low, almost hushed tones. There were no more slaps or shouts.

Over the following days and weeks, it became apparent that the husband had gotten the message: if he threatened his wife again, his tough young neighbor would give him a dose of the same. The beatings stopped.

Arthur graduated from Robert Morris High School, built in 1897 as the first public high school in the Bronx, and the education he received in the soaring Gothic brick structure complete with turrets and spires was rated as one of the finest offered by any of the city's public high schools. In the school's sprawling auditorium, Arthur and the rest of the student body gathered for daily assemblies amid the hall's ornate columns and a commemorative World War I mural that would earn the school a place on the National Historic Register. Arthur saw that masterpiece daily for four school years. The mural had been rendered by renowned French artist August Gorguet and entitled *After Conflict Comes Peace*. At the time, the vivid images of war-scarred France did not matter much to the teenager.

After his 1936 graduation from Morris, Arthur immediately began working; any thought of college was out of the question with the Depression still battering the nation and the family needing every dollar. He sold electrical fixtures for Jack Meyerowitz, his uncle, and doubled as a receiving and shipping clerk and supervisor of ten men for a wholesale lampshade company in Brooklyn for three and a half years. Although fortunate to have any work in the midst of the Depression, in 1939 Arthur was employed only for twenty-eight weeks, earning $400. Fortunately for the family, his father worked all fifty-two weeks and brought home $1,560, but there was never much left over after the bills were paid.

Wanting to contribute more and finding his life too sedate despite his busy social calendar, Arthur began to think about other avenues for a steadier and more exciting financial future. He had always been interested in airplanes and yearned for the chance to fly, and in late 1940, he spoke to an Army recruiter in Manhattan about the Army Air Corps. The sergeant told Arthur that a college education was not mandatory for aviation cadets so long as they had graduated from a good high school. The recruiter added that once Arthur completed basic training, he "could transfer to the Air Corps if he passed the physical and mental examinations."[2]

Filled with excitement, Arthur, who had never traveled beyond New York and New Jersey, signed a one-year enlistment paper on January 8, 1941. He was formally inducted at Fort Dix, New Jersey, and was soon on his way to basic infantry training at Fort Bragg, North Carolina.

Once he completed basic, Arthur made two requests to his commanding officer: a pass to attend Seymour's Bar Mitzvah in New York and the application to transfer to the Army Air Corps. The officer turned down the Bar Mitzvah pass brusquely and then set Private Meyerowitz straight regarding aviation training—Arthur had signed up for one year, and the Army did not allow such enlistees to waste its time and money in flight school. The recruiting sergeant had lied to him, and Arthur, furious but trapped, started counting the days until January 8, 1942, when his assignment would be complete. Meanwhile, he sent Seymour one month's Army wages as a Bar Mitzvah present. He earned stellar reviews from his superiors first as a rifleman and then as a .50-caliber machine gunner.

On December 7, 1941, about a month before his enlistment was up, Arthur was stunned by the news of the Imperial Japanese Navy's strike against Pearl Harbor. He immediately signed up for three more years, out of patriotism, out of the certainty that he would be drafted anyway, and out of hope that he could now transfer to the Air Corps. He wrote to Seymour that "my life expectancy as a machine gunner will be about thirteen seconds, so I want to fly and fight that way."[3]

Arthur, hard-nosed and keenly intelligent, possessed just the sort of nerve and leadership skills required in the cockpit. On June 8, 1942, his first step toward becoming an aviation cadet came when Lieutenant Colonel E. O. Lee, the commander of the 60th U.S. Regiment, 9th Infantry Division at Fort Bragg, rated him as an "excellent soldier" and recommended that his request for transfer to the Air Corps be accepted, with three nonfamily character references from people who had known "the candidate for no less than five years." All three letters, from respected New York businessmen, testified that Arthur was a young man "whose character is of the finest . . . is reliable and trustworthy . . . an asset to any branch of the service he might choose."[4] All he could do now was wait it out and hope that he would not be shipped off to North Africa or the Pacific as an infantryman before a transfer could arrive.

On July 16, 1942, Arthur was told to report to Lieutenant Colonel Lee. His heart racing as he hurried to his superior's office, he knew the reason. A few minutes later, Arthur stepped outside and headed to his barracks—with the news that his transfer "for an Aviation Cadet Appointment to the Air Corps [had] been officially accepted."[5] Elated, he was no longer a "dogface" with Company H. He wanted to give his family the news immediately, but because only one neighbor had a phone, he had to call that number and ask that they tell Rose, David, and Seymour that Private Arthur Meyerowitz was now an aviation cadet, with the opportunity to earn his wings.

The opportunity came more slowly than Arthur would have liked. Before he could claim a spot as a flight cadet, he was required to complete physical training, classroom training, and hands-on runway instruction; if he came through the regimen successfully, another physical exam awaited. Cadets had to undergo a grueling work-up that washed out any number of candidates for everything from punctured eardrums to vertigo. Only then could Arthur make it all the way from the ground to the cockpit.

After a processing stint in Columbia, South Carolina, to await his initial assignment in the Army Air Force, Arthur was transferred for a few months to the Army air base in Nashville, Tennessee, and then near Biloxi, Mississippi. He performed well both in the classroom and on the ground at the Air Corps Technical School, where would-be pilots, airmen, and ground crews—"Paddlefeet"—alike were indoctrinated in aircraft technology and mechanics from nose to tail.

The most nerve-racking moment of Arthur's training so far came in August 1942, when he underwent the dreaded physical and classroom examinations for aviation cadets, the last hurdles before flight training. Strapped to a mechanized tiltboard, he was tipped in different, dizzying angles at varying speeds to measure his capacity to endure sudden dives, climbs, rolls, and loops in a fighter plane or a bomber. With no way to tell in which direction the board would move, many recruits threw up within a minute or passed out as the board's pitching and gyrations increased or decreased. If a cadet could not stand up within a few seconds after the tiltboard was stopped, he was dropped from ("washed out") pilot training. The cadets who managed to wobble from the board and stay on their feet were hustled immediately to an eye chart and ordered to read each line as fast as possible so that the doctors could determine how quickly each man's eyesight could recover from severe vertigo. If the flight candidate failed to complete the lines within one minute, he was out.

Once the vertigo and eye tests were done, Arthur was poked and prodded from head to toe as the doctors searched for anything from a slight hearing imperfection to slow reflexes, any of which would disqualify a man. He winced as a doctor inserted a long probe into his nostrils to rule out any hint of a deviated septum or sinus anomalies. Still feeling the effects of the tiltboard, Arthur and his fellow candidates had to run a mile in the sweltering Mississippi heat and have their heart rates and pulses measured.

After Arthur made it through the physical, the results of which were sent for review to an Army Air Force medical board at Wendover

Airfield, Utah, he faced the Graduation Field Test. This was the final examination to measure how much flight candidates had absorbed in the classroom. Any grade less than the eightieth percentile meant dismissal from the program. Arthur scored an 82, just above the 80 he needed to continue. Now he had to wait several days for the final results of his physical.

On August 2, at Wendover, an Army medical board deemed the young man from the Bronx qualified to fly. He wrote home that he would always consider it to be "one of the best days of his life."[6]

Arthur was assigned to the flight-training base in Laredo, Texas, a dust-choked, rough-and-tumble ranching town that still evoked the Wild West. Intrigued by the sight of genuine cowboys and wranglers on horseback, the city kid and several of his fellow cadets decided to give the saddle and reins a try on a pass into town. It certainly could not be as difficult as learning to handle a plane, Arthur reasoned.

He managed to stay atop his horse during his first lesson. Then, as he was tying the reins to a hitching post, the horse snapped its head back toward him just as he was leaning forward to finish the task. With a sickening thud the horse's snout slammed against Arthur's left eye.

Arthur staggered for a moment and sank to his knees, his eye closing fast. The impact sent blood pouring from his nose. His friends helped him to his feet, laid him in the back of a jeep, and sped back to the base infirmary. Groggy from the impact, Arthur gazed with his good eye at the white-coated Army doctor who appeared in front of him. The physician was Japanese. With Japanese Americans rounded up in the wake of Pearl Harbor as potential threats to the nation and languishing in heavily guarded camps on the order of President Roosevelt and Congress, Arthur had reason to balk at treatment from the doctor.

Before he could say a word, the doctor said, "I may be Japanese, but I am *American*. Your eye needs to be operated on, and you won't find anyone better than me for the job."[7]

Awash in pain, Arthur simply nodded. He felt sick to his stomach at the realization of what the crack of the horse's massive snout against his face likely meant. If his eyes had not already been watering from the blow, he would have had a hard time holding back tears.

The doctor proved as good as his word, performing a retinal procedure and draining the fluid and blood pressing against the eye and the orbital socket. For an aspiring pilot, however, 20/20 vision was nonnegotiable. The lingering damage to Arthur's eye was slight, but even that killed any cadet's chance to take the throttle of a bomber or a fighter. Even if perfect vision eventually returned, a nation at war and in dire need of combat pilots as soon as possible could not wait for such an injury to heal.

Arthur did not want to return to the infantry, but he didn't want to sit on the sidelines either. The attack on Pearl Harbor and the rumors of Nazi atrocities that had seeped into Jewish communities across America in the past few years filled him with an anger he could barely describe. He wanted to fight for his country, and if he could not do it in the cockpit, he had to find a way to stay in the air, to "do his bit" aboard a bomber. He did not have much time to figure something out.

On November 13, 1942, Arthur was ordered to appear in Wendover before an Army Air Force Faculty Board, which informed him that he was "physically disqualified for further flying duty because of physical disability."[8]

Arthur then requested that he be considered as an Army Air Force Officer School administrative candidate, noting his stellar record in Air Technical School and in all phases of his training up to his accident. It was a long shot because men with at least some college experience were first in line.

Impressed with "the record of Aviation Cadet Arthur Sidney

Meyerowitz," a board officer asked that if his request was "not favorably considered, is there any type of technical training you desire?"[9]

Arthur was ready with his answer, one he had formulated over the weeks of his recovery. "Sir, in that case, I would like to be considered for training as an airplane flight engineer."[10]

The board members conferred and quickly reached a decision, acknowledging that Arthur's removal from flight training was due to physical reasons, not performance. They assigned him to training as a flight engineer. Since he was already a skilled .50-caliber machine gunner and B-24 flight engineers doubled as the bomber's top-turret gunner, he stood out as an ideal candidate.

Once Arthur fully recovered from his surgery, his second round of flight training began, but this time as an engineer. The classroom training over the following months proved as intense as the training for an aspiring pilot; Arthur spent long hours in lectures for maintenance fundamentals, hydraulic systems, engines, electrical systems, fuel systems, aircraft instruments, propellers, engine operation under all sorts of duress, and aircraft inspection. He soon learned that pilots and flight engineers were required to know more about the planes they flew than bombardiers, navigators, or anyone else aboard a B-17 Flying Fortress or a B-24 Liberator.

In October 1943, with his eye healed, Arthur completed two intensive weeks of training as a top ball-turret gunner and was promoted to staff sergeant. Assigned to the 715th Squadron, 448th Bomber Group, he entered the third and last phase of his training, at Sioux City, Iowa. All that remained before he was sent overseas were several B-24 practice flights from the airfield at Herrington, Kansas, and final classroom examinations for flight engineers. Unless he performed below required standards in both the air and on the ground, he would soon be heading off to the war. The big question was whether he would be sent to the European or the Pacific theater of operation. Pilots and crewmen were told their destination only after they shipped out.

On October 30, 1943, just four days before flying out from Sioux City, Arthur sat down to compose a letter to his parents.

||||||||||||||||||||||||

As the steam radiators of the third-floor apartment hissed and clanged, Rose Meyerowitz wiped an early November-morning frost off the apartment's front window. Findlay Avenue began to appear below with each rub of her cotton cloth against the glass. The street was packed with commercial panel trucks and a handful of cars beeping incessantly. People bundled up against the gusts that occasionally rattled the apartment's windows bustled along the street. David had left for work at 7 a.m., and Seymour had scampered out the door for school a half hour later.

Spotting the mailman walking down the building's front steps, Rose laid her cloth on the windowsill. She walked downstairs to the row of metal boxes on the lobby wall, inserted her key, and pulled out several letters. Among a few bills was an envelope embossed with the logo of the Hotel West, Sioux City, Iowa; she immediately recognized Arthur's handwriting on the envelope. She rushed upstairs, settled into the worn fabric of her reading chair next to the window, and stared at the letter. Taking a deep breath, she opened it to find three pages of stationery:

Dear Dad & Mom,

I am writing you just before I get ready to leave the States. This is one thing I would rather not have to write you both. I know how you feel about me. All I can say to that is I feel the same way about you. Ever since I can remember you were always swell parents. You gave me every chance to make something of myself. I have no kick coming.

I am about to go overseas. I knew it was coming a long time ago. It's something I have been training a long time for. I think I have a

*darn good chance to see this thing through & come back to you all safe
& sound. My biggest worry is your worrying about me. Please don't.
You don't have to.*

*You will see nothing is going to happen to me. If I knew you won't
carry on, I would feel so much better. All I ask of you, Dad, is take
good care of mom & Seymour. I guess you know what I mean. I don't
want to write any more on the subject. Just tell mom not to worry &
everything will come out ok. From what I heard today, I am going to
a place I want to. It looks like it will be China. I will fly all the way. I
am glad it won't be by boat.*

*There will be times you won't get mail from me. Don't worry. It
will have to take a longer time to get to you now. So try & understand
above everything don't worry about me. That's about all I can say
for now.*

Just take good care of mom for me.

All my love to you.
Artie[11]

Rose tucked the letter into her apron pocket and closed her eyes.
Arthur's bravado conjuring a slight smile for an instant, she silently
prayed for Arthur's return, as she made Seymour do every morning
and evening. She not only worried about Arthur, but also about Seymour and Esther. They, too, saw the newspapers filled with grim
news of massive battles and losses in Europe and the Pacific.

Rose got up from the chair, picked up the cloth, and began to
dust again.

After logging a scant forty-eight hours and thirty minutes in the air
aboard B-24s, Arthur flew aboard a C-47 transport plane to Morrison Army Air Field, in West Palm Beach, Florida, on November 11,

1943. Every pilot and airman knew what the assignment meant: They were shipping out for combat. With the highest casualty rate of any branch, the Army Air Corps had no choice but to rush pilots and airmen into action.

At Morrison, thousands of air personnel were assembled for their overseas dispositions by the U.S. Army Air Forces Ferrying Command. The more fortunate bomber pilots and crews flew out to Europe or the Pacific on new bombers; when B-24s or B-17s fresh from the factories were not available, thousands of pilots and airmen were crammed aboard troop transports or converted passenger ships. Eighth and 15th Air Force crews headed to England or Italy would spend two to three weeks in storm-tossed Atlantic waters where Nazi U-Boats prowled the convoy routes. Some of the vessels leaving Palm Beach never made it more than a few miles from Florida before German torpedoes sent them to the ocean bottom. The grim gibe was that if a ship lumbered straight out of Palm Beach Harbor and kept going straight, "you were heading into U-Boat Country, so kiss your ass good-bye."[12]

To Arthur's relief, he and his crewmates would not make the Atlantic crossing by ship. They had been ordered to fly out to war on a new B-24 named *Maid of Tin*. They would not know their destination until they were in the air, and they opened a sealed envelope.

Arthur and the other men of the 715th were rousted from bed at 3 a.m. on November 19, 1943, and told by an orderly that they were to ship out aboard *Maid of Tin*, with all their gear. Before climbing into the bomber with fourteen other men of the 715th, including two pilots, Arthur headed to a 5 a.m. briefing. William Blum, a pilot in the squadron, wrote: "It was still dark and very humid when we were told to report . . . the briefing room was crowded and we were all conscious of the long flight before us. The briefing was short, a roll call of the crews scheduled to take off, the order to take off, photographs of landing fields along the route, a detailed account of all landmarks and aids to navigation, emergency ditching procedure, and finally a thorough weather briefing."[13]

After a quick breakfast at the mess, Arthur and the others flying out boarded jeeps to the bombers lined up on the airstrip. Blum recalled that "everyone gathered for a last cigarette in our homeland before the big hop."[14]

A few days earlier at the Morrison processing center, Arthur had been required to make out a will and was given a quick medical examination. He named his mother, Rose, as the beneficiary of the $10,000 government death insurance accorded to the men of the 8th Army Air Corps.

When *Maid of Tin*, laden with 2,500 gallons of gas, soared above the airstrip and headed southwest through drizzling rain and a low cloud cover toward Puerto Rico, the pilot turned over the controls to the copilot. The skipper then reached into his flight jacket and removed a sealed envelope marked *SECRET* in bold type, and switched on the intercom.

"Men," he intoned, "I'm about to inform you of our destination."

As every crewman fell silent, the sound of the pilot tearing open the envelope could be heard faintly above the drone of the engines.

The pilot said, "Your destination—the British Isles."

Blum's words echoed the thoughts of Arthur: "No one said a word. We all had hoped for a tour of China. The British winters meant bad weather and the Jerries were hot pilots."[15]

The South Atlantic Crossing to Great Britain took nearly two weeks, with *Maid of Tin* making required fueling stops and layovers at Puerto Rico, Trinidad, Brazil, and Dakar and Marrakesh, both in North Africa. From there, the B-24 landed at Seething Airfield, Station 146, on December 3, 1943.

When Arthur first set foot at Seething on December 3, 1943, he was uncertain about what to expect. As a jeep wove across frozen mud and rutted paths to rows of barracks, several airmen waved. "You'll be sorry!" a few shouted.

Another crewman bellowed, "Here comes the fresh meat!"[16]

Not exactly a reassuring welcome, Arthur thought. He later learned that both greetings were an 8th Air Force tradition for arriving crews.

Arthur and his comrades were soon dropped off at their new home, the 715th's aluminum Nissen hut, whose uninsulated, tarpaper-covered walls housed rows of thin-mattressed cots with only three feet separating them. The reek of the coal-fired stoves that supplied warmth against the English chill merged with cigarette smoke and the odor of wet woolen blankets and uniforms. As Arthur would soon learn, those smells seemed more fragrant to airmen each time they survived another mission and returned to Seething.

Before he could fly out on an actual mission, nearly three weeks in Seething "lecture rooms for precombat orientation and theater indoctrination" awaited. The collective eyes of Arthur's fellow rookie crewmen and pilots often glazed over from their instructors' long-winded sermons and their exhortations that no mission was ever a "milk run," a bombing run in which there was little or no flak or enemy fighter planes. Arthur and other city boys stifled laughter as young men from rural spots stared wide-eyed when lecturers sternly pontificated about venereal disease and "loose women" around the British airfields where the rookies would be based.

There was one lecture that proved different for Arthur, as well as the other rookie airman. He heard the harsh warning about the odds against pilots and airmen surviving the required twenty-five missions over Hitler's Europe: "On an average, the 8th Air Force loses four out of every hundred planes on every mission . . . Of course, some missions will be a disaster due to very aggressive enemy action."

This being the case, the instructor reasoned, "A crew that flies twenty-five missions has almost a hundred percent chance of being shot down by its last mission."[17]

Arthur and the others sat utterly silent. It hit them full force that, in all likelihood, many of them would never see home again.

Unlike some airmen, Arthur had already prepared himself for that grim possibility. Before leaving for war, he had told his younger brother, Seymour, "If I'm going to die, I'd rather fly. I don't want to die on the ground."[18]

As he had told his brother, neither the eye injury nor anything else was going to stop him from fighting the Nazis. He was willing to die for his country, and as part of a B-24 crew, he knew and accepted that he was likely to do just that. Still, saying it and having air-combat veterans tell it were two different things. The reality first riveted and then haunted B-24 and B-17 bomber crews, and Arthur proved no exception.

Now, less than a month since he had made the long, harrowing flight from Florida to England aboard *Maid of Tin*, that harsh reality hit him. It had begun moments after he had been pulled out of bed at 3 a.m. and had swelled by the time the preflight briefing ended. To fill out crews slated to fly a mission but shorthanded by casualties, squadron leaders routinely drafted pilots and airmen who were supposed to have a "day off." Arthur fully understood the necessity. What he could not quite shake was Colonel Thompson's grim visage at the briefing. Thompson had laid it out bluntly and candidly: the mission ahead would be the last for many of the crews flying out in a few hours. From the moment that the colonel had concluded the briefing with the words "kick their asses," Arthur's stomach had been churning.[19]

It had gotten even worse after he stepped into the mess hall for 5:30 a.m. breakfast, right after the briefing. He only picked at the scrambled eggs, ham, sausage, and toast that cooks piled onto the airmen's tin trenchers. Everyone in the mess hall could tell who was flying out that day and who was off duty. Men who downed endless mugs of coffee and ate little or nothing had just come out of the briefing room. They also toted thermoses of coffee to help ward off the fifty-below-zero temperature of a B-24's cabin at twenty-eight thousand feet above the ground.

As Arthur reached the bomber he saluted the pilot, Second Lieutenant Philip Chase, and the copilot, Second Lieutenant William H. Thomas. A couple of cocky college boys, he thought, but decent enough guys. Still, he had no doubt that he would have been better in the pilot's seat than either of them.

He stopped near the front of the bomber, slowly running his fingers across the fuselage's cold steel skin and the colorfully painted image of a buxom pinup girl clad in a white bikini top and grass skirt cradling a bomb—her *Harmful Lil Armful*. For the second time before flying into combat, he inspected a B-24's 67-foot 8-inch length, its 110-foot wingspan, and its four powerful Pratt & Whitney R-1830 turbo-supercharged radial engines, 1,200 horsepower each. German flak and fighter planes had rocked both his plane and his "rookie" nerves aboard *Consolidated Mess* on December 24, but at least now he knew what to expect over France.

As he began his inspection, he grew concerned by the pounding *Harmful Lil Armful* had taken from antiaircraft fire on her third mission, the previous day, December 30. He was wary of the chance that any damage to the aircraft less than a day earlier might not be fully repaired. He did not have to remind himself to pay special attention to the bomber's engines.

From talking with other engineers, he had learned that the B-24 Liberator could not match the B-17 Flying Fortress's capacity to endure heavy damage and that crews had dubbed the B-24 the "Flying Coffin" because it possessed only two exits. The escape hatch was located near the tail of the aircraft, and a fire anywhere in front of the exit could trap the crew. The only other escape was the bomb bay, whose doors often jammed from flak's concussive waves.

The aircraft was highly susceptible to fires as well. Luftwaffe fighter pilots had learned to rake several fuel tanks mounted in the B-24's upper fuselage with machine-gun and nose-cannon rounds and set the bomber ablaze. Once the flames spread, the B-24's gravest flaw appeared, as the wings would often buckle and crumple. On his first mission, Arthur had witnessed several doomed B-24s plunging past his bomber, their flaming wings folded upward like fiery butterflies.

As Arthur and his fellow engineers and mechanics continued their preflight inspections, some crewmen tossed footballs in the semidarkness between the planes and on the fields' edges; other airmen hurled baseballs, the staccato slaps of horsehide into leather gloves toted from all corners of America a poignant reminder of home, of better days. Cigarettes glowed everywhere.

Dozens of trucks packed with massive five-hundred-pound bombs lumbered up to the planes surrounding the runways. The bombardier of each crew would arm the bombs with detonation pins once the B-24s neared their French targets. Other trucks laden with steel containers that held gleaming .50-caliber machine-gun belts surrounded eighteen bombers arrayed along Seething's three runways.

Arthur worked his way around the plane, meticulously going over each of his checkpoints twice while the rest of *Harmful Lil Armful*'s crew arrived in the back of an open truck. They clambered out and huddled around the bomber. When he finished his inspection of engines one and two and emerged from beneath the left wing, he spied Staff Sergeant Thomas M. McNamara, a veteran of four missions already and an older-brother figure to several of the younger crewmen. McNamara's hand rested on the shoulder of nineteen-year-old Staff Sergeant William D. Dunham, an Ohio farm boy whose gaunt face was creased with worry.

Arthur stopped and nodded at them. Although *Harmful Lil Armful*'s crew was not his own, Arthur had spent a lot of time at Seething with McNamara. A square-jawed, wide-shouldered, Irish New Yorker with a raucous, infectious laugh, he regaled his crewmates with a bottomless font of hilarious stories from his tough upbringing in Hell's Kitchen to his family's move to Grand Rapids, Michigan. McNamara knew every inch of the B-24 and B-17 alike. Before enlisting in the Army Air Force, he had worked in Henry Ford's B-24 plant in Willow Run, Michigan.

Whether he was in the freezing barracks where the six crews of the 715th Bomber Squad slept, the mess hall, or the briefing room, McNamara's confidence and experience always reassured his own crew and other airmen in the unit. Even the pilots sought his counsel when it came to the literal nuts-and-bolts workings of the bombers.

At the sudden backfire of a truck's tailpipe or perhaps even a firecracker, since it was, after all, the final day of 1943, Dunham stiffened and cursed softly, his eyes wide. "He's just nervous," McNamara assured Arthur.

"He'll be fine," he added with a smile.

Arthur smiled at the two men, walked over to the other wing, and crouched beneath the number three engine. All around the plane, other crew members were making their own preflight checks. Navigator and second lieutenant Harry K. Farrell and bombardier and flight officer Edward E. George, a pair of Ivy Leaguers with the innate confidence of their upper-class pedigrees, quietly conversed and looked up to say hello to Arthur. Despite the difference in their background from the rest of the crewmen, they were, as McNamara said, "good eggs."

Radio operator Staff Sergeant Joseph Defranze, a wavy-haired, gregarious nineteen-year-old kid from Hyde Park, Massachusetts, grinned at Arthur. "Make sure we've got all four propellers," he joked.

Arthur retorted, "Colonel Thompson told me we only need one."

Tail gunner and staff sergeant Howard R. Peck, who said little but had proven a deadly marksman with his .50-caliber Browning on his first two missions, chuckled.

Arthur barely heard the laughter. He had already spied several large dents from German flak that had bent parts of the engine's casing close to the propeller—too close for his liking. There were at least a dozen holes in the casing and the underside of the wing from where Messerschmitt 109 fighters' machine guns and nose cannons had found their mark. Knowing how vulnerable the B-24's wings were, Arthur rushed over to the two pilots.

Saluting, he explained the damage he had found. "Sir," he said to Lieutenant Chase, "the ship is unfit to fly—the engine needs to be fixed."

For a moment, Chase and Thomas stared at him. Then Chase's angular features tightened, and he glowered at Arthur. "This is a milk run—quick and simple, Meyerowitz. She'll get repaired when we get back."

The pilot started to turn his back to Arthur.

Arthur understood Chase's thinking: Every flight brought them closer to the magic number of twenty-five. They wanted to fly.

Any mission was dangerous even without a damaged engine. Still, it was the flight engineer's duty to raise the alarm if a bomber was too damaged. Chase and Thomas, like all B-24 and B-17 pilots, had been taught, as B-24 pilot William E. Carigan Jr., recalled, that "the flight engineer, with his wide knowledge of the plane, must always get your ear, and any warning he gives must be seriously considered."[20]

"Lieutenant Chase," Arthur said.

Chase wheeled around, scowling again. Thomas's stocky shoulders tensed, and he shook his head, his thin lips clenching.

"The repairs shouldn't take more than a day."

"That's enough, Sergeant," Chase snapped.

Arthur knew he should shut up now before risking a charge of insubordination to a superior. He could not do so. He knew what he had seen. If he were the pilot, he would never endanger his men like that.

"Fix the ship!" he shouted before he even realized the words came out of his mouth.

Chase's blue eyes narrowed. "You're not the pilot, and you're not in charge. *Harmful Lil Armful* will fly today with the engine as is."[21]

Arthur slammed his clipboard to the ground, turned his back to the two pilots, and joined his staring crewmates. From behind him, neither Chase nor Thomas said a word.

CHAPTER 2

||||||||||||||||||||||||||||||||||||||||||

PURPLE HEART CORNER

Piercing the gloomy gray skies above Seething at 8:15 a.m., the roar of eighteen B-24s' engines could be heard ten miles away in Norwich. At full strength, the 448th Bomb Group's four squadrons had once stood at sixty-four Liberators, but German flak and fighters had thinned Colonel Thompson's command to forty-eight, with thirty undergoing repairs. If Lieutenant Chase had heeded Arthur's warning about *Harmful Lil Armful*'s damaged number three engine, that number would have been thirty-one. Arthur and the other men in the B-24s taxiing onto all three runways knew that some would not return from today's mission and silently prayed that their "number was not up."

At other airstrips all across England, Wales, and Scotland, a similar scene unfolded as B-24s, B-17s, and squadrons of P-38, P-47, and P-51 fighter planes began rising one by one at minute intervals into the dense winter clouds and starting the dangerous process of forming the "box" that would stretch some 150 miles at altitudes of eighteen to twenty-eight thousand feet.

As Arthur and every bomber crewman understood, stacking bombers in murk so thick that pilots could literally see only the plane in front of them caused deadly collisions; on Arthur's first mission, on December 24, two planes had clipped each other but had managed to land safely. Only when the formation pierced through the cloud ceiling did crews feel safe. That relief was fleeting. It ended the moment that the formation banked on its flight path toward the waiting Luftwaffe and the 88-millimeter antiaircraft cannons on the ground.

Arthur tensed as the B-24 in front of *Harmful Lil Armful* rattled down the strip and took off. *Harmful Lil Armful* shuddered the moment that Lieutenant Chase pushed the bomber's four throttles forward, her wings vibrating and shaking every inch of the fuselage. Adrenaline surged through Arthur. Chase took his foot off the brakes, and the B-24 lurched forward and picked up speed. She hurtled down the six-thousand-foot runway and, at seemingly the last moment, climbed above the ambulances parked near the strip's edges. Arthur glimpsed the control tower, three runways, and snow-swathed pastures and farmland for a few instants. Then a wall of gunmetal-gray clouds enveloped the plane.

"Gear up!" Chase barked to Thomas.[1]

Arthur's second mission—a flight he was not supposed to be on—had begun.

▬▬▬▬▬▬▬

The B-24s and their escort took nearly an hour to stack up in formation, banked southeast over the English Channel around 9 a.m., and set course for the southwestern coastal region of France. *Harmful Lil Armful*'s target, La Rochelle Laleu Airfield, lay some 600 miles southeast of Seething, and at a cruising speed of 215 miles per hour, the bomber would reach the drop zone close to noon.

Harmful Lil Armful maneuvered into the "Purple Heart Corner," the number two position of the stack's third element, the uppermost and most vulnerable part of the formation. Aware that his bomber's spot exposed her to increased flak because German gunners always aimed their first salvos at the highest part of formations and worked their way down the stack, Chase was taking a huge gamble that the damaged number three engine could withstand the relentless concussive waves from German antiaircraft cannons. In the third element, machine-gun fire from the two lower elements could hit the bombers as the first and the second fired upward at German fighters.

At first, Arthur took comfort in the drone of the bombers and at the presence of their fighter escort, as if nothing could blunt such a massive collection of force. Soon, though, he thought about the questionable engine. A B-24 could fly on three engines, but had no business beginning a mission with an engine that could quit at any instant and force the bomber out of the stack. The third element was vulnerable to enemy fighter planes able to strike from above without worrying about defensive fire from the first and second elements below. German fighters would pounce on a bomber with an engine suddenly acting up over German airspace and force a B-24 to drop out of an already susceptible spot in the formation.

For the moment, Arthur immersed himself in his flight engineer's duties to tend to the aircraft's many electrical and hydraulic systems. As soon as *Harmful Lil Armful* reached its position, he and the other flight engineers in the formation moved to a position on a pedestal behind the pilot and copilot and remained there until the bombers reached Nazi airspace. Arthur served as the third set of eyes scanning the dials and instruments on the cockpit's front panel. He also had to use a series of switches to move fuel between tanks, as needed, to keep the plane balanced.

As the formation neared the French coastline, Arthur communicated constantly with Chase and Thomas to update them on the flight engineer's required readings of engine and navigation instruments, reporting that the engines were not showing any signs of malfunction. The pilot and copilot merely nodded at his words, or ignored them. They were paying little attention to Sergeant Glevanick's temporary replacement.

Despite the front panel's initial indicators that the plane was functioning smoothly, Arthur continued to worry about number three, checking its performance over and over. He was concerned that if the engine's propeller sheared its weakened shaft, it could be flung through the plane's fuselage. Just because number three thrummed steadily on the crossing did not mean it would stand up to Nazi flak.

As the B-24s drew ever closer to France at high altitude, Arthur had to take longer to garner accurate readings from the cockpit panel because the frigid temperatures inside the unheated bomber frosted over gauges and dials. He wiped the frost off the glass surfaces and tapped them gently in case the indicator needles had become stuck.

Chase's voice burst across the intercom: "Entering enemy airspace!"[2]

Arthur climbed into the top turret and strapped himself behind the Martin Electric Upper Deck top ball turret's twin .50-caliber machine guns. Surprisingly, he had found that the bubble's seat and footrest were roomy enough to prevent cramping. The top turret was more comfortable than the bottom bubble, which gunners dubbed the "hell seat."

He adjusted his oxygen mask and plugged the cord of the airman's standard-issue twenty-four-volt rheostat flight suit into one of the outlets along the inside of the fuselage just beneath the turret to ward off the cold at twenty-eight thousand feet. Underneath, he wore a pair of long johns. Because a short in the plane's electrical system could ignite the flight suit, pilots and crewmen would yank out the cord at the first sign of flak.

All the while he braced himself for the dizzying and gut-churning duels with German fighters and the lethal wall of flak from one of the war's most fearsome and accurate weapons: the German 88mm antiaircraft cannon. In lecture rooms, Arthur had learned that the *Acht-Acht* Flak 18 cannon could hurl fifteen to twenty shells per minute up to thirty-thousand feet high, but until he had experienced the weapon above La Broye on his first mission, he had not grasped just how frightening the 88 was.

As every mile brought *Harmful Lil Armful* closer to the 88s, Arthur's head was low in the turret, his field of vision limited at the turret mechanism's bottom rim. He wore tinted goggles to ward off the constant glare of sunlight against the Plexiglas, but other than those hindrances, he had sweeping views from the frameless cocoon.

Arthur peered down through occasional breaks in the clouds at distant, murky gray-and-white patches—glimpses of Nazi-occupied France. Beneath the formation, German radar and "spotter stations" were picking up the oncoming bombers. They were tracking their speed, course, and altitude so that the German gun crews could swivel their 88s skyward, lay in their settings, and wait for the right moment to pull the dreaded cannons' lanyards. Every now and then Arthur spied silvery shafts rising from "chaff," strands of Christmas-tree tinsel cut into varying length and dangling from the open ports of the bomber's waist guns. The tinsel sent confusing readings to German radar operators, designed to buy formations just a few more minutes before flak gunners found the range.

The gunners patiently awaited just the right moment to hurl twenty-pound shells above, below, behind, and in front of the formation to create a "kill zone." Allied bomber crews dreaded the 88s even more than the Luftwaffe fighters—with good reason, as Arthur had learned on his first mission. The 88 shells burst in a spray of metal that tore through planes and men alike, with skilled gunners "leading" their shells to detonate in front of bomber cockpits and kill the pilots. Brilliantly designed, the antiaircraft cannon ejected fired shells quickly and recoiled smoothly. A gunner simply had to insert a new shell into a firing tray again and again. Unlike almost every other antiaircraft gun used by either the Allies or the Japanese, the 88 rarely, if ever, jammed. Its crews could go about their lethal business with total confidence and efficiency. An English pilot called the 88 a "semiautomatic cannon."

The German antiaircraft crews knew that Allied bombers locked on to their target runs thirty miles out. At that point, experienced flak gunners zeroed in on the formations.

Approaching the primary target, La Rochelle Laleu Airfield, the formation found the site obscured by heavy cloud cover. The lead command pilot, Captain Heber II. Thompson, ordered the bombers to head for the secondary target, Châteaubernard Airfield. Second Lieutenant Chase always tried to exude coolness, but this was only his second time in combat. His voice quavered when he switched on the intercom as the formation neared the target. He ordered the bombardier, Flight Officer Edward George, to "take her in" for the target run. George's task was to fix his Norden bombsight on the airstrip twenty thousand feet below, and drop some eight thousand pounds of bombs. Every other bomber pilot in the dense stack did the same. Far beneath them the Gironde River looked like a twisted silvery path in the snow, a trail leading the bombers straight to their targets.

Arthur's heart started to race, his breath quickening in his oxygen mask. He checked the belts on his .50-caliber and fired a quick burst into the gap between *Harmful Lil Armful* and the bomber on its left to make sure the weapon would not jam. The other machine gunners on each bomber did the same. They all knew what was coming—clumps of black smoke swirled beneath the formation. The 88s were almost in range. The Luftwaffe's Me 109s and Focke-Wulfs were not far behind.

Again, Arthur thought "shit luck" to be flying out on December 31 instead of getting ready to toss back a few beers and know he would actually see the dawn of the New Year.

Within minutes, flak erupted everywhere in blinding bursts,

pilots straining to hold their rocking bombers steady. Metal shards hissed in all directions around *Harmful Lil Armful*. Arthur instinctively ducked as shrapnel smacked into the thick laminated glass-and-plastic canopy of his top-turret gun. The metal did not penetrate this time, but if a shell burst closer, he was a dead man.

Pushing down the thought, he scanned in every direction. As several grayish-brown specks appeared in the distance and grew bigger fast, he plugged the jack of the small microphone fastened to his flight suit's collar into the intercom box just below the Plexiglas bubble and clicked it on. He shouted, "Bandits—three o'clock!"

All anxiety drained from Arthur as his reflexes and training took over. From the hundreds of Luftwaffe fighter planes converging from every direction, he spotted an Me 109 knifing through the blur of dogfights. He had immediately identified one of the Luftwaffe "killers"—pilots selected for both their marksmanship and nerve to head straight for the bombers. Training his sight on the 109, he poured a long burst at the German's engine and the cockpit.

As his .50-caliber Browning roared to life, Arthur was already braced for the machine gun's tremendous kick and noise in the turret. The longer he fired, the more smoke would pool at the top of the turret and cloud his vision, so he had to take brief breaks to try to disperse the cloud with a gloved hand.

As the Messerschmitt peeled away, Arthur kept firing—another Me 109's silhouette rose from behind the B-24's tail with its machine guns flaring. The German pilot darted off to the left of the bomber and then angled in at the bomber's cockpit. Arthur swiveled his turret and raked one of the fighter's wings. The Me 109 burst into flames and spun down. In an instant the plane exploded. Only falling bits of metal and smoke remained—no sign of the pilot or a parachute.

Arthur felt nothing; he just kept firing in all directions at swooping fighters. *Harmful Lil Armful*'s nine other .50-caliber Browning M2 machine guns chattered away at Me 109s and Focke-Wulfs.

Arthur winced as incoming 88 shells detonated faster and faster above and around the B-24. He tried to ignore the increasing slaps of shrapnel against his turret's canopy. He continued to fire bursts at fighters he could barely see through the smoke and flak. If his turret took a direct hit from an 88 high-explosive shell, the Plexiglas, his head, and upper torso would disintegrate. This was the nightmare that top ball-turret gunners called the "Headless Horseman."

As Arthur fed one belt after another into his Browning, Flight Officer George strained at his throttle to hold the plane level, trained never to break formation unless the bomber was hit and going down. In the second element, beneath Arthur's plane, the lead B-24, commanded by Lieutenant M. R. Jordan, took a direct hit from flak and exploded, virtually disintegrating in one bright flash. No one had time to jump.

Suddenly another flash, to *Harmful Lil Armful*'s starboard side, blinded Arthur for a few moments. As he shook his head hard to try to clear the yellowish-orange haze from his eyes, a sound like hailstones slamming against a car's metal roof echoed throughout the plane. Shrapnel ripped through the fuselage. The impact of the 88 shell's detonation violently shook the starboard wing, and just as Arthur had feared when he had inspected the damaged number three engine, the wallop proved too much for it. In the cockpit, the bomber's oil-pressure warning light flickered on the control panel and blinked steadily. The number three engine was sputtering. As Arthur had told Chase and Thomas, *Harmful Lil Armful* never should have taken off that day.

Arthur heard the straining engine and muttered, "Son of a bitch—I warned him . . ." He swiveled his turret to open up on another Me 109 pouring machine-gun rounds at the bomber.

Flight Officer George guided the plane in on three engines and alerted the pilots and crew that he was opening the bomb-bay doors. Arthur had to stop firing immediately because the bomb-bay hatch was directly below his turret. If his hot empty shell casings dropped into the stacked five-hundred-pound bombs beneath the hatch, *Harmful Lil Armful* would disintegrate. As he sweated it out, George dropped the payload on the target and returned control back to Chase and Thomas. Arthur opened up again on the German fighters.

Thirty seconds later near-blinding yellow explosions ignited the target, Châteaubernard Airfield, far beneath the formation. Chase held the bomber steady in the formation as the B-24s made a slow, wide turn and set course back to England. The Germans promised to make every mile back a nightmare. Arthur just hoped they made it.

He and his fellow gunners continued to unleash withering blasts at the fighters swarming all through the formation. Volleys ripped into *Harmful Lil Armful* as flak shook the bomber with teeth-rattling thuds. Razor-sharp bits of shrapnel tore through the fuselage and hissed through the open ports of the waist gunners. Several shards ripped through McNamara's thick leather flight jacket, slicing through flesh and bone along his rib cage and opening his abdomen. Across the intercom, he groaned, "I'm hit . . ."

Arthur heard Dunham, the other waist gunner, shout to McNamara, "Are you okay?"

"Don't worry about me," McNamara grunted, as he kept firing.

In the top turret, Arthur grimaced, hoping that McNamara was not hurt badly, and kept on firing his Browning at the seemingly endless swarm of fighters dogging the B-24 and separating it from the formation like a hobbled animal from the herd.

The plane lumbered along for an hour and a half. Then a sudden jolt nearly pulled her out of the formation. Arthur knew instinctively that this jolt was different, the harsh crash of an 88's direct hit. The number three engine stalled and sputtered for an instant. As oil poured from the casing, small flashes flared across the slowing propeller. Flames engulfed the engine within seconds. Moments later, another engine, number four, began to fail as the manifold oil pressure plunged, and its propeller slowed and then stopped. Arthur was gripped by nausea for a moment, and then rage. He wanted to shout: *You stupid son of a bitch, Chase!*

It did not matter now. Arthur had to keep his head.

Chase's voice crackled across the intercom: "Number three's out. We'll try to hold the plane in formation and make an emergency landing once we cross the English Channel." Every crewman heard the tremor in their pilot's voice, his words raspy, even his rapid breathing audible, not a comforting sound.

Within a minute or two, thick, acrid smoke from the engine billowed into the cabin. Chase and Thomas started coughing and were nearly blinded. Flames immersed the right wing. The bomber shuddered, stalled again, and, slowly, fell out of and behind the formation. *Harmful Lil Armful* was losing altitude and becoming vulnerable to fighters from beneath as the distance between her and the third element steadily increased.

Chase realized that the plane was finished. "Abandon ship!" he croaked across the intercom of the smoke-clotted bomber. There was no mistaking the terror in his voice now.

Two Me 109s appeared above the bomber, dove past her, and climbed back up to make a pass at the plane's underside with machine-gun blasts, rounds shearing through the plane's thin skin with a sound like scissors tearing at curtains. Bullets clanged against the bomber's aluminum-and-steel ribs with deafening clangs. Aware of sudden movement beneath his turret, he looked down to find Chase, Thomas, and the radio operator, Defranze, staggering through the shaking plane to the sole escape exit, in the tail.

"Where are you going?" Arthur shouted.

A few moments later they leaped into the frigid sky, followed by the bombardier and tail gunner, Arthur spying their chutes amid orange bursts of flak. The B-24, with no one in the cockpit and just two engines functioning, jerked every which way as its nose turned downward. At that moment, Arthur would not have cared if an 88 burst ripped apart Chase's and Thomas's chutes—any pilots who jumped before their crew deserved the worst. If he got out, Arthur vowed to confront both men on the ground, insubordination be damned. They were cowards, not worthy of leading a crew.

In the third element's number three slot closest to *Harmful Lil Armful*, B-24 pilot Lieutenant A. L. Northrup, wrote in his postmission report that he could only watch helplessly as "[Chase] kept straggling back out of formation. His #3 engine was seen to be smoking, probably from a flak hit, and two Me 109's were seen to be making determined attacks from below."

Gefreiter (corporal) Siegfried Schulmeyer, one of the two Me 109 pilots, would be credited with downing the B-24.

According to Northrup, crewmen in other B-24s within view of *Harmful Lil Armful* "report[ed] seeing [her] go into a steep dive, then climb, stall and then dive. Several (4–9) chutes were observed when last seen."

Arthur unstrapped himself, grabbed his chute, and slid from the bullet- and shrapnel-pocked turret into the cabin.

He crawled through the black smoke toward the tail, still seething that the two pilots "hit the silk" before anyone else. He shoved aside his anger and kept crawling toward the tail. He felt like he was moving as fast as he could, but had barely reached the halfway point when the heat in front of him increased.

He shouted as loudly as he could, "Is anyone still here?"

Through the smoke and noise came McNamara's voice, faint, nearly a groan:

"Help! Help!"

Arthur crept along the catwalk, blinded by smoke as he felt the steel-ribbed walls of the fuselage. The heat burned him right through his leather gloves. As he reached the waist-gun port, McNamara moaned.

Still strapped behind his Browning, bleeding from the shrapnel that had ripped into his stomach, he was completely entangled in wires.

Arthur tore at the snarled wires, which sliced through his gloves and slashed his fingers. He kept pulling, but could not pry them off.

Above the thunderous vibrations of the plunging bomber, McNamara screamed, "Get outta here, kid! I'm done for!"

"No way!" Arthur yelled back, straining to free him.

McNamara cried, "You gotta get outta here, Arthur!"

Arthur calculated that the B-24 had descended to about twenty thousand feet. Once her wings buckled and folded upward and her nose turned straight down, she would plummet the rest of the way, too fast to attempt a jump from the bomb bay.

For a moment, through a gap in the smoke, the two men's eyes met. With his one free hand, McNamara pulled Arthur's hands away from the wires. He nodded at Arthur, who could feel the rosary beads entwined around McNamara's fingers. "Make sure Dunham got out," McNamara rasped. "The kid panics sometimes . . ."

Fighting back tears, Arthur turned and crawled back the way he had come.

The bomb bay offered his only hope to escape burning to death. As he reached the opening, he was met by a blast of freezing air. George must have opened the doors when Chase had ordered them to abandon ship. The other waist gunner, Dunham, was perched at the bomb bay and clutching a railing at the open doors' frame.

"Let's go!" yelled Arthur.

Dunham did not stir. Arthur lunged at him and cried, "Go!"

Dunham stepped aside and shoved him away. As Arthur stumbled to his knees, Dunham tried to push past him toward the waist-gun port where McNamara was trapped. Arthur grabbed one of Dunham's ankles and held on.

The plane shuddered again, and her nose turned sharply downward, both men sliding closer to the gaping bomb bay.

Arthur snatched at Dunham's parachute harness to haul the man with him through the opening. At the same instant Dunham unclipped his harness buckle, and it slipped from Arthur's hand. Dunham's parachute dropped to the floor. Arthur grabbed one of Dunham's ankles again, and Dunham kicked at him with the other foot, loosening Arthur's grip. Arthur lunged at Dunham's ankle again, but suddenly Dunham kicked him out of the plane.

As he fell backward, Arthur stared back up for a fleeting moment at Dunham, who was holding fast to a strut near the bomb bay and looking back at him. Then Dunham vanished back inside the plane. The sight would haunt Arthur's dreams for the rest of his life.[3]

CHAPTER 3

HIT THE SILK!

After counting to ten, Arthur, surprised by how quickly the distance was increasing between him and the plane, "hit the silk"—pulling his rip cord. The chute jerked out of its pack and snapped him upward for a few seconds. A tight pull and then pressure against his armpits and thighs almost took his breath away. If he had counted too fast, he might not have put enough distance between himself and the blazing B-24. His chute billowed fully open, and he hovered for several seconds. Then, as his slow descent into Occupied France began, relief flickered through him. A lot of airmen's chutes failed to deploy. That relief vanished just as fast with the realization that the cumbersome chute responded poorly, if at all, to a jumper's tugs on the lines.

He knew that maybe three other men—Chase, Thomas, and Defranze—had gotten out of *Harmful Lil Armful* and were drifting down in the afternoon sky among dozens of other chutes from doomed bombers and fighters. A hellish but spellbinding and surreal scene unfurled around him, a savage tapestry of Allied and German planes splintering into pieces in midair, plunging toward the snow-shrouded French woods and countryside, the dark smudges and orange explosions of flak everywhere. He suddenly noticed that his gloves were scorched, with dark red stains on the discolored leather. The spots were blood—he didn't know if they belonged to him or to McNamara.

Though terrified as he descended, Arthur thought about his parents, Seymour, and Esther. As he floated ever downward, his thoughts raced back to what lay below him. Would the wind carry him into trees where the Germans would find him dangling in his harness and shoot him on sight? Even if they took him prisoner, the Gestapo executed many Jewish airmen on sight. Sometimes, if regular German Army troops were the first on the scene, they treated Jewish Allied airmen and soldiers according to the Geneva Conventions and took them to standard POW camps. Other times, however, soldiers treated them no better than the Gestapo or the SS did.

None of that would matter if he landed awkwardly against the trees and the impact snapped his neck or broke his back. Even worse, if he was injured on touchdown and lay there in the brush, he could freeze to death. His family and Esther would never know what had happened. He would literally vanish.

As the wind pulled him closer to a stand of pines, he decided that the trees were still a better option than touching down in an open field or too near a town. He steered toward them. Chase's words—"This is a milk run"—rushed back to him just seconds away from the trees. Then, with a harsh tug, his lines snagged on a limb, ending his jump. He hovered some thirty feet above the ground. Somewhere—perhaps close by—the Gestapo and Vichy police, who collaborated with the Nazis in the southern regions of France, certainly had seen the B-24 going down and were converging on the crash site and then fanning out in all directions to round up any survivors. He could only pray that if anyone found him, they would be French Resistance or even the German Army. Anything but the Gestapo or Vichy police.

In the distance, the shouts of German patrols echoed. Fighting panic that Germans would arrive to find him trapped in the trees, he fumbled for the Army-issue knife strapped to his right boot, yanked it from its sheath, and sawed away at the thick leather harness and the limp cords. The blade cut through the first strap. He slipped down just a few feet, still hanging from the chute for a moment. He hesitated before cutting the other strap and the cords, pondering how hard the fall would be. He took a deep breath and started to saw again. Suddenly he slid from the harness, plunged straight down, and slammed against a frozen patch of ground peeking through the snow. The jolt sent a searing pain through his lower back, and for an instant he thought he had been shot. Then, for another instant, he lay there afraid to move, praying that he had not shattered his spine.

He gingerly forced himself to his feet, and his legs nearly buckled as new waves of pain tore through his back. He somehow stifled a scream. As he had been trained to do, he climbed the tree to cut down his chute despite the endless waves of agony. Then he slid down the trunk, nearly passing out. He buried his chute and harness in a snowbank to conceal his landing and staggered deeper into the woods to hide. His uniform and boots were already sodden with nearly frozen water.

Shivering, Arthur dug a hole in the snow behind a tree-flanked road, his bare knuckles getting redder by the second through his shredded and bloodied gloves. He looked at his watch again. It was 3:30 p.m.

He had no idea where his crewmates were, no idea if they had made it. Still, he was trained not to search for them. His chief task was to evade capture on his own unless he happened upon one of the other survivors, and to seek help from locals, as risky as that was. He only knew the fates of McNamara and Dunham. Tears came again, and he brushed them away.

As he lay in the hole, his teeth chattering, pain punctuating even the slightest movement, he wondered if fate had put him on *Harmful*

Lil Armful or whether it was just bad luck. Maybe McNamara and Dunham were the luckier ones, he thought with anguish before chasing away that thought.

Arthur lost track of time, not certain if he passed out several times from the pain, only to awake wet and shivering in his hole. As gray twilight gave way to darkness and the temperature dipped to freezing, he was startled by the thrum of bombers' engines high above him and the all-too-familiar thumps of the 88s. The Brits' nighttime strikes were under way.

He rolled over to take a look at the night sky flaring with powerful German searchlights and arcing yellow trails from the muzzles of antiaircraft batteries. Gasping as hot spasms ignited throughout his lower back, he spotted smaller, multihued explosions, lots of them, beneath the torrents of flak. He was transfixed, not sure what they were. Then he suddenly remembered that it was New Year's Eve and that the more diminutive blasts must be fireworks set off by French families in stark defiance of the Nazi blackout. If the locals had the guts to set off banned incendiaries in plain view, maybe, he thought, they would have the same courage to help downed Allied airmen.

The sight of those fireworks unleashed an anguish he could not hold back. Checking his watch again, he realized that in less than six hours, it would be New Year's back in the Bronx, where Arthur's extended family and Esther had undoubtedly gathered. In Manhattan, no fireworks would burst above the skyline. No crowds of revelers would gather in Times Square or anywhere else; there would be few vehicles on the city streets. Few restaurants were open, as curfews were enforced by air wardens even though the prospect of German bombers appearing over New York was virtually nonexistent. The blackout restrictions' chief aim was to prevent German U-boats from honing in on American ships that would have been illuminated by the city's lights, making them easy targets for the submarines. On New Year's Eve of 1943, the entire Atlantic seaboard was darkened.

For the Meyerowitz family and the Loews, Esther's family, wartime strictures would mute the New Year's celebration, but without any idea of whether Arthur was on base, in the air, or even alive to see the first day of 1944, he knew that the family gathering would be somber. He was certain, though, that they were thinking of him and would certainly raise a toast to him at midnight and pray for his safe return. Arthur was alone.

He reached for the survival kit, called the "aids box," that every pilot and crewman was ordered to fasten to his belt if he had to parachute from a doomed plane. Taking inventory in the snow, he ate several of the chocolate bars in the kit as he checked the rest of the contents: Benzedrine tablets, an amphetamine to stay awake; matches; water-purification tablets; and white medical adhesive tape to bind any cuts or wounds. Arthur thought that a few Band-Aids would have worked better than the tape if he had been cut.

He could use the chewing gum and was glad to find a large compass that he fully intended to use, but did not think he would find the sewing kit in the bag much of a help. Examining the box further, he found a large red purse containing small, folded maps and several thousand French francs. He tucked the purse into one of his pockets and the Benzedrine, water-purification tablets, gum, and compass into another.[1]

Again, he exhorted himself to stay calm, to *think*. He had never been the sort of person who panicked, and prided himself on keeping a cool head no matter how much pressure he faced. Those were the attributes that had earned him a spot—all too briefly—as an aviation cadet. Now he had to rely on those traits more than he could ever have imagined.

CHAPTER 4

"WHAT'S IN HIS HAND?"

As Arthur pondered his next move in his snowy hiding place, Chase, Thomas, Peck, Farrell, and George had touched down the previous afternoon to find themselves in a nightmarish spot. The other survivors of *Harmful Lil Armful* had landed within a few hundred yards of each other near the town of Lesparre on December 31.

The Americans had removed themselves from their chutes and buried them in the snow, as Arthur had done. Gestapo and French Vichy police who had been alerted by the B-24's fiery crash had rushed to Lesparre and rounded them up. The Germans stripped the prisoners of their flight suits, gloves, caps, jackets, wool shirts and pants, and boots and bound their hands behind their backs. Then they shoved the Americans against the stark stone wall of the local Gestapo headquarters and forced them to sit on the icy ground.

An hour crawled by, then another. The men sat, shivering, with no idea if Arthur, McNamara, and Dunham had made it out and where they were now or if they were even alive. Farrell tried to say something to Chase. A German guard cursed and slammed his rifle butt against Farrell's skull with a sharp crack. "No talk!" the guard shouted.

Blood trickled from Farrell's hairline, the drops freezing before they even reached his eyebrows.

As the skies darkened, the Americans languished in the cold in just their T-shirts, skivvies, and socks, teeth chattering too much to even think of defying the sentry's order. Farrell was slumped against the wall, groaning intermittently as he lapsed in and out of consciousness.

Shortly after nightfall, an open-backed transport truck pulled up in front of the prisoners. An officer jumped from the passenger seat and strode over to them, his hobnailed boots crunching against the snow and ice.

Peck leaned toward George and whispered, "What's in his hand?"

The Gestapo officer snarled for silence. He loomed over the prisoners and halted directly in front of Chase. In passable English, the German asked if Chase was the pilot.

Chase nodded.

The German leaned down, opened a clenched, gloved fist, and waved two sets of charred dog tags in Chase's face. In the glint of the truck's headlights, Chase could make out the names—*S/Sgt. William B. Dunham* and *S/Sgt. Thomas M. McNamara.*

Chase said nothing to the officer and looked away. The crewmen against the wall all knew that their pilot and copilot had hit the silk first, and all likely blamed them for not sticking with the crippled B-24 until the crew had a chance to bail out. Some five miles away, Arthur, alone, injured, and unable to get McNamara's and Dunham's faces out of his mind, "was mad enough to kill Chase and Thomas if he ever got the chance."[1]

Over the next hour, the officer interrogated each cold and dazed prisoner except for the semiconscious Farrell. Finally, he gestured to several guards. They prodded the Americans to their feet, their cold limbs and muscles flaring with pain after hours on the ground. Then the Germans dragged them over to the truck and shoved them into the back for transport to a POW camp, Stalag Luft 1, Barth-Vogelsang, in Prussia. They huddled together under several foul-smelling, thread-bare woolen horse blankets that the guards tossed at them.

CHAPTER 5

MARCEL

Arthur crawled from his hiding spot shortly before dawn on New Year's Day 1944. He straightened for a few moments, testing his back. Still hurts like hell, he thought, but at least he could move. He began to brush snow and caked ice off his clothes. Suddenly he ducked as a truckload of prisoners guarded by the Gestapo clattered past him and down the road.

He could not see the faces of the slumped captives.

To get a better view of the landscape, he climbed a tree, no easy feat with his nearly frozen fingers and the searing stabs of pain throughout his back. He clutched a massive limb, his eyes watering from the effort and agony, and gauged the terrain—a small town (Lesparre) in one direction, open fields and scattered farmhouses in another. He decided quickly that the town was out of the question, likely teeming with Gestapo and French police.

From the direction of the farms, a dog was barking. Arthur's breath caught for a few seconds as he wondered if the Gestapo was prowling the area with a search dog. He listened more intently and decided that the bark did not sound like the deep-throated voice of a German shepherd or a Doberman, but could be a farm dog. He could not stay in the tree much longer and made a choice. If the dog did belong to a farmer, he thought, perhaps the farmer might be one of the locals who had set off New Year's Eve fireworks in defiance of the Nazis.

He struggled down from the limb and back to the ground, every movement excruciating. He crossed the narrow road as fast as his back would allow and gingerly lowered himself over a four-foot-high stone wall he could crouch behind to hide if necessary. He limped in the direction of the barking dog, toward a secluded farmhouse down the road and away from the town.

Nearing the squat house, whose whitewashed stone walls appeared cracked and ancient, he hunkered down behind dense brush and pondered his next move. He needed food and water as well as shelter, and would have to risk an approach to a local soon, even though he spoke no French.

Freezing and hungry, Arthur rested awhile as a wan sun broke across the snow-cloaked field. Then a woman emerged from the farmhouse. She was alone. Arthur decided he had no choice but to gamble.

He stepped out of the brush and warily approached her. A middle-aged woman in a kerchief, a thin winter coat, and old boots, she spotted Arthur and stiffened for a moment. Then, to his near shock and then relief, she smiled warmly and beckoned him. In broken but easily understandable English, she said, "Please, come in."

Arthur hesitated, then blurted out, "I'm an American—Jewish. I don't want to put you in danger . . ."

He unzipped his flight jacket and pulled out his *chai*.

She smiled again, took his arm, and led him inside. "We will take care of you," she said.

For all Arthur knew, she would bring him inside and send someone to fetch the Gestapo right away. Still, he had no choice but to trust her and hope for the best.

She brought him into the kitchen, where her husband was sitting at a table sipping weak coffee. As soon as he saw Arthur's flight uniform, he smiled, stood, and clasped Arthur's hand. The farmer, also in broken English, told him he was welcome. Then he insisted that Arthur remove his uniform, dog tags, boots, and airman's watch. Arthur hesitated. Along with the small snapshot of Esther, which he would not hand over, the *chai* was his only vestige of home, and if the man intended to betray him, Arthur would just as soon hang on to his keepsake. The couple had already seen the necklace, so it wouldn't matter if the husband turned it in to the Gestapo or not.

The woman disappeared for a minute and returned with a sweater, patched work pants, and battered field boots. She placed them on a chair and nodded at Arthur.

Arthur hesitated again, still worried that the man planned to run to the Gestapo with items proving that a Jewish American airman was at the farmhouse.

The woman reached into a pantry drawer, rummaged around in it for a few moments, and removed a thin chain with a small medal attached. She walked over to Arthur and pressed it into his right palm. "It is a Saint Christopher medal, the patron saint of travelers," she said. "He will see you home safely."

Still, Arthur paused. He fingered the *chai* at first, and then clutched it, unable to let it go. Slowly, as her intense look reassured him, he loosened his grip. He unclasped the *chai*, handed it to her, and placed the Catholic medal around his neck. Then he removed a small leather pouch from an inside pocket of his flight jacket. The pouch contained the compass, a card inscribed with his name, rank, serial number, and rights as a POW, and several thousand Vichy francs. He removed five hundred francs, which downed airmen were supposed to dole out to anyone who helped them. He reached for her hand and placed the francs in it. At first she shook her head, but when Arthur insisted, she nodded and accepted the money, tucking it into the hip pocket of her drab woolen sweater.

She asked him, through her fractured English and through gestures, if he had any other forms of identification. He shook his head. Before leaving on a mission, all pilots and airmen were required to fill out tags with their name, rank, and unit, and leave their wallet, letters, any jewelry, and any personal belongings with a purser who placed each man's belongings in a small burlap bag, tied the tag to it, and handed each man a receipt.

After every bombing mission, many never returned to gather their items, which would be mailed home to families after the yellow Killed-in-Action telegrams arrived from Western Union.

As the woman discreetly left the kitchen for a few minutes, Arthur took the hint, undressed, and put on the farm clothes. The man put on a cap, scarf, and coat and said that he would return soon with a friend who could help the American.

After her husband vanished out the back door, the woman returned and assured Arthur that their friend was a leader of the local French Resistance. Arthur sagged into a chair while the woman broke two eggs into a cast-iron pan with sliced onions and tried to explain that she wished she could give him more, but they were subsisting on food rations, and the Germans had seized most of their crops and livestock.

As he gulped down water and then his eggs, the relief that he was warm and fed for the moment dissipated into fear again that the farmer might return with the Gestapo or the police, not with this mysterious man.

Arthur scanned the kitchen for any weapon he could grab if the Germans burst into the house, and found a cutting knife in a half-open drawer beneath the tabletop. He quickly removed it and slid it beneath the napkin the woman had given him.

She asked Arthur if he would like to lie down and rest, but he shook his head. He remained at the kitchen table, staring at a small windup clock on the counter.

After a few of the longest hours of his life, Arthur was startled by the sudden growl of a motorcycle engine outside. As the engine slid into idle, the back door was flung open and the farmer rushed in with a second man. Arthur's fingers tightened around the concealed cutting knife.

Standing mere feet from him was a compact, dapper man with a thin, dark mustache and slicked-back black hair. He had the bearing of a military officer; the farmer might have betrayed Arthur to a Vichy policeman or a Gestapo collaborator.

The man looked directly at Arthur, and in accented but polished English assured the anxious American that he had no reason to be afraid. The Frenchman's eyes moved to the knife Arthur was gripping. Slowly, Arthur's fingers unclenched.

"I am Marcel," the man said in flawless English. "That is all you need to know for now. Come with me." Arthur would not learn Marcel's last name—Taillandier—for several weeks, and just how important a figure in the Resistance he was.

Arthur balked, still seated. It was full daylight now, and the roads would be filled with Germans and police.

Taillandier added, "It is not safe for you here. We must go at once."[1]

Instinctively, Arthur rose from his chair as quickly as he would have for an officer at Seething. The farmer's wife hugged him and kissed both his cheeks, and her husband shook Arthur's hand again.

Arthur followed Taillandier, who wore an elegantly cut black overcoat, white silk scarf, and black fedora. Outside, Taillandier suddenly stopped and turned to him with a speed that surprised him. In one hand the Frenchman held a gold cigarette lighter, and in the other, two *American* cigarettes. Arthur had not even seen Taillandier's arms or hands stir—he was that fast and agile.

Taillandier radiated a quiet menace. He was just the sort of man Arthur needed if he had any hope of seeing his family again.

CHAPTER 6

THE SHED IN THE WOODS

In his ill-fitting farm boots, Arthur slipped several times as he trailed Taillandier across a snowy back pasture toward an opening in a chest-high hedgerow. A motorcycle with a sidecar was parked near the gap.

Taillandier strode up to the motorcycle, a French Army Gnome-Rhône, and turned to Arthur. With a tight smile, Taillandier pointed at the sidecar. The Frenchman's narrowed eyes made him appear nothing less than sinister. The American had encountered countless tough guys from the Bronx to Seething, but something about Taillandier unnerved him. Beneath the beret the farmer's wife had given him, Arthur shivered and lowered his eyes for a moment. He nodded.

Taillandier nodded back, his smile vanishing as quickly as it had flared. He picked up a leather helmet and goggles from atop a canvas tarpaulin that shrouded the sidecar's opening. As he put them on with one hand, his other pulled the tarp halfway off the sidecar.

Arthur did not need to ask what Taillandier wanted. The airman immediately crawled into the opening and wedged himself into a near-fetal position on the floor beneath the sidecar's seat. A few seconds later he lay in darkness inside his musty cocoon while Taillandier fastened the tarp's snaps to bolts on the sidecar's exterior.

The Gnome's 500-cc engine sputtered and caught, the cylinders emitting a reddish light that had earned the motorcycle its nickname—"the glow worm." The motorcycle shot forward, pain slashing through Arthur's lower back as he bounced against the sidecar's shaking walls and floor and tried futilely to brace himself with his hands. Disoriented, fighting nausea, he was certain of only one thing: the motorcycle was racing along at high speed.

With no wristwatch, Arthur lost all sense of time. The unmistakable clank and vibration of steel treads from passing German tanks and armored personnel carriers eclipsed the roar of the Gnome's engine several times. Each time, Arthur prayed that the motorcycle would not be stopped and the sidecar searched by German soldiers or even worse, Gestapo.

Unable to tell how long he and Taillandier had been on the road, Arthur clutched the shaft of the small, padded-leather seat with one hand and braced himself with the other against the wall as the sidecar rocked and bounced. His ears throbbing from the engine's clamor, he could barely sense anything except pain and swelling and the dizzying twists and turns that flashed him back to the mechanized tiltboard tests in flight training.

The motorcycle swerved suddenly to the left and came to a sharp stop. Arthur's head slammed against the sidecar's steel wall. As a new flash of pain surged through him, light flooded the sidecar, blinding him for a few moments. He blinked and squinted blurrily up at Taillandier, who had removed the tarp halfway.

"Out," the Frenchman said calmly.

Grasping the sidecar wall, Arthur pulled himself out only to slip and crumple to the snow-slicked ground. His legs had gone numb in the cramped confines.

Taillandier helped the American to his feet and held his right arm as he steadied himself. They were standing by a dense hedgerow, the motorcycle concealed from the road by the brush.

Taillandier pointed across a long, open yard in the direction of another farmhouse, stone-walled and low-roofed like the one Arthur had approached earlier that day.

"Can you walk?" Taillandier asked.

Arthur nodded. At the distant door stoop, a man and a woman waved their hands frantically.

The man shouted, *"Vite! Vite!"* Quickly.

Down the road a rumble grew steadily louder and closer.

"Troop carriers," Taillandier hissed.

His arm still locked around Arthur's, Taillandier dragged him to the farmhouse. They lurched into the house scant seconds before the first truck crammed with Wehrmacht—German Army—infantry rolled past and kept going, followed by at least ten more.

The farmer helped Arthur to a battered sofa and introduced himself as "Jean Barbot." As his wife brought Arthur and Taillandier a pitcher of water, a small wedge of cheese, a few bread crusts, and a cold compress for Arthur to press against the "goose egg" that had arisen on his head when it struck the sidecar wall, Taillandier snapped off several rapid bursts of French that sounded like orders.

Barbot nodded deferentially.

Turning to the American, Taillandier said, "I must leave immediately, but will return for you in several days after I've made arrangements. Monsieur and Madame Barbot will look after you."

<hr />

Over the next four days, the Barbots and their large family tended to Arthur. Food was in short supply because of Nazi rationing, but the

Barbots made sure that he received the same share as everyone else. As he had done for the couple at the first farmhouse, he gave Jean Barbot a few hundred francs.

The Barbot children smiled at Arthur or ignored him, seemingly accustomed to strangers suddenly showing up in their midst. Because no one in the family spoke much English, Arthur could do little except hide out in a ramshackle woodcutter's shed in the nearby woods. He understood that the Barbots could not risk the Nazis or the police discovering an American airman in the farmhouse. If he was captured in the woods, the family could deny any knowledge of a stranger in a woodland shed.

For Arthur, the wait for Taillandier's return proved to be composed of equal parts of boredom and fear. Shivering beneath several blankets that did little to ward off the winter gusts whistling through the shed's two broken windows, he tensed every time footsteps sounded in the snow and brush outside. Relief spread through him every time those footsteps turned out to belong to one of the Barbots, but he lay awake much of the nights listening for the heavy, hobnailed crunch of German or Vichy police boots.

Arthur had two visitors on his third day in the woods. Along with a tureen of hot soup and bread and a change of shirt, sweater, trousers, and socks, Jean Barbot showed up with a middle-aged woman and a pretty teenage girl. He introduced them as "Madame Michel and her daughter Christiane." The sight of the mother and daughter, who smiled shyly at him, reassured Arthur.

Arthur figured that the clothes meant he would be on the move again soon. In halting English, Madame Michel, whose careworn features still hinted at past beauty, explained to him that she was from the town of Lesparre and that he would be staying there with friends of hers and Taillandier. They were all members of the French Resistance.

As Arthur, sitting on the earth floor with his shrieking back against a wall, gulped down the soup and devoured the bread, he strained to follow her heavily accented English. When she leaned down and patted his shoulder, however, he smiled up at both the mother and the daughter.

Madame Michel said, "We will take care of you. Marcel will be here soon."[1]

While Arthur had guessed that Taillandier was an important figure, he did not know Taillandier was a key Resistance leader in the run-up to the looming Allied invasion of Fortress Europe. General Charles de Gaulle, leader of the Free French forces, in Great Britain, had issued a direct order to Taillandier not to risk his cover by aiding downed Allied airmen unless absolutely necessary. Even in that case, Taillandier was to hand them off to Resistance groups whose chief mission was to help Allied airmen escape the Nazis.

Alone most of the time for four pain-racked days and nights in the woods, Arthur sensed that his best chance to see his family and Esther again rested somehow with the enigmatic Taillandier.

⸻

As Arthur hid and waited for Taillandier's return in the first week of January 1944, uneasiness about her son filled the thoughts of Rose Meyerowitz. She wondered where he was, if he was safe, when the war might finally end and he could return home. Each week, she went to the movies with David, Seymour, and Esther, who worked during the week as a secretary, hoping for a fleeting glimpse of Arthur in the newsreel footage from the war fronts.

The last they had heard from him was a military postcard with a brief message that he was stationed "somewhere in England." The airmailed card had arrived in early December, nearly a month ago.

A brown car slid up to the curb directly beneath 1205 Findlay Avenue. An elderly man in a brown cap and a drab overcoat emerged from the vehicle, lugging a weather-beaten satchel with a strap. Rubbing frost from the living room windows, Rose saw him, dropped her cloth, and clutched the windowsill with both hands. The satchel and cap were those of a Western Union courier.

He dug into his bag, removed a yellow envelope, scanned it, and looked directly up at 1205 Findlay Avenue. Swooning for a moment, Rose blinked and steadied herself as the courier headed toward the building's front steps. Her heart throbbing, she walked to the door and waited as the footsteps on the staircase thudded louder and closer.

For a few seconds she tried to remember who else in the building had someone in uniform.

But her mind went numb.

"It's Arthur . . ." she murmured.

There were two firm raps on the door. She opened it to face the courier, whose rheumy eyes met hers beneath his snow-sodden cap. He handed her the damp envelope and averted his gaze, knowing all too well that the message was either an MIA (missing in action) or a KIA (killed in action) War Department telegram. "I'm sorry," he said, his shoulders slouching.

He wheeled around and headed back toward the stairs.

Rose remained in the doorway, her hands shaking. She labored to get her breath back. Then she closed the door, staggered over to her chair, and tumbled into it. She sat there for over an hour, fighting to summon the strength to open the envelope. Finally, she willed her fingers to move. She opened it slowly and began to read:

Casualty Message

MR & MRS DAVID MEYEROWITZ

1205 FINDLAY AVE NYC

THE SECRETARY OF WAR DESIRES ME TO EXPRESS HIS
DEEP REGRET THAT YOUR SON STAFF SERGEANT

ARTHUR S MEYEROWITZ HAS BEEN REPORTED MISSING
IN ACTION SINCE THIRTY ONE DECEMBER OVER FRANCE
PERIOD IF FURTHER DETAILS OR OTHER INFORMATION
ARE RECEIVED YOU WILL BE PROMPTLY NOTIFIED
OFFICE OF THE ADJUTANT GENERAL[2]

The words seemed to swirl in front of her, making her dizzy. There was not even an official's name at the bottom of the message.

Stifling a shriek, she quivered and cried quietly. If she dissolved emotionally, her husband and Seymour might do the same. Then, slowly, a glint of hope pierced her fear. How could she grieve when Arthur was still *missing*? The War Department had not sent a Killed-in-Action telegram, so there was no evidence, none whatsoever, that Staff Sergeant Arthur Meyerowitz was dead.

When David and Seymour returned late in the afternoon, Rose showed them the telegram. Father and son stared at the note for a minute before sobs began to rack Seymour and David tried to fight back his tears. They all knew that this moment might come, but had blocked it out as best they could.

Rose reminded them that Arthur was missing in action and that they still had to tell Esther. Planning to write a letter to the War Department the following day and every few weeks until she had an answer, Rose refused to give up hope.

That night, few words were said in the Meyerowitz home, everyone lost in their own reveries about Arthur, their own fears.

When David and Seymour trudged with bleary eyes to the kitchen table for breakfast the next morning, they were startled to find that Rose's striking coal-black hair had turned white. She had no intention of doing anything about it until Arthur came back. David had no choice but to go to work, but when Seymour balked at heading to school, Rose tersely told him to grab his book bag and report to class because there was no excuse for cutting class except illness or a death in the family. No one had died, she emphasized to her silently skeptical younger son. Seymour knew better than to voice his doubts. "I did it [prayed]," he says, "but I did not believe completely, did not accept internally that he would ever come home."[3]

CHAPTER 7

WAR IN THE SHADOWS

As Arthur continued to languish and wait in the woods near the Barbots' farm, Marcel Taillandier intended to comply with his orders from London. He was already making arrangements to entrust Arthur to the Brutus Network, a Resistance band whose chief mission was to spirit Allied pilots and crewmen out of Occupied France to safety in neutral Spain. Taillandier was the founder and leader of the shadowy and deadly Resistance group Morhange; his reason for choosing the name was unclear, but various connotations of *Morhange* mean "unconditional love" and "truth." Taillandier's specialties were intelligence, counterintelligence, ambush, sabotage, and ruthless assassination of Gestapo agents, collaborators, and agents of the German military intelligence agency known as the Abwehr ("defense"). Taillandier's trademark was cutting down enemies in broad daylight for maximum psychological effect. He had little time for Allied escapees even if he wanted to help them, and had done so only a few times for high-value pilots.

Still, Taillandier had noted that despite severe pain from a back injury and a pronounced limp, the American had not hesitated to cram himself into the sidecar and never once cried out as the motorcycle bounced down the road. By the time he left the airman with the Barbots, he realized there was nothing weak about the American. When he had reached for the napkin-covered knife at first sight of Taillandier, the Frenchman strained not to smile—the airman was a fighter.

Taillandier decided he would make sure that Sergeant Meyerowitz would be treated as a high-priority escapee, even if the Frenchman needed to stay involved a bit longer before Brutus orchestrated an escape plan. He had no intention of taking too many liberties with his orders from de Gaulle—at least not yet.

||||||||||||||||||||||||||||

Marcel Taillandier was born on March 25, 1911, in Condat-en-Combraille, in the central French province of Auvergne, the son of Jean-Baptiste and Marie (Debas) Taillandier. The family moved to the picturesque medieval village of Châtel-Guyon for three years and then to Châteaugay, a town founded by the Romans and surmounted by a fortress once inhabited by the Knights Templar. For an energetic boy like Taillandier, the rivers and ridges flanking the town offered boundless opportunities for adventure.

Taillandier grew up with his two sisters, Margaret and Mathilde, in a France reeling from the carnage of World War I. The region's male population was composed heavily of boys and old men. Most families in the region had lost men on the Western Front during World War One and harbored a deep hatred of the Germans.

Intelligent, athletic, and a natural leader among his classmates, Taillandier loved military history and was "attracted very young to the profession of arms."[1] In 1924, at the age of thirteen, he joined the Troupe Billom, a military-style club for schoolboys; he relished the group's calisthenics, discipline, marching, hiking, and bivouacs and looked up to the troop's instructors, former officers in the French Army. He especially loved working with military radios, excited to learn codes and to see the ways in which communications and intelligence played key roles both on and behind the front lines.

In 1928, Taillandier had a decision to make. A talented artist, as well as a top student in mathematics and science, he qualified for university study but leaned toward a military career. Knowing that the French Army offered bright young men a course of study in engineering that could provide a career path as an officer and later as a highly paid professional in civilian life, Taillandier made his choice. He enlisted in the 8th Engineers.

After sailing through basic training, he began his engineering studies at the garrison of Versailles, just outside Paris, specializing in radio communications and electronics. His deft drawing ability and his painstaking eye for detail on blueprints and schematic diagrams earned him the attention of his instructors. He had no idea how crucial his artistic skills would prove in the coming conflict.

Taillandier spent many of his off-duty hours wandering through the Louvre to study the paintings and drawings of masters from the Renaissance to the Impressionists and Modernists, from da Vinci to Chagall. He also loved to walk along the Left Bank to view and often admire the works of the artists clogging the walkways adjoining the Seine River. A dashing figure in his uniform, he evoked admiring looks from women of all ages.

Taillandier became a full-fledged engineer over the next several years, was promoted to chief warrant officer, and was assigned to the French Army's prestigious Counter-Espionage Unit, in the Department of War's Radio Service. Only the toughest and most capable engineers were chosen for the unit, for if war broke out, Taillandier and his unit would be deployed behind enemy lines to gather and relay intelligence on everything from mass troop and armor movements to the names of suspected spies and infiltrators.

In 1935, Paris offered vibrant distractions for a single young officer on the rise despite the ongoing hardships of the global Depression and the ominous rearming of Germany, especially since Hitler's blatant, belligerent disavowal of the Versailles Treaty in 1934. Paris teemed with musicians, artists, sculptors, writers, playwrights, poets, foreign journalists, and thrill-seeking expatriates from all over the world. On the surface, the city still throbbed with the pulse of the Roaring Twenties and the jazz age, men and women of all ages embracing a live-for-today philosophy and straining to push away the encroaching shadows of Nazi Germany, Fascist Italy and Spain, the Soviet Union, and Imperial Japan. Somehow, in some way, Europe would pull back from a second conflagration, millions believed. Hitler or Mussolini might posture and threaten, but they would back down on the brink of any repeat of World War I.

Taillandier and his friends immersed themselves in the city's nightlife and reveled in its jazz clubs, cafés, restaurants, and seemingly infinite parties. Many of France's military leaders swallowed whole the notion that not even Hitler craved another ruinous conflict with France and Great Britain.

War was likely the last thing on Taillandier's mind at the moment that he was introduced at a Christmas dinner party in 1935 to a beautiful young Parisienne named Simone Dupontheil and was immediately smitten. Never a man to hesitate and acutely aware that Simone had a veritable legion of suitors, the courtly, confident young warrant officer, *sous-officier*, proposed within a few weeks. To the surprise of no one who knew Taillandier, Simone said yes, and after a spring wedding in 1936, the couple settled in Paris, where he was stationed at the famed nineteenth-century fortress Mont-Valérian.

Even among the thousands of men in uniform in the French capital, the dashing, dark-eyed engineer, still clean-shaven and yet to grow his trademark pencil-thin mustache, stood out in his visored Foreign Legion–style *képi*, tan tunic with shoulder bars and insignia, and cavalry-style jodhpurs, or riding pants, tucked into knee-high, polished black boots. The covered holster on his right hip held a .32-caliber MAB-D semiautomatic pistol. If war did come, he would also carry a 7.65-mm MAS *modèle* 38 submachine gun.

Within a few years, Taillandier and Simone had two daughters, Monique and Christiane. Then their run of nearly five idyllic years and the lives of everyone in the nation were shattered with the Nazi invasion of Poland, on September 1, 1939.

France and Great Britain soon declared war on Hitler's Germany and Mussolini's Italy, and Taillandier was ready. As with most of his fellow officers, he remained confident in the state-of-the-art Maginot Line, a vast network of linked fortresses, tunnels, and bunkers that stretched along the entire border between France and Germany and ended where the dense, supposedly impenetrable Ardennes Forest began in northeastern France and stretched into Luxembourg and Belgium. Deployed behind the allegedly impregnable defenses were French aircraft, armored divisions, and artillery ready to blunt the Nazi onslaught. With the British Expeditionary Force (BEF) and the Royal Air Force (RAF) pouring into France, Taillandier did not envision any prospect that the Nazis could win.

What neither Taillandier nor his fellow officers could anticipate was the new form of warfare that Hitler's generals had devised. No one in the French and British high command was ready for the coming blitzkrieg—"lightning warfare," coordinated and rapid assaults by armor, mechanized infantry, aircraft, and artillery. The Allied strategy was mired in the past, a repeat of World War I's trench warfare—static defense lines along the Western Front. France and Britain were about to pay for that approach.

From September 1939 through April 1940, the armies stared each other down in a stalemate dubbed the "Phony War." The French and British expected that the Nazis would attempt to skirt the Maginot Line and flank it by striking through the Low Countries, the Netherlands and Belgium, to the north but above the forests, ridges, and hills of the Ardennes. The British Expeditionary Forces were dug in along the French–Belgian border, but only a few French and British divisions were emplaced along the Ardennes.

On May 10, 1940, the Germans unleashed Fall Gelb (Case Yellow), the expected strike through the Netherlands and Belgium. The French and British surged into Belgium to meet the Nazi onslaught. Awaiting his orders to the front, Taillandier was still stationed in Mont-Valérian, but now as a member of the army's top Special Services unit, Counterintelligence Section Five Office, monitoring both Allied and German radio transmissions crackling along the Maginot Line. Unexpectedly, flurries of messages started to come in from the lightly defended Ardennes sector.

For the next forty-eight hours, Taillandier had a front-row seat to a catastrophe unfolding hour by hour. He and his fellow operatives could not believe what they were hearing at first. German panzers, tank columns, were pouring out of Ardennes forests so thick that French and British reconnaissance planes had been unable to spot them through the tangled canopy of towering pine and fir trees over the previous weeks. No one had even considered sending foot patrols into the woods despite distant, muffled rumbles within the Ardennes for several weeks. According to German general Erich von Manstein, commander of the attack through the Ardennes, "through strenuous maneuvering and planning, the forest was selected as the primary route of mechanized forces of Nazi Germany . . . for the Invasion of France. The forest's great size could conceal the armored divisions, and because the French did not suspect such a risky [Nazi] move, they [the French commanders] did not consider a breakthrough there [the Ardennes]."[2]

Now the impossible erupted with every message streaming through the transmitter of Section Five. Taillandier and everyone else in the unit's air-raid bunker deep beneath Mont-Valérian's massive granite walls and floors knew that only two French divisions stood behind the

Meuse River and Manstein's tanks. If the panzers overran the defenders, the Germans would cut the Allied forces in half and trap hundreds of thousands of British and French troops between Manstein's armor and the German forces bearing down through Belgium.

Taillandier monitored radio traffic without sleep and for two days was heartened that the badly outnumbered French divisions in the Ardennes put up a savage fight, desperately trying to buy time for reinforcements to arrive. The Luftwaffe's brand of blitzkrieg destroyed hundreds of Allied fighters and bombers before they even got off the ground, and the Germans seized near-complete control of the skies as Stuka dive bombers and Junker Ju 88 high-altitude bombers tore up French and British airstrips from the Belgian border to fields just outside Paris. The bunker in which Taillandier agonized over the disheartening messages from every front shuddered from the wallops of heavy Luftwaffe bombs pounding airfields just a few miles away.

On May 12, Section Five fell silent for a long minute or two. Taillandier and the others were receiving the first communiqués the unit had been dreading. The 7th Panzer Division was crossing the Meuse in force and rolling into northern France. Leading the armored columns that plunged Section Five into momentary shock and despair was Major General Erwin Rommel, who would later command the Afrika Korps and earn military immortality as the "Desert Fox."

Taillandier quickly recovered his composure, readjusting his earphones and listening in to the messages coming in with heightened urgency. No matter what, he was certain that the fight was far from over and equally certain that Section Five would soon be ordered north to operate behind the German lines. He was wrong in both assumptions.

llllllllllllllllllllllll

On June 3, 1940, the drone of hundreds of Luftwaffe bombers reverberated above the spires and rooftops of Paris. Bombs poured down as the Nazis pounded the French capital for the first time. As explosions rocked Mont-Valérian, deafening vibrations tossed chairs, tables, wire-less radio sets, and the men of Section Five in all directions. Although Taillandier's first thought was to get Simone and the girls out of the city as soon as possible, he forced himself to tamp down his emotions and focus on his duty.

As the Luftwaffe pummeled Paris throughout the day and the air-raid sirens blared endlessly, grim news from the Northern Front filled Taillandier's headset. Operation Dynamo, the desperate effort to rescue Allied troops trapped on the beaches of Dunkirk, was over. The last boatloads of more than 100,000 French and 224,686 British Expeditionary Force (BEF) troops were on their way to England, miraculously evacuated by every available ship from battlewagons to fishing boats and even yachts in late May and early June. The Luft-waffe had turned the shoreline into a slaughter pit, but strangely, Hit-ler had held his panzers behind Dunkirk. Among the Frenchmen who had escaped to fight another day against the Führer was a tall, haughty colonel named Charles de Gaulle, who was determined to drive the Nazi invaders from France and restore the nation's shattered pride.

Taillandier told Simone to drive the following night with their daughters from Paris to Toulouse, some four hundred miles south, where the couple had family. Taillandier soon followed them, ordered to abandon Paris with Section Five and set up a new communications and listening post just outside Toulouse. The counterintelligence unit hastily loaded their equipment onto Chenillette Lorraine 1937L sup-ply carriers and piled themselves into Renault UE trucks for the retreat south. The convoy rattled toward Toulouse with headlights off at night to evade Luftwaffe sorties similar to those that had turned the roads to Dunkirk into a tangle of debris and dead or wounded soldiers, civilians, and animals. To Taillandier's relief, Simone and the children had made it to Toulouse safely.

On June 13, Hitler's legions marched triumphantly into Paris, their jackboots' rhythmic thumps echoing along the Champs-Élysées as

massed Parisians watched in silence and tears. Shame and rage seethed
jointly in many. The seeds of resistance were already stirring. With
several hundred thousand Frenchmen remaining under arms, Taillandier expected that a final, desperate battle for the rest of the nation
loomed. He relished the chance to fight until the end and knew that
many of his comrades embraced that same resolve.

Taillandier was now stationed with Section Five at the Château de
Brax, an abandoned thirteenth-century castle with jutting turrets
perched atop a thickly forested ridge some ten miles southwest of
Toulouse. The fortress offered a perfect spot for the powerful radio
transmitter that Taillandier helped install, the reception strong
enough to pick up Allied communications from London and intercept
Nazi messages anywhere in France.

At 1:35 a.m. on June 25, 1940, Taillandier felt as though someone
had landed a thunderous blow to his chest and stomach. For a few
moments, his vision seemed to swim. The official news that France
had just surrendered to Germany overwhelmed Taillandier and the
other counterintelligence operatives at the Château de Brax with feelings of fury, betrayal, and despair. All they could do for the moment
was to wait and wonder what would happen next, and as the next few
weeks passed, Taillandier resolved that no matter what, the war was
not over for him. He would never accept the surrender or forgive the
politicians and the military leaders whose cowardice had shamed
France.

For Taillandier, any French citizen who collaborated with the
Germans would be judged a traitor. He did not yet know how, but he
did know that he would never accept German rule or anyone who did.
If not for his wife and children and his determination to protect them,
Taillandier might have envied his countrymen who had escaped
Dunkirk and would keep fighting under the command of the recently
promoted General Charles de Gaulle, now commander of the Free
French forces in Britain.

The effects of the Franco-German Armistice of June 22, 1940, washed over Taillandier and the rest of the nation in the following weeks. The pact divided France into two "zones": the German military would fully occupy the nation's north and west, but not central and southern France, including Toulouse. Instead, Vichy France, as the zone was named for the town selected as the capital, would be governed by French officials and military working with the Nazis. On the surface, Vichy France retained a level of self-government; however, the Nazis would pull the proverbial strings, especially with the ominous presence of Gestapo, Abwehr (counterintelligence), and a horde of spies and collaborators salted throughout the zone. The division of France into two sectors made sense for the German military, which was marshaling every possible resource for the unfolding Battle of Britain and for the eventual Operation Barbarossa, the ill-advised invasion of Stalin's Soviet Union.

Infuriated by the very idea of Vichy France, Taillandier did not yet know that he had caught the attention of Colonel Paul Paillole, a highly placed French counterintelligence commander who saw a chance to hit back at the Germans under the cloak of "cooperation" with the new order. Paillole was impressed by Taillandier's prowess at interception of German communications, his skill having earned him a reputation as a "pianist," the highest compliment a radio engineer could garner in the intelligence service. Meanwhile, Taillandier was still wearing the uniform of the French Army, expecting any day to be told that his unit had been disbanded and pondering how he could still fight for France.

Taillandier soon learned that Article IV of the armistice decreed that a French force dubbed l'Armée de l'Armistice would be installed by the Nazis in the unoccupied zone and in French colonies in North Africa and elsewhere. According to the treaty, "the function of these forces was to keep internal order and to defend French territories from any Allied assault while remaining, in theory at least, under the overall

direction of the German armed forces." Under no circumstance would
Taillandier take up arms against the Allies and fight for the Nazis. He
prepared to resign from the army.

There was just one problem: both the new Vichy government
and the Nazi victors ordered fifty thousand French soldiers to remain
in uniform until sufficient volunteers came forward to fulfill the
quotas for the Vichy Metropolitan Army and the paramilitary Gendarmerie were filled. Taillandier received orders to remain at his post
at the Château de Brax.

Chafing at the directive but uncertain of his next move, Taillandier was summoned sometime in early summer 1940 to Vichy to meet
with Colonel Paillole. As with everyone in Section Five, Taillandier
knew that Paillole was a rising star in the army's counterespionage
unit, or secret service, the Fifth Bureau, to which Taillandier's unit
was attached. The thirty-six-year-old Paillole, whose father had died
in action in World War I, loathed the Germans with an almost patho-
logical intensity; he also despised the British and derided de Gaulle as
an opportunist. Paillole confided to trusted friends that "although
Germany was 'enemy number one,' Britain was 'enemy number two.'"[3]
In France, he was hardly alone in his dislike of the British. Many
French officers believed that the British had fallen back to Dunkirk
too fast, denying France an opportunity to regroup and possibly stop
the Nazi advance. The British countered that it had been the Maginot
Line that had collapsed, not the British Expeditionary Force.

In a dreary concrete office building converted into a headquarters
of sorts for the Vichy version of the secret services, Taillandier was
escorted into a small, windowless office where a man with short, neatly
cropped black hair and penetrating brown eyes sat behind a steel desk-
top crowded with tidy stacks of documents, folders, and photographs.
Colonel Paillole, puffing on a cigarette and dressed in a dark blue
tunic, a white shirt, and a black tie, did not rise to greet him. He ges-

tured for Taillandier to take a seat in one of the two folding chairs in front of the desk.

On the drive to Vichy, Taillandier had grappled with the best, most respectful way to decline any order by Paillole that he join the new clandestine unit. Although uncomfortable as the colonel scrutinized him through swirls of smoke, Taillandier met the man's gaze.

Paillole was immediately impressed by the twenty-nine-year-old Taillandier's "clear eyes [and] his bright demeanor . . . his thinking."[4] Paillole also realized suddenly that he had met the man before—at the town of Montrichard during the retreat from Paris. In his memoir, Paillole recalled: "We reached Montrichard through some smaller and empty roads. Garnier [one of Paillole's operatives] had set up his files and unpacked the intelligence archives in a requisitioned building. The phone operators tried to reopen the lines and a young warrant officer set up a field telephone in the office. I noticed how exceptionally smart and well prepared that man was. His name was Marcel Taillandier and later, in 1943, he was to set up and lead the *Morhange* Resistance group."[5]

The initial reports that the colonel had received about the younger man appeared accurate: Taillandier possessed innate nerve. Two questions Paillole needed answered were whether the "pianist's" steely demeanor would hold up during dangerous, spur-of-the-moment covert missions and whether he would hesitate to kill a man—or a woman—given the operations Paillole had in mind.

Before the colonel even got to those questions, he had to gauge the depths of Taillandier's patriotism. Paillole himself planned to operate in a way that would reassure Vichy officials of his loyalty to the fledgling regime; at the same time, he intended to hamper the Nazis in every way possible without arousing suspicion. His approach would lead many historians to brand him as a collaborator, others to revere him as a friend of the Resistance, and others, more accurately, to view him as something between a pragmatist and a patriot. He espoused the view that "the work of [his] services was to defend [Vichy] sovereignty and to prevent unauthorized individual acts of collaboration [with the Nazis] on the part of ordinary French citizens."[6] Playing his dual roles deftly, Paillole would be tapped by Vichy to command the government's top counterespionage body, the Service de la Sécurité Militaire.

In Taillandier, Paillole hoped to find a man who, wearing the Vichy Army uniform, could use his position and his wits to root out collaborators and Nazi spies. As the colonel hurled rapid-fire questions designed to elicit information and test Taillandier's ability to "think on his feet," Taillandier sagely realized that blunt answers were his best approach because the intimidating intelligence professional would see through any attempt to mask his genuine beliefs. He did not hold back expressing his hatred of the Nazis, his desire to find a way to fight them, and his contempt for the puppet government that Paillole now served.

The colonel did not change expression when Taillandier affirmed his intent to help the Allies—including the English—in every way he could. Most importantly, he confirmed a key point that Paillole's inquiries had suggested: Taillandier was willing to sacrifice his life without hesitation for a free France.

Paillole, who had wanted to be a field officer but whose superiors judged his photographic memory, icy demeanor, and ruthlessness as the ideal traits for intelligence and espionage, now revealed what he wanted from Taillandier. The colonel wanted to maintain a veneer of collaboration with the Germans to prevent occupation of the Vichy zone; however, he wanted to use handpicked clandestine operatives in the Vichy military, police, prisons, courts, and government to arrest or sometimes "eliminate" German agents and French collaborators. That was why, he told Taillandier, he needed men willing "to hide in plain sight," in Vichy uniforms, and ferret out spies and traitors.[7]

Taillandier agreed to take on the mission, but insisted on one condition. Refusing to perform any duties that could aid the Nazis or Vichy collaborators in any way, he would only take on a role that would secretly undermine the Germans and traitors.

Paillole suppressed a smile at the warrant officer's courage in the presence of France's "chief spymaster." He nodded.

As Taillandier rose from the chair and saluted, everything changed for him. Pierre Saint-Laurens writes, "So began his second life in Toulouse, his war in the shadows."[8]

CHAPTER 8

||||||||||||||||||||||||||||||||||||||||

"CRAZY-MAD"

On January 1, 1944, Taillandier's delivery of Staff Sergeant Arthur Meyerowitz to the Barbots reflected the minute-to-minute danger of the Frenchman's "war in the shadows." Speeding off on the Gnome through the dissipating mist, Taillandier was plotting the last-minute details of an ambush set for later that afternoon. This planned strike against the Gestapo was one of the most audacious and important of his lethal career in the Resistance.

Taillandier's path from his first meeting with Colonel Paillole to his first glimpse of Arthur stretched nearly three and a half years. In that span, Taillandier had risen from a gifted radio "pianist" to one of France's most ruthless, brilliant, and feared Resistance leaders. All that the Germans and the Vichy police knew about him were his code name, "Ricardo"; his unit's name, Morhange; and the unit's lethal daring and efficiency, which prompted another Resistance leader, Pierre Saint-Laurens, to write: "*Morhange* group members were deemed to be 'crazy-mad' [slang meaning "afraid of nothing"]. It is to them we

assigned the most hazardous and dangerous missions, including infiltrating groups in collaboration and German institutions (Gestapo),
because the group did not hesitate."[1]

Taillandier remained in the uniform of a French Army warrant
officer in and around the Château de Brax from June 1940 until December 1940, when the Vichy government officially disbanded his unit;
during that time, he sized up and recruited fellow soldiers to help him
amass and hide stockpiles of small arms, explosives, and radio equipment for future use against the Nazis and their Vichy allies. Taillandier
and his men concealed the materials in the forests between the Château
de Brax and Toulouse. From the castle tower, he used the powerful
transmitter to monitor, or "strum," Nazi transmissions from the occupied city of Bordeaux, secretly passing on messages for Paillole to send
to de Gaulle and the Free French intelligence service in London. By
the end of 1940, de Gaulle and his staff were well aware that the warrant officer at the Château de Brax was a huge intelligence asset.

The dissolution of his unit, Section Five, in December 1940, freed
Taillandier to pursue more aggressive action against the Germans and
Vichy collaborators with the team he had assembled. All of them were
chafing to hit back at the Nazis and collaborators. To Taillandier's surprise, Section Five's radio transmitter and equipment were simply
abandoned at the Château de Brax. With several high-ranking Toulouse police officers and officials in his evolving network, Taillandier
felt comfortable enough to establish his fledgling operation at the
remote castle. If his planted operatives in the Vichy forces could not
persuade officers to ignore the Château de Brax, Taillandier would
simply kill them.

Colonel Paillole was ready to turn Taillandier loose on the Abwehr,
the Gestapo, and collaborators. In a January 1941 meeting with Captain d'Hoffelize, Paillole's head of counterintelligence in the Toulouse
Station, the two officers discussed undercover operations. Paillole said,
"I have more important news. I'm in contact with Taillandier again."

The captain responded, "He's [Taillandier] the man we need in my area. He wants to work with us [the Toulouse police and Vichy counterintelligence] on condition that he not be tied to a desk and can slug it out with the Krauts and their friends. Do you agree?"[2]

Paillole concurred. They were about to unleash a nightmare named Marcel Taillandier upon the Nazis and their Vichy minions.

Throughout 1941, Taillandier donned a suit and tie and toted a briefcase each weekday to his new "job" at a Toulouse purchasing bureau for engineering equipment—which included explosives. As he walked past brick buildings whose hue had earned the ancient city its nickname, *la ville rose*, the pink city, Toulousains saw just another young business-man making his way to work in the Vichy regime. He strode into his office, along the Garonne River and the Canal du Midi, and went to work for a Nazi operative named Otto Brandl. Brandl, duped by Paillole into thinking that Taillandier was a fervent collaborator, entrusted him with procuring building materials and explosives that were to be used for the construction of Hitler's Atlantic Wall, the Nazis' vast defensive complex to blunt any Allied invasion. Taillandier's mission for Paillole was to gather intelligence on the German defenses and to siphon off any and all materials that could be used in sabotage operations. At night, Taillandier stole up to the Château de Brax to monitor Vichy and German communications and report them to Paillole.

Taillandier's position with a Nazi company allowed him to travel with few restrictions between Vichy France and the Occupied Zone. This allowed him to cultivate contacts through whom he obtained front-wheel-drive Citroën sedans, gasoline, explosives, small arms, and forged documents. With wartime gas rationing in effect, few people could use their cars; however, Taillandier not only hoarded large amounts of gasoline, but also planned to use the black Citroëns for Resistance business.

Using his position, his charm, and his fluent German, Taillandier applied another of his talents to gain access to Atlantic Wall construction sites. Morhange member Pierre Saint-Laurens, in *Conte de faits, X15, Réseau Morhange*, writes: "In addition to his professional qualities and his extraordinary courage, Taillandier had a talent for drawing and such manual dexterity that it was possible for him to reproduce any official stamp [Vichy or Nazi] with paper, cork, rubber, and ink and to counterfeit the most complex documents."[3]

It was impossible to distinguish between Brandl's signature and Taillandier's forged version. That signature proved to be the entry point for Taillandier's boldest counterintelligence gambit yet.

In January 1942, he was dispatched to Solomiac, a town in the Midi-Pyrénées foothills, to set up future Resistance supply and escape routes across the mountains into Spain. He received a message there from two of his radio operatives, known as "strummers," that they had intercepted Nazi communications about a large, heavily guarded blockhouse outside Paris. Inside the bastion were blueprints for the intricate bunkers, tunnels, minefields, beach obstacles, garrisons, and gun emplacements for the entire Atlantic Wall. Taillandier did not hesitate for a moment.

He dyed his hair and eyebrows blond and put on a pair of rimless, nonprescription "Heinrich Himmler–style" glasses for a fake identification photo. Then he crafted false papers with both a Vichy and an official Nazi eagle-and-swastika seal, placed two large valises and a bulky briefcase in the trunk of his Citroën, and drove to Paris. At the Vichy-Occupied Zone border, Nazi guards scrutinized his papers, and he was quickly allowed to resume the drive to Paris. In the Tourville section of the city, he handed counterfeit identification cards to the two strummers and told them to head to Toulouse and lie low until he came back.

On the following day, Taillandier strode into the offices of the Todt Company, a contractor with access to both the blockhouse and Atlantic Wall construction site. Easily able to pass himself off as an engineer and collaborator with impeccable references, he was hired.

He worked as a supplies procurer for the company for several weeks, and when he was sent to the blockhouse for a three-day inventory of items that the architects and engineers had on hand or needed, he was given a tour of the building. As he was escorted past two massive, reinforced steel doors, his guide explained that all of the plans for the outfit's projects were stored on several tables inside. He led Taillandier to a small, windowless office near the doors.

Taillandier noticed over the next day or two that security outside the blockhouse and at the building's sole entry and exit was tight, with armored cars, soldiers, and attack dogs ringing the structure. Inside, however, proved another matter. Engineers, architects, and clerks moved around at will, unchallenged. When Taillandier saw that each night at twelve, the third shift replaced the second and the steel doors to the planning room were left open for the midnight-to-8 a.m. employees, he knew what his next move would be.

On his third and final night at the blockhouse, he waited in his office for the planning room to clear, put on his coat and hat, picked up his briefcase, and walked over to the steel doors. As he had hoped, they stood slightly ajar.

He pulled one open a little more, his heart pounding, and peered inside. It was empty. He slipped into the low-ceilinged room. His breath caught at the sight of three long tables flanking the concrete walls. Neatly stacked blueprints covered the tabletops. Without the slightest hesitation Taillandier quickly scooped up as many papers as he could and stuffed them into his briefcase. He left just enough piles on the table to try to buy a few minutes before anyone realized that a batch of blueprints was missing.

He hurried back to the doors, stopped, and listened. There were voices, but still down the hallway. Under no circumstances could he let himself be spotted exiting the room. He waited and froze as footsteps came closer. Holding his breath, he flattened himself against the wall next to one of the doors. As soon as the footsteps faded, he exhaled, slipped out the doors, and forced himself to walk at a normal pace to the exit, where two steel-helmeted sentries awaited him. His luck held. One of the Germans recognized him and waved him through without even asking for his identification card.

Taillandier walked quickly to his car, started it up, and drove to the final checkpoint at the gate. Again, he was not challenged. He drove down several streets and pulled into an alleyway where a man in a dark overcoat and low-slung fedora waited next to a small car, a Peugeot. Paillole's man was right on time, as planned. Taillandier climbed into the Peugeot, removed the rimless glasses, and drove to a safe house on the outskirts of the city.

Once inside, he washed out the blond dye and slicked his hair down. He burned the papers and identification card he had used to dupe the people at the Todt Company and get into the blockhouse, and drove out of Paris. At several checkpoints, German guards studied his new photo card and papers and opened the trunk of his car, where his two large suitcases were packed with clothes and hidden compartments containing the blueprints for the Atlantic Wall. Only once did a soldier order Taillandier from the car and make him open the suitcases. After a cursory glance at the meticulously folded shirts, pants, undergarments, and socks, the sentry grunted at Taillandier to close his luggage and get moving.

When Paillole's network smuggled the blueprints through Spain and to London, Taillandier's reputation soared not only in French but also in British intelligence circles. De Gaulle now viewed the former "pianist" as an indispensable asset behind Nazi lines. Taillandier's daring and opportunistic theft of the plans for the Atlantic Wall set off a frantic Nazi manhunt for a blond man with glasses. He was long gone, though, having pulled off one of the greatest counterintelligence coups of the war.

Some ten months after Taillandier's daring gambit, on November 11, 1942, the growl of German Panzer Divisions' tanks and self-propelled cannons, followed by endless convoys of troop carriers, echoed above the border of Vichy France and the Occupied Zone. The Allies had invaded North Africa, exposing southern France to future strikes by the Americans, the British, the Free French, and their comrades from other nations. Suspicious of the Vichy regime's loyalty to him in France and North Africa alike, Hitler had decided that all of France must now fall under occupation.

Colonel Paillole, tipped off that the Gestapo and Abwehr already suspected that his true allegiance lay with the Free French, fled to Spain and then to London, one step ahead of capture and execution by both the Germans and the Vichy government. In London and later from Algiers, he made certain that Marcel Taillandier would remain one of the most important leaders of the Resistance. Now, with the Gestapo and the German Army seizing Toulouse and southwest France, Taillandier embraced his opportunity to do what he had craved since the fall of France: to take the fight to the Nazis and collaborators in a ruthless, personal way.

Taillandier, now known to French, British, and American intelligence by his code name, "Ricardo," began his campaign in earnest against the Nazis and collaborators in and around Toulouse. From de Gaulle and Paillole, orders came for Ricardo and his twelve most trusted operatives—including a woman named Lilli Camboville—to infiltrate the Toulouse Gestapo, Abwehr, and police. The effort would uncover and execute collaborators, gather intelligence, conduct sabotage missions, and kill German operatives. Taillandier was also ordered to help other Resistance groups to set up escape routes for downed Allied airmen across the Pyrénées, but de Gaulle personally emphasized that Taillandier's primary duty was counterintelligence and guerrilla warfare. He was not to risk his life and mission to take part in an escape unless it was utterly necessary.

With Vichy now under Nazi rule, Otto Brandl summarily discharged Taillandier, but had no inkling that the former procurer was a member of the Resistance. German intercepts of transmissions from London sometimes turned up mentions of a "Ricardo." No one knew who he was or what he looked like.

Taillandier, in need of a job that would aid his Resistance activities, found a near-perfect position as the manager of the Frascati Bar and Café, which was nestled in the center of Toulouse. He turned the café into a meeting place where he and his team met and planned their operations. In a real-life scenario reminiscent of "Rick's Café" in the classic film *Casablanca*, the bistro was packed with local partisans, collaborators, Gestapo, and Vichy police. The Frascati also featured an upstairs brothel, with prostitutes who proved to be patriots by passing useful tidbits of information from Nazis and collaborators to Taillandier.

As part of an effort to blackmail Vichy officials into providing the names of collaborators and intelligence about upcoming Gestapo operations, members of Taillandier's unit frequently wriggled into a crawl space above the brothel. They snapped photos of prostitutes and clients in bed through strategically bored holes just large enough for a small camera lens. Taillandier never took the photos or blackmailed the subject himself, as keeping his identity secret from the police and the Gestapo was crucial. He knew how to use the incriminating images, though.

The Frascati was a place where ideologies blurred and backroom intelligence was swapped. Everyone had an agenda. The café was one of the few spots in Nazi-occupied Toulouse where the Germans and police fraternized with locals and looked the other way—something Taillandier knew and used to deadly advantage. By May 1943, he and his team had executed at least thirteen collaborators, the traitors often unmasked through information gleaned in the Frascati or between the bedsheets of the upstairs brothel.

The Toulouse Gestapo, determined to find and kill the Resistance members who were taking out valuable informers, had eyes and ears everywhere. Through informers and the torture of several people of

divided loyalties, the Germans came up with several last names—
Gardiol, Pointurier, and Candau—as likely candidates for the spate of
assassinations of collaborators in plain view on their doorsteps, in their
cars, or on the city streets.

That same month, Taillandier ordered the execution of a reviled
informer named Platt. Taillandier, wearing shades, a beret, and a
mask, with one of his operatives at the wheel of a nondescript Citroën,
knocked on Platt's front door on the afternoon of May 21, 1943. When
the traitor answered, Taillandier pulled a pistol from his overcoat
pocket and wordlessly fired two shots between his eyes. The traitor
was dead before he crumpled to the floor. The screech of the fleeing
sedan's tires and the screams of neighbors who had witnessed the
lightning-fast and merciless shooting were the trademarks of Ricardo's activities.

On June 24, 1943, Gardiol, Pointurier, and Candau all received
calls from a trusted friend to meet Ricardo at the Frascati. It was a trap
set by Gestapo Obersturmführer Müller. Awaiting the trio at the café
were Gestapo operatives who had been ordered not to seize the Frenchmen until a fourth man—the mysterious Ricardo—joined them.

Gardiol, Pointurier, and Candau walked into the characteristi-
cally crowded bar around noon, spotted Lilli Camboville alone at a
table, and joined her. A few minutes later, Taillandier entered, suddenly realized that there were even more Gestapo inside than usual,
and walked past his friends without looking at them. Because Taillandier was familiar to the Nazis as the bar's manager, they had no
reason to suspect that he was in fact Ricardo. Müller and his men paid
no attention as he walked to the back, climbed the staircase leading to
the brothel and the rooftop, and kept going. He climbed from the
attic annex onto the roof and made his way across several rooftops
until he came to a fire escape. There, he lowered himself to an alley
and vanished.

Müller and his men waited for several more minutes. When the three men and the woman at the table rose to leave, he and the Gestapo pounced. They arrested them and hustled them off to the city center, where a giant red-and-black swastika flag was draped above the Gestapo headquarters. Agents in black uniforms and skull-and-crossbones-adorned caps and others in dark suits and low-brimmed black fedoras bustled in and out of the entrance to the thirteenth-century bastion with its narrow-slit windows, parapets, and two steel front doors.

Müller and his agents had missed any connection between the Frascati's manager and the four people who had just been arrested. Frantic to extract Ricardo's identity from the prisoners, the Gestapo went to work immediately on the Frenchmen and Lilli, who was three months pregnant. According to Morhange member Pierre Saint-Laurens, who knew them all, Lilli was Taillandier's mistress, and the child was his.

Taillandier hid in a friend's attic annex, unable to flee the city because the Gestapo and the police were stopping, searching, and questioning anyone who even attempted to leave Toulouse by bus, train, or car. He could only agonize over the plight of his captured friends and hope that somehow they would not crack under torture.

For several days, the Gestapo beat the three men with fists and chains. They did not break, not even when the Nazis used pliers to tear off their fingernails and rip out their teeth. They were shocked with electrodes taped to their testicles, but still did not give up Ricardo.

Lilli's pregnancy ended with several thunderous punches and kicks to her abdomen. When she miscarried, the Gestapo simply tossed the lifeless fetus into a wastebasket. Then they stripped her naked, bound her hands, and hauled her to a bathtub filled with ice water. They blindfolded her and shoved her head beneath the water. After a few seconds, they yanked her head out. She gasped for breath. Again and again, the men shoved her head back into the frigid water and removed her only when she was an instant away from drowning. She revealed nothing about Taillandier and their unit.

Three days after the Frascati raid, Taillandier received word from one of the operatives who were staking out Gestapo headquarters for him. Just before dawn, the Gestapo dragged the four Resistance prisoners out of the fortress, threw two of them into the backseat of a waiting sedan and the other two into another, and drove them to the train station. As sunrise seeped across Toulouse and the city's ancient bricks emitted their famed roseate hue, Gardiol, Pointurier, Candau, and Lilli were thrown into a cattle car already crammed with men, women, and children. The train slowly pulled from the terminal, the engine's clamor not loud enough to muffle the sobs and screams from the windowless cattle car. Taillandier's friends were on their way to concentration camps, but his identity remained hidden from the Gestapo. Only Gardiol would ever see France again.

Taillandier returned to the Frascati after "falling ill" for a few weeks. He "resigned" as the café's manager, but the Gestapo did not yet know that he was the Resistance leader Ricardo. Musee departemental de la Resistance (Toulouse) director Guillaume Agullo says, "As far as I could find, Marcel never used again the Frascati the same way; it stopped becoming his everyday place, he had to be more prudent. . . . But he therefore continued to go there, more or less, depending on the periods. But from now on, the operational PC [headquarters] became the Chateau de Brax."

Taillandier's network had been dismantled, but Ricardo was far from finished. He began putting together a new network he would call Morhange, embarking on a personal reign of terror that would strike fear into the Gestapo, the police, and anyone who dared to cooperate with them. Pierre Saint-Laurens, in his history of Morhange and Taillandier, writes: "This fierce repression [the Frascati raid], far from damaging the morale of Taillandier, led him to decide to move to the attack. He gathered around him those who had escaped like him. He created *Morhange*."[4]

The Gestapo soon learned to its fear and fury that Ricardo was not only alive and well, but had reconstituted his hit squad. From August to September 1943, under direct orders from Paillole alternately in London and Algiers, Taillandier and his men kidnapped at least six Vichy intelligence agents who worked for the Gestapo, and brought them to the Château de Brax, where Taillandier still operated a powerful radio transmitter.

Taillandier and Morhange, unlike the Gestapo or the police, did not torture prisoners. Instead, they were subjected to rigorous verbal interrogations by former civil and military justices who had joined the Resistance. The interrogations were actually cross-examinations in which the prisoners were allowed to defend themselves, but Taillandier and his associates had compiled irrefutable proof that the accused had collaborated or worse with the enemy.

Pierre Saint-Laurens, one of Taillandier's operatives, writes that in the cavernous great hall of the château, the collaborators were "considered traitors to the nation, [and] were judged on the military tribunal code."[5]

As Taillandier watched all of the proceedings, the death penalty was handed down, but if the prisoners had provided confessions and information, they were assured that no retribution would be taken against their families. Taillandier gathered the information in folders and later transmitted the intelligence to a Free French transmitter in Barcelona, from where it would be sent to London or to Algiers.

The executioner was a strange young man known only as Pierre. Saint-Laurens writes: "Then came the gruesome part of the case, the 'funeral' of the castle. A gravedigger always prepared three graves in advance in case of need; they rarely remained long unoccupied. There is even an executioner, Pierre, aged less than 20 years, a disturbing character who takes pleasure in his duties and complains when there is no hurry to execute collaborators."[6]

Pierre's method of execution was to force the condemned man to kneel in front of his grave. He then pressed the tip of a revolver against the man's forehead and ordered him to keep his eyes open or he would make him die slowly. Sometimes, Pierre would hold the gun in place for several agonizing minutes, reveling in the sobs and quivers of the doomed prisoner. Always it ended the same way. A shot pealed above the grave, and the collaborator toppled backward into the hole.

On October 15, 1943, Taillandier struck again. He had received an order from London to eliminate Colonel Jean Sénac, a German plant in the former Vichy Intelligence Service. Stationed with the police now in Toulouse and working with local Gestapo chief Wilhelm Redzeck, Sénac infiltrated numerous Resistance units in southwest France, and his agents had set up many French men and women for ambush, arrest, torture, and execution by the Nazis.

Sénac, in a topcoat, scarf, and white fedora, emerged from Gestapo headquarters, adjacent to Toulouse's elegant and palatial Capitole, on the brisk fall morning of October 15 and walked down the steps. The Place du Capitole teemed with people headed to work and with Gestapo and police. Suddenly a black Citroën pulled up alongside Sénac. Two men sprang from the car, grabbed him, and flung him into the backseat. Then the car sped away.

That night, Sénac was tried at the Château de Brax and summarily executed by Pierre as Gestapo and police mounted a futile door-to-door search in Toulouse. Redzeck, enraged by the kidnapping of Sénac in broad daylight under the nose of the authorities, had no doubt that Ricardo was behind the operation and ordered the Gestapo to use all means necessary to identify and track down the elusive, enigmatic Frenchman. Taillandier had no intention of lying low in the wake of Sénac's "removal." From Paillole came another order, one that Taillandier knew would inflame the region, but one that he had long wanted to undertake. In September 1943, a British submarine had secretly picked up Free French intelligence agent and assassin Alphonse Alsfasser in Algiers. The sub had broken the surface several nights later in a remote inlet near Marseilles. Alsfasser rowed to shore in a rubber safety raft and was met by two men in dark berets and long black over-coats. One of the pair was Taillandier. Their mission was to bring the assassin to Toulouse and kill Toulouse police superintendant Barthe-let, a notorious collaborator and Nazi sympathizer who handed over hundreds of French patriots to the Gestapo.

For Taillandier, the directive was personal. Barthelet had been instrumental in setting up the Frascati raid that nearly nabbed Tail-landier himself and sent four of his most trusted and valuable opera-tives to concentration camps. As any good officer would do, he was preparing the operation's groundwork over several months after a communication from Paillole, who warned "my Toulouse comrade [Taillandier] against that police official and alerted the *Morhange* group to be very careful." Paillole described "the head of the Tou-louse police [as] a man whose brutally repressive policies against Resistance fighters . . . led us to put him on the list of dangerous indi-viduals deserving D measures."[7]

The *D* stood for death, and Taillandier was eager to carry out the order. Throughout the war, Resistance units all across France often received coded messages with simply a name and a *D*.

Taillandier immediately understood why Paillole had trusted Als-fasser to do the job: "Alphonse Alsfasser was a strong young man, a loner with intense patriotic feelings . . . and was a repentant gangster."[8] Like Taillandier, he would not hesitate to kill a man face-to-face.

For weeks, Taillandier and his Morhange operatives staked out Barthelet's every movement. He would leave his office in the city's Place Saint-Étienne near eight o'clock every night and drive to his house "at the crossroads of two streets far from the center of town." A police car always traveled ahead of him, and to his rear was a sedan with several Gestapo agents. They would remain at his house until he parked in the adjoining garage and entered his home from an entryway inside the garage. The three vehicles took the same route each evening "down deserted avenues, the Allées Verdier and the Place du Grand-Rond."[9]

The planned execution was brutally simple. When Barthelet and his escort reached the empty Place du Grand-Rond, Taillandier, Alsfasser, a third shooter, and a skilled Morhange driver would race up alongside the superintendent's car. Then Taillandier and Alsfasser would rake the official with submachine guns and speed off before the escorts could react.

At 7 p.m. on October 16, 1943, just one day after the kidnapping and execution of Sénac, Taillandier, Alsfasser, and two Morhange men parked a Peugeot 402 behind the soaring rose-hued, Romanesque expanse of Saint-Étienne Cathedral. Barthelet always turned down the narrow street behind the church on his way to the Place du Grand-Rond. Taillandier and the others waited.

To the gunmen's shock, Barthelet's car appeared on the road at 8:30 p.m.—alone. They let him pass and trailed him, all but the driver cradling Thompson .45 submachine guns delivered by Allied bombers to secluded drop zones in the countryside. The weapon's speed and killing power made it Taillandier's favorite.

Barthelet appeared oblivious to the car to his rear as he approached the Place du Grand-Rond. Still no escort, Marcel noticed. The police official slowed down, and as the Peugeot drew within a few feet of his rear bumper, Barthelet suddenly hit the gas and veered in the wrong direction down a tight one-way street.

The Morhange driver shot past the street and slammed on the brakes. As he threw the transmission into reverse, Taillandier, suspecting a trap, shouted at the driver not to follow Barthelet and drive away as fast as possible. In the backseat with Alsfasser, Taillandier turned and looked out the rear windshield for any Gestapo or police cars bearing down on them. To his relief, the street was empty. He "cancelled the operation until another date could be set when it would be carried out differently."[10]

Taillandier already had a backup plan prepared. Before Alsfasser's arrival, he noticed a small, vacant lot in front of the police chief's house.

Several thick bushes along the lot could easily hide two men. Taillandier also discerned an ideal parking spot some 360 yards from Barthelet's home and completely out of sight from both the home and from the route the official took every evening. He chose Saturday, October 23, for the hit.

At 7:45 p.m., Taillandier and Alsfasser stepped from the Peugeot's parking spot onto the nearly pitch-dark street and half walked, half ran to the bushes near the house. Their long, baggy overcoats concealed their Thompsons. Crouching in the thicket, they peered at the street.

Nearly thirty seemingly endless minutes dragged by. Finally, at 8:15, the sweep of headlights washed the street in front of them; the police car appeared first and stopped just past the house. As Barthelet turned into the garage, the Gestapo sedan pulled up in front of the short concrete driveway and waited.

Barthelet got out of his car, walked the few steps to the entrance, and waved at his escort. The two cars slipped down the street.

As Barthelet went back to his car, opened the driver's door, and removed his briefcase from the passenger seat, Taillandier and Alsfasser sprang from behind the bushes and ran across the street. Barthelet stared for a moment and tried to reach the door from the garage to the house. The two gunmen stopped a few feet from him and leveled their Thompsons. For several moments, they waited, letting Barthelet fully realize it was over for him, daring him to accept it like a man and face them or try to run and get shot in the back like a coward. Just a step from the door, he exhaled and did face them. They opened up with two long bursts, chunks of plaster and wood chips from the door flying in every direction. Bullets raked the traitor from head to toe, nearly cutting him in two.

Sprinting back to the Peugeot, they sped off into the night.

Paillole wrote: "The execution had a huge impact on the region. The authorities ordered a curfew from 9 p.m. to 5 a.m. The feeling that no one could hide from [Morhange's] revenge was now real to the top administrative echelon, including the police, the Abwehr, and the Gestapo leadership. London radio mentioned that execution as a warning to French collaborators that treason carried harsh consequences: the Morhange group was now wound up and ready to continue its retribution."[11]

Over the following weeks, the Gestapo, the Abwehr, and the police scoured Toulouse and the countryside for Ricardo and his operatives, rounding up hundreds of men and women whose neighbors suspected they might be involved with the Resistance, then beating and subjecting them to the same water torture that Lilli had endured. Most were innocent people who were victims of local grudges. No one provided information that led the Germans or the police any closer to unmasking Ricardo and his operatives.

Alsfasser was betrayed by an informer a few weeks later. On the evening of November 26–27, 1943, he left a farm with local Resistance fighters escorting him and several other men to a remote stretch of beach near Saint-Tropez, in southeastern France. There, he was supposed to board a submarine for the return trip to Algiers.

One of the Resistance members, sixteen-year-old Monique Giraud, would tell Paillole what happened on the dark shore: "At 11 p.m. our team, including the intended passengers of the submarine along with the mail carriers [couriers], went out into the night. Two columns of Resistance were on either side, about 40 yards away. That walk through the shadows and the outlines of other people was hallucinating. We stopped from time to time to listen to the faintest of sounds, then we would start walking again, hunkering over. Finally we reached the sea. We thought we were safe, when just 100 feet from the water we heard, 'Halt!' cried out in the silence mixed with the sound of waves. Shots rang out. That's when Alsfasser was killed."[12]

When London informed Taillandier of the grim news, he radioed a terse answer to Paillole and de Gaulle: "He [Alsfasser] will be avenged!"[13]

Over the next few months, Taillandier and Morhange eluded the Nazi curfew again and again to kidnap and execute collaborators. Taillandier received a tip in late December that the Toulouse Gestapo, so alarmed by Ricardo's success and correctly suspicious that his agents had infiltrated the police and the Gestapo, planned to send its most sensitive files for safekeeping to Nice. Five Gestapo cars were scheduled to make the run on the evening of January 1, 1944, under the command of one of Redzeck's top aides, Obersturmführer Messak. Afraid that a full-fledged convoy with troops and armored vehicles would draw too much attention, the Gestapo opted for a quick and hopefully inconspicuous dash from Toulouse.

Taillandier, whose reason for being in Lesparre was murky but certainly involved a Resistance matter, was not about to pass up such an opportunity. Eight hours or so after leaving Arthur Meyerowitz at the Barbots' farm and racing some three hundred kilometers back to Toulouse, he led twelve Morhange operatives in an ambush of the Gestapo contingent on the road between Toulouse and Carcassonne. In what became known as the "Courier de Nice Raid," he and his men executed five Gestapo agents and made off with a literal treasure trove of Nazi and police files with the names of enemy agents, double agents, and collaborators. For many, their death sentences were imminent from the moment that Morhange seized the documents.

Due in large measure to the savage success of Morhange, the region into which Arthur had parachuted from *Harmful Lil Armful* had never been more dangerous. His fate rested largely in the hands of Ricardo, the man whom the local Gestapo, Abwehr, and police wanted to unmask and kill more than any other Resistance leader in southwest France. Arthur actually knew the man's real first name, which was more than the Nazis and their collaborators did.

CHAPTER 9

||||||||||||||||||||||||||||||||||||||||||||||

AKA GEORGES LAMBERT

On the evening of Friday January 5, 1944, Dr. Pierre and Gisèle Chauvin anxiously awaited a "guest" in their Lesparre home. They knew only that he was an American airman whose aircraft had crashed in flames on the Médoc Peninsula a few miles north of the town on New Year's Eve. The Chauvins' home, tucked amid the medieval stone houses, stores, and cafés of Lesparre's main street, stood directly across from a small Gestapo headquarters; Gisèle, a chemist, ran a pharmacy on their house's first floor, with the family's quarters upstairs.

From their back window, which faced Gestapo headquarters, Pierre and Gisèle had watched in silent, helpless fury on January 1, 1944, as the Gestapo stripped five American airmen of all clothing except their undergarments, left them shivering in the snow against a wall across the narrow street for several hours, and finally carted them off in an open truck.

When a courier delivered the Chauvins a coded message from

"R"—Ricardo—that the pharmacy would receive a "delivery" on the afternoon of January 5, the Chauvins assumed that their guest was another survivor of the downed bomber. He was hardly the first such visitor. The family had hidden twelve to fifteen Allied pilots and airmen at various times for over a year, and the Chauvins not only fed and clothed the strangers, but also trained them in skills that could save their lives once they attempted to make the grueling, hazardous passage out of Nazi-occupied France to Spain. That Pierre and Gisèle did so literally in plain sight of the Nazis testified to their courage and their contempt for the Gestapo, the couple taking defiant pride in aiding Allied airmen right across the street from the Germans.

Some neighbors supported the Chauvins quietly; potential local collaborators who might have turned in the physician and the pharmacist did not dare to do so because they feared the Resistance—especially Morhange—more than the Nazis and the police.

In November 1943, as Arthur Meyerowitz completed his flight training and still thought he would be fighting in the Pacific theater, Pierre and Gisèle Chauvin were visited in Lesparre by the doctor's cousin Pierre Dupin. Dupin was a top operative of Réseau Brutus, which until December 1943 was led by André Boyer and operated in and around Bordeaux. Boyer had been arrested by the Gestapo that month and would die in confinement. Now, Dupin recruited patriotic men and women into Brutus throughout southwest France.

The Lesparre-Médoc region seethed with hatred for the Nazi occupation and for French collaborators, and Dupin knew that no one loathed the Germans and the traitors more than the Chauvins, especially Gisèle. At church one Sunday, she bit her lip as the parish priest launched into a sermon that tore not only at her faith, but also at her patriotism. As he half implored, half demanded that the locals accept the Nazi occupation and submit to the Germans' decrees and orders, she stood and shook her head. Then she stepped from the pew into the aisle, turned her back to the priest, and strode out of the church.

The surprised stares and frowns of several parishioners followed her; so, too, did suppressed smiles and almost imperceptible nods of approval from others.

Gisèle agreed to serve as a sector chief for the Brutus Network. Discovery by the Germans meant death, and with collaborators and the Gestapo everywhere, the slightest mistake or bit of bad luck would prove fatal, as it would for Boyer. Gisèle, however, loved her country fiercely and was determined to do anything that would help her own children grow up in a liberated France. Dr. Pierre Auriac, a key Brutus operative, lauded Gisèle as "dynamic, and [she] never hesitated to host and manage American airmen shot down over the Médoc on the escape route through Spain."[1]

As they always did, the Chauvins made preparations on January 5, 1944, for an Allied airman on the run. Earlier that day, Pierre took their young live-in maid, Simone Blanchard, back to her family's home on the pretext that her room needed to be cleaned out because it was suddenly rat-infested, yet again. Gisèle and Pierre always told the same story to their two older children, nine-year-old Jean-Claude and six-year-old Monique, warning them to stay away from the maid's quarters or risk being bitten by rats.

Gisèle and Pierre grew concerned around 8:30 p.m. when there was no sign of their guest and his escort. At nine, the German curfew took effect, and anyone on the street would be stopped and questioned; the airman had no identification papers and stood no chance if he was seized. Having put the children to bed and placed her infant, seven-month-old Patrick, in his crib in his parents' bedroom, Gisèle set the dinner table. Pierre appeared with two bottles of wine.

As he placed the wine on the table, insistent knocks on the front door pounded upstairs. Gisèle and Pierre exchanged a tense look—everyone in the region understood that any knock could be black-uniformed Gestapo at the door. Pierre walked over to an arched window, pulled up one of the shutters' slats a little, and peered down at the street. He smiled wanly at Gisèle. Their other dinner guests had arrived. All were Brutus sympathizers or operatives. The group would spend the night at the Chauvins' due to the curfew. They would also be pivotal in helping with the airman.

Gisèle went downstairs to let them in and scanned the street behind them. It was empty except for a Gestapo agent turning the corner to the headquarters less than fifty feet from her back door.

She checked her watch. It read nearly 8:40 p.m. She shivered and reached for a shawl from a nearby coat stand. Wrapping it around her shoulders, she remained behind the slightly ajar door. She wondered if something had gone wrong, if Gestapo agents were about to spill from the old prison that served as their headquarters and swarm into the house.

||||||||||||||||||||||||

Staff Sergeant Arthur Meyerowitz, in a shabby brown overcoat and a beret pulled low across his brow, was huddled in the backseat of a black Citroën driven by one of Taillandier's men, a chain smoker with several deep scars gouged across his cheeks and a harsh glint in his dark eyes. The Morhange operative had thrown open the dilapidated door of the woodcutter's shed an hour earlier. Arthur, lying beneath a scratchy horse blanket against the ramshackle rear wall, never heard the approaching footsteps in the snow and did not have time to do more than stare as the door flew open. He thought that the Germans had found him.

Before Arthur could open his mouth or even stir, the stranger grunted in guttural English, "Come with me, Sergeant." The man's hands were hidden in the pockets of his long, belted overcoat.

Arthur did not budge under the blanket except to grasp the handle of the knife he had taken from the farmer's kitchen near Lesparre before Taillandier brought him to the Barbots.

"I am with Marcel," the man said, removing his hands from the pockets to show they were empty.

Arthur warily rose to his feet, ignoring the now-familiar pain that ripped through his back anytime he moved suddenly. He followed the slightly stooped but wide-shouldered man in dim twilight through the woods to a car parked along a dirt path wide enough for just one vehicle. Thick stands of trees flanked the sedan. Gnarled, leafless branches that had grown on both sides of the path over the centuries were entwined like giant skeletal fingers above the trail. Arthur shuddered at the sight, which seemed right out of horror movies or even the haunted forest in *The Wizard of Oz*. He was glad that he was not superstitious; at that moment, however, he wished he had his *chai*.

When the man opened a rear door, Arthur climbed into the backseat. The nameless operative slid behind the wheel and in a few seconds was speeding without the headlights on down the nearly pitch-black road.

Everything was happening so fast that Arthur had no time to worry as he was jostled around the backseat every time the sedan hit a bump or turned suddenly. At some point, he realized that they must have turned onto a paved road because the ride grew smoother. Then the car started to slow down. Arthur spotted the outlines of a large, square tower, the Tour de l'Honneur, an imposing remnant of a fourteenth-century castle.

"Lay down," the driver ordered in his hard-to-follow English. The car snaked down a long street, Arthur certain that he could hear the staccato thumps of his own heart. The car slowed and stopped.

"Wait here," the Frenchman muttered.

As the operative slipped out of the car and closed the door carefully and quietly, Arthur's heart raced even faster, and his temples suddenly pulsed with pain and pressure. The door nearest his head opened slightly, and the man hissed, "Out."

Arthur shifted into a crouch, suppressed a cry as his back flared again, and pushed himself out the half-open door. A few steps across a tiny sidewalk stood a three-story, stone building with a ground-floor, plate-glass window with the words *Pharmacie, 33, Rue Jean-Jacques Rousseau* painted in red.

The door rested slightly ajar, a shaft of light spearing the front steps and sidewalk. A woman's voice said, "Come inside now."

Without hesitation Arthur entered the house and stepped into a foyer where framed photographs and several small paintings adorned wallpaper with a delicate floral pattern. He grimaced at the mud stains his boots tracked on an expensive-looking Oriental carpet.

The door closed softly behind him, and the woman turned, smiled at him, and told him in almost flawless English not to worry. In the Bronx, everyone would have called her "a stunner," Arthur thought. She was perhaps in her late twenties or early thirties, with dark hair and eyes and delicately contoured cheekbones.

He was right about thirty-three-year-old Gisèle Chauvin's age, but he would never have guessed that she was the regional chief of Réseau Brutus.

As she took Arthur's arm and guided him upstairs, his stomach growled at the unmistakable scent of a simmering stew and fresh-baked bread. Smiling again at the American, Gisèle explained in her fluent English that fresh bread was hard to come by because of Nazi food rationing, but that if one knew one's way around the black market, there were ways to obtain a little meat and bread to augment the usual fare of hard biscuits, eggs, old vegetables, and bruised fruit. Butter was nearly impossible to come by since the German Army had seized and slaughtered nearly every cow in the region.

Arthur balked for an instant as she nudged him into a dining room where a group of people rose from chairs behind the table set with elegant china and crystal and several bottles of wine. Gisèle assured him that everyone there was his friend now. A tall man with neatly parted black hair and a serious expression walked up with his hand extended and introduced himself as Dr. Pierre Chauvin. Pierre guided him to a chair at the long dinner table, where recognition and relief flowed through Arthur at the sight of the Chauvins' neighbors Charlotte and Christiane Michel. Martial Michel—Charlotte's husband and Christiane's father—and Charlotte's brother and sister, Pierre and Mimi Delude, who shared Charlotte's good looks, also welcomed the American with wide smiles.

He could not help but note that despite the occupation and its privations, everyone in the dining room was well dressed, the men in jackets and ties, the woman and young Christiane in skirts and blouses. His hosts looked as though the war had changed nothing in Lesparre and as though the Gestapo were not coming and going across the street.

Arthur winced as he considered his threadbare sweater and baggy trousers. As if reading his thoughts, Charlotte said in her limited English that they had dressed up for a "special guest."

Gisèle disappeared for a moment when a baby's squalls echoed from down the main hallway, and soon returned with little Patrick in her arms. She sat at one end of the table, gently rocking him, and urged Arthur to eat.

He needed little prompting. As he tried not to gulp his first genuine dinner—a beef stew with just enough meat for flavor but teeming with potatoes, onions, and carrots—since the mess hall at Seething, he started to relax. His hosts, all of whom knew at least a smattering of English, regaled him with conversation about themselves and questions about him and his family back in the States. They made sure his wineglass, as well as their own, was refilled several times.

Eventually Gisèle turned serious and told Arthur that he would need to become "deaf and dumb" if he was to have any chance of escape. Puzzled, he asked what she meant. It was Pierre who answered that they planned to teach him how to behave like a mute if he was spotted and questioned by Germans or collaborators. Meanwhile, Gisèle slipped from the table to place the baby back in his crib.

Arthur listened half dreamily and with bemusement, aglow both from the wine and from his relief at the camaraderie of the dinner table.

A sharp and sudden crack right behind him sent him leaping from his chair, knocking it over. Having slipped behind him, Gisèle had clapped her hands hard.

"No good!" exclaimed Gisèle, who had just come back into the room, with a good-natured smirk. "You must practice!"

Arthur immediately grasped the lesson: he could not afford to let his guard down for an instant. The smallest mistake could doom both him and his rescuers.

The Michels and the Deludes assured him that, along with the Chauvins, they would do everything they could to help him on his long journey home. They would accompany him as he moved between towns and hiding places and on the furtive trek to the Spanish border. The realization that all these people were risking everything for him comforted and even awed Arthur, who vowed to himself not to let them down.

Gisèle told him that his stay with them in Lesparre was to be brief. The Resistance was already forging his "ICs," identification cards, without which he could be arrested or worse by the Gestapo. Her next words reinforced just how much danger he was in and just how courageous his helpers were: "The Gestapo headquarters is directly across from our backyard. It is not safe for you here."

If his bomber had not gone down so close to Lesparre, Arthur would not have been in so much danger. The local Gestapo, however, had not only captured five of his comrades and found the bodies of two others, but also knew how many crewmen a B-24 contained. At least one airman, possibly two if a bottom-turret gunner had been aboard, was unaccounted for from *Harmful Lil Armful*; if casualties had thinned the pool for replacements, the bottom turret was the spot left unfilled. The Germans were still looking for another airman, and the Chauvins needed to move Arthur as soon as possible.

They told him that as long as he was in France, there was no "Arthur Meyerowitz." Gisèle informed him that he was now the man on the forthcoming identification card and paper. "Your new name will be Georges Lambert."[2]

She did not tell him that the expert forger creating those documents was none other than Marcel Taillandier. For the moment, that was more information than they needed to share with Arthur in case he was discovered by the Gestapo or the police and might give up the Morhange leader's name under torture. The Chauvins had never known Marcel to craft papers for an Allied airman.

Later that night, Arthur settled into a real bed—that of the maid—for the first time since touching down on French soil. A small crucifix was affixed to the wall, and on the nightstand were a Bible and a set of ivory rosary beads, items that a Jewish airman from the Bronx could never have envisioned in his own bedroom. Pierre and Gisèle had loaned him a pair of Pierre's pajamas and given him a painkiller to numb the excruciating pain in his lower back. Tomorrow, they told him, they would drill him without respite until he could convincingly play the part of the deaf and dumb Georges Lambert.

CHAPTER 10

||||||||||||||||||||||||||||||||||||||

A LONG SHOT AT BEST

On January 6, 1944, near 8 a.m., Arthur was awakened from a deep sleep by several soft knocks. As he blearily opened and rubbed his eyes, Gisèle nudged the door open and entered. As he sat up in the maid's bed on the third floor of the house, she handed him a neatly pressed dark suit, a white shirt, a light blue tie, and a new beret and asked him to wash up, get dressed, and come downstairs as soon as possible.

He shot her a hesitant look. She immediately understood and told him that her children were at school and would spend the night with the Michels, who lived at 16 rue du Palais de Justice, a short walk down the street from the Chauvins and just across the street from Pierre and Mimi Delude. No one would be in the house except Gisèle; her husband, Pierre; and Arthur.

He quickly did as she asked and joined her and Pierre, who was holding a camera, in the kitchen. To his surprise, the suit, one of Pierre's, fit him fairly well.

"We have a gift for you," she said. "Are you ready to have your picture taken, Georges Lambert?"

She reached into an apron pocket, pulled out a small booklet and a piece of stationery, and placed them in Arthur's hands. They were his identification card and a letter bearing the forged signature of the mayor of Soulac-sur-Mer, near Lesparre, and attesting to the fact that the man with the papers was indeed Georges Lambert.

"You are an agricultural worker and were born on May 4, 1915, in Algiers, Algeria," Gisèle continued. "You relocated to Soulac-sur-Mer"—northwest of Lesparre—"on July 20, 1942, and your address there is the rue Bremontier. Your profession is farmer."

Chuckling, she added, "Just play the part." Her expression tightened in an instant. "Never, ever, say a word to anyone in public, whether you are inside or on a street. We will teach you a few signs and gestures, and you must practice them until they are perfect."

His stomach constricting, Arthur nodded.

"Now, your photo," she said. "We will paste it on your card."

She added that Arthur's forged documents were special, crafted by one of the finest counterfeiters in the Resistance—who rarely, if ever, created papers for downed airmen.

The Chauvins led Arthur downstairs into the cellar, opened a bulkhead door shielded by an overhang, and posed him a few steps past the door. Pierre closed the door, moved a few feet in front of Arthur, explained that the Vichy officials often took identification photos outside, and readied the camera. Arthur realized that no one could spot them from the adjoining buildings.

"Do not smile," Gisèle told him. "No one in France has much to smile about these days."

Arthur knew the feeling and stared tight-lipped at Pierre. Pierre snapped several shots, and they quickly returned inside. Pierre excused himself to race off on his motorcycle to see "Carl," a Brutus sympathizer who developed photos quickly for the Chauvins.

After a cup of watery, bitter coffee that made Arthur long for the strong cups of joe at Seething, and a few slices of bread and jam, his education in convincingly demonstrating that he was stone deaf and unable to utter a word began in earnest. Gisèle was relentless—he must never flinch at loud noises from any direction; he must never make a sound in public unless he had to cough, sneeze, or clear his throat; he must never appear to understand what anyone was saying to him or near him; he must avoid eye contact with police, Gestapo, soldiers, or anyone in a suit and coat who looked remotely official or suspicious.

She warned him that he would be stopped and challenged by the Germans and Vichy police many times before his escape could be arranged. When that happened, she instructed, he was to act as "stupid and slow" as possible, no matter how aggravated or aggressive the inquisitor became. Even if they struck him, Gisèle said, he must never respond. He must take the abuse, play his part, and limp away.

Gisèle apprised him of the Germans' pet tricks to trip up a man they suspected was feigning deafness. They might grin and amiably ask him if he had a cigarette or a light. If he automatically reached into a pocket or even shook his head, he was finished.

Another danger was women. As Gisèle said with a teasing smile, Arthur was a handsome man, and if an attractive woman noticed him and said even a casual *bonjour*, he must refrain from answering or even returning her look. Gisèle glowered when she advised him to especially ignore "loose women" who were collaborators and traitors. They would give him up in a minute to the Gestapo or the police.

If Arthur was on a street anywhere and heard a cry for help from anyone, even a child, he must not "hear" it and not respond.

When Arthur asked if it might not be easier to conceal him and move him from spot to spot until an escape could be attempted, Gisèle emphatically told him no. There were so many collaborators spying on their neighbors throughout southwest France that Brutus had found it easier to hide airmen in plain sight.

She took him to a window facing the home's backyard and opened the shutters just enough to see across the street. Pointing at the Gestapo headquarters, she advised him to study the way the Germans dressed and moved so that he knew not to look just for the men in the black uniforms, boots, and visored caps, but to recognize how they looked in civilian garb such as brimmed hats, trench coats, and dark suits.

She pulled a chair over to the window and told Arthur to watch everyone who came and went from the building and to familiarize himself with how they moved, how they acted, even how they lit their cigarettes.

Whether in Lesparre, Bordeaux, or Toulouse, she said, there was a sameness to the Gestapo officers' appearance and behavior. She left Arthur in the chair for at least an hour while she went downstairs to fill orders at the pharmacy.

While he waited for her to return, Arthur followed her instructions: he studied his enemy.

Focused on a pair of plain-clothed agents rushing from the headquarters, Arthur strained not to jump from his chair at a sudden smack a few feet behind him. His back flaring with the effort, he sat still.

"Much better, Georges," he heard Gisèle say.

Pierre came back around 5 p.m., having made his rounds and visited several patients in the town. From an overcoat pocket, he removed an envelope and spread its contents on the dining room table. Several photos of a somber-looking Georges Lambert lay there.

Gisèle tapped one with her finger. "That one," she said.

Pierre pasted the image onto Arthur's identification card, gave him a pen, and told him to sign the box in the right-hand corner of the document—but just remember to sign "Georges Lambert," not "Arthur Meyerowitz." Arthur knew the man was not kidding. From here on, Arthur Meyerowitz *was* Georges Lambert.

Dinner that evening was early, at 6 p.m., a bland porridge and a batch of small carrots. Shrugging and smiling, Gisèle said that the previous night's dinner had been a special occasion for a new friend. This was how they normally ate.

Arthur wanted nothing more than to go to bed right after dinner, worn out from the ordeal of the past few days. A knock on the front door startled him, but he relaxed when Pierre and Mimi Delude stepped into the dining room with several bottles of wine.

"Not yet, my friends," Pierre Chauvin said with a smile. "We still have a few hours before curfew, and our American guest still has a few lessons left."

For the next hour, Gisèle and Pierre fired a barrage of questions at Arthur in French, German, and English. "Who are you?" "What is your name?" "Who is helping you?"

Every time his face twitched, Gisèle would admonish, "No! If you show anything, the Germans will know you can hear."

Pierre and the Deludes took turns ambushing Arthur by dropping books and metal pots and pans behind him from time to time. If he flinched or started to duck, all four reminded him to control every reaction of a man who could hear.

"Concentrate!" Gisèle chided him firmly.

Pierre Chauvin thrust a piece of paper and a pencil in front of him. "Sign," the Frenchman growled in a commanding way.

Arthur picked up the pencil.

Again, Pierre Chauvin snapped, "Sign!"

Arthur stared woodenly at him. A book slammed against the floor somewhere close behind Arthur. He did not stir.

Pierre leaned close to him and scowled, pointed at the pencil, and then pointed at the paper.

Arthur did not react for a moment. Then, slowly, he took the pencil and began to write.

Gisèle snatched the paper from the table. Again, Arthur did not budge.

Scanning the paper, she smiled and handed it to her husband. Arthur had written "Georges Lambert."

"Your lessons are over for the night, Georges," she said.

Arthur did not move or react to her words.

"Very good," she said softly.

She excused herself for a little bit to take care of a few things in her pharmacy downstairs, and her husband went with her.

Pierre Delude opened one of the wine bottles and poured a glass for Mimi, Arthur, and himself at the dining room table. Pierre raised his glass and toasted in a quiet but defiant tone, "To victory and to our American friend's safe escape."[1]

They all took a sip.

Gisèle and Pierre would have liked to spend another day or two instructing him, but they had to get him on the move as fast as possible because the local Gestapo would keep up their search for the B-24's missing airman.

Before Arthur went upstairs to the maid's room, Gisèle pressed two pills into his hand to relieve his pain and hopefully help him get some sleep. Arthur swallowed them, the medication calming his back a bit. He dozed from time to time, but never fell fully asleep that night.

CHAPTER 11

PLAYING THE PART

Pierre woke Arthur before dawn and he dressed quickly in the same clothes he had worn for his ID photo. Most of the townspeople, including the nearby Gestapo and police, had not yet stirred.

He took a last look at the iron-framed bed and began to straighten the rumpled sheet and bedcovers. Pierre told him to leave it and come downstairs.

In the kitchen, Gisèle and Charlotte and Christiane Michel were sitting at the table. Jean-Pierre Dupin, his long Gallic face tight and tense, was standing against a counter; he nodded at Arthur and asked if he had any questions before they set out for the autobus stop in the town center. Arthur drew a deep breath and shook his head.

Jean-Pierre reached into an inside pocket of his coat. He pulled out a pair of dog tags, and when Arthur realized that they were his, taken from him by the helpful farmer on January 1, he was confused. Jean-Pierre's reassurance that he had been entrusted with the tags so that one of his radio operators in Bordeaux could relay Arthur's name, rank, and service number to London eased Arthur's concern.

After a cup of weak coffee and a slice of nearly stale bread with a small smear of apple jam, Arthur followed Jean-Pierre and the Michels to the front door at 6 a.m. for the 6:30 autobus to Bordeaux. Gisèle hugged him tightly, kissed him on both cheeks, and whispered, *"Bonne chance."*

When she released him, Pierre handed him sturdy fleece-lined gloves and a wool overcoat that could not have been more than a year old, given its near-immaculate condition. Arthur hesitated, knowing that the coat was the doctor's and probably the best one he still owned. Pierre and Gisèle both smiled at him. Arthur, his eyes moist, put it on and donned his beret. He reached into his pocket and offered them several hundred francs, as he had been instructed to do with those who aided him. Gisèle smiled and accepted—for the Resistance.

He headed down the front steps with Jean-Pierre, who wore a worker's cap and scarf with his heavy coat, and the Michels, both of whom wore winter coats, wool hats, gloves, and boots. Arthur fought an overwhelming urge to look back. Pushing away his emotions, he concentrated on his new mission—life as Georges Lambert.

As Arthur and Jean-Pierre, along with Charlotte and Christiane, walked through a steady snowfall toward the bus stop along Lesparre's main street, they blended in with a handful of locals starting their morning rounds. Glad to have the beret keeping his head dry, Arthur glanced at the Church of Saint-Trelody, whose brooding Gothic towers and buttresses evoked memories of the architecture of Robert Morris High School, back in the Bronx. He ignored the pang of homesickness and kept moving. Farther down the street, they passed the nineteenth-century Palace of Justice and a nearby prison. A German soldier stood at the entrance with a Schmeisser submachine gun slung from his right shoulder. Arthur avoided any eye contact.

At the end of the street, a knot of people was lined up at the door of a battered green autobus that looked at least twenty years old to Arthur. A policeman, in a dark blue caped overcoat and a Foreign Legion–style cap, or *képi*, was checking the IDs and documents of everyone who wanted to board the vehicle. Arthur slipped behind his escorts so that if he was challenged and discovered, the officer might not realize they were together.

He scanned the papers of the Michels and Jean-Pierre and quickly waved them onto the bus. Arthur stepped up to the policeman and, as the Chauvins had instructed, met the man's eyes benignly. "Do not avert your eyes or else someone might think you are trying to be evasive," the couple had told him.

The officer, a thin-lipped, pallid man, barely glanced at Arthur, gave his photo and papers a cursory examination, and handed back the documents. Arthur hoped his hands were not shaking as he took his papers and stepped into the bus. He walked past the Michels and Jean-Pierre without looking directly at them and settled into a ripped leather seat toward the rear, unsure whether the moisture on his brow and upper lip came from the snow or from sweat. He had no illusions that future checks of his photo and papers would prove so easy.

At 6:45 a.m., fifteen minutes late because of the identification checks, the door clanged shut and the autobus shifted from a grinding idle into rasping motion. It rattled out of Lesparre and southeast onto a divided highway for the thirty-nine-mile trip to Bordeaux. The vehicle was shaking badly, and if there was a heater on board, it was working poorly or not at all. Arthur gratefully pulled Pierre Chauvin's warm overcoat tighter around himself.

Leaning to the window, Arthur scraped enough frost off it to glimpse the landscape, mostly ancient, gray-stone walls marking the snowcapped boundaries of farms and vineyards. Magnificent châteaus with gables, turrets, and massive windows even more splendid than the manors of England dotted the terrain.

Once, Christiane turned around and smiled at Arthur, but an

instant before he returned her smile, he caught himself—he did not want anyone on the bus to link him to the Michels and Jean-Pierre in case he did not pass inspection when they reached Bordeaux. He winced as Christiane's smile faded and a flash of hurt spread across her young face before she turned around.

The countryside waned about an hour into the trip as towns and then large neighborhoods emerged outside the bus's windows. On road signs, *Bordeaux* appeared with growing frequency. Arthur then spotted a wide, gunmetal-gray river, the Garonne. The autobus rattled across the Pont de Pierre, a long-span bridge, and onto the rue Sainte-Catherine, the longest pedestrian street in France, clogged with cars, buses, and military vehicles.

As the autobus slowed to a virtual crawl, Arthur stared at the array of medieval and more modern buildings. On the Place de la Bourse, there stood a mammoth equestrian statue of King Louis XV. The bus passed the Grand Théâtre, a sprawling eighteenth-century neoclassical edifice. Cathedrals seemingly soared everywhere, and when the remains of the Palais Gallien, a late-second-century Roman amphitheater appeared, he was reminded of photos from high school textbooks about ancient history. It dawned on him just how old this city was, how there was nothing in New York that even came close.

The occasional remnants of medieval turrets and defense walls hammered home the fact that this was a city that had seen warfare for over a thousand years. Now the German tanks, half-tracks, and *Kubelwagens* (small Volkswagen staff cars) that were parked at points along both sides of the vast boulevard testified to the reality that war was once again afflicting Bordeaux.

The bus turned onto the Esplanade des Quinconces, the largest square in Europe. German artillery ringed the thirty-one-acre plaza, the barrels pointed at the buildings of the surrounding city. Scanning the extensive tract, Arthur marveled at the symmetrical rows of trees, known as quincunxes and the origin of the esplanade's name. The trees were arranged in rectangles with one at each corner and one in the middle.

The plaza was packed with people and soldiers, and Arthur observed Jean-Pierre, a few aisles to the front, glowering out his window at a group of Frenchwomen strolling arm in arm with Nazi officers past two white-marble rostral pillars that faced the nearby Garonne River. Studying the crowds more closely, Arthur realized that there were many other women who were escorted not only by German soldiers but also by black-uniformed Gestapo. Soon he would learn that in Occupied France, the sight of women in the company of Germans was not always what it seemed: many of the Frenchwomen were working for the Resistance and gathering intelligence from their German "friends."

Shortly after winding past a sprawling monument whose pedestal was decorated with bronze horses and surmounted by an allegorical statue of a female "Liberty," the autobus lurched to a stop at a busy bus station at the curved edge of the esplanade. Each time a bus pulled up, a uniformed Gestapo officer holding a clipboard, and a police officer stepped in front of the exit to check the documents of every passenger boarding or debarking. Arthur closed his eyes for a minute and silently urged himself to concentrate as he had been taught.

He opened his eyes as the bus stopped. Ahead of him, Charlotte, Christiane, and Jean-Pierre left their seats and stepped into line with the other passengers. Arthur waited until they were near the door and then moved into the aisle, his heart pounding beneath the thick overcoat.

One by one the people in front of him stepped from the bus, a minute or two passing each time they did. The Michels and Jean-Pierre exited in turn and were waved through after brief inspections of their papers. Five passengers remained in front of Arthur. As each one's turn to exit came, a blank expression settled across their faces. They revealed nothing—not fear, not annoyance, not anger. No one wanted the police or the Gestapo to detect the slightest flicker of emotion that could arouse suspicion.

As Arthur reached the doorway and watched the woman in front of him hand her documents to the two officials, he saw his companions clustered on a curb some twenty feet away, waiting for him but ready to vanish into the crowd if he was detained.

"*Prochain!*" the French policeman barked.

Arthur stood on the top step, utterly still.

"*Prochain—vous!*" the officer yelled, his eyes narrowing and his face flushing.

The Gestapo agent, a stocky man with a ruddy face behind the haze of the cigarette in his raised left hand, fixed his light blue eyes in a feral stare on Arthur.

He jabbed his right index finger at Arthur. "*Vous!*"

Arthur did not even nod. He stepped off the autobus and waited. If he reached too soon for the documents in the inside pocket of his coat, either man might shoot him on the spot for making a suspicious movement.

The German continued to glare at him and flicked the cigarette just inches past his head.

"*Vos papiers,*" your papers, the policeman ordered, leaning in close to Arthur.

Arthur looked blankly at him.

The Nazi's right hand moved to the holster belted to his black, shin-length greatcoat. He opened the cover and rested his hand on the exposed Luger pistol.

The police officer took a step back and thrust out his right hand, his eyes now dark slits. "*Vos papiers . . .*"

Slowly, Arthur unbuttoned his overcoat and held out the inside flap for both men. He reached slowly into the interior pocket and pulled out his ID card and papers. The Frenchman leaned forward and snatched them. He pored over the photo and the papers and, cocking his head suspiciously at Arthur, gave them to the German, who examined them for nearly a minute. While the two men muttered to each other in French, their eyes darted back and forth from the photo and papers to Arthur. He recognized a few words that Gisèle and Pierre Chauvin had insisted he must know—*muet*, mute, and *sourd et muet*, deaf and dumb, as well as his phony birthplace, Algiers.

Because Arthur's identification card stated that he was from Algiers, no Nazis or Vichy officials could check out "Georges Lambert": the North African city had been liberated by the Allies. The Germans and their French collaborators had either fled the city or had been arrested. Now Marcel's canny forgery gave Arthur an even better chance to pull off his role as Georges Lambert.

The policeman pointed to the photo and the signature, then at Arthur. Arthur nodded. The German's mouth twisted into a sneer as he held out his clipboard and a pen and shoved them into Arthur's hands. Again, the Frenchman pointed to the identification card's signature and then at the pen.

The Chauvins had prepared Arthur for just such a challenge. Deliberately, but not so slowly as to appear hesitant, concentrating so that his hand would not shake so much that the two signatures might appear different, he signed "Georges Lambert."

As he did so, the German moved a few steps behind him.

"Turn around!" the Gestapo agent bellowed in French.

Arthur kept his back to the man, finished signing the clipboard, and handed it to the police officer, who was peering at him for any hint that he had heard the shout.

The German walked back, and both men examined the signature. The officer returned Arthur's documents. Arthur started to walk toward the curb where his friends waited, his hand trembling and sweaty as he slipped the ID card and papers back into his pocket.

Jean-Pierre and the Michels did not say a word when Arthur joined them. He had played his part perfectly, convincing the German and the policeman that a deaf mute named Georges Lambert had stepped off the autobus. He would need to display that kind of

nerve under pressure, a trait that all too many downed airmen under-
standably lacked for the nightmarish cat-and-mouse tactics necessary for any hope of a successful escape from Occupied France. It
was especially true now, with the Allied invasion of France imminent
and the Nazis on their highest state of alert throughout the region.

Jean-Pierre led them to another bus, a smaller one near the curb.
Several others were parked behind it, and police officers were stationed in front of each. Perhaps assuming that most of the passengers
lining up in front of the vehicles had already undergone inspection
from the just-arrived autobuses, Jean-Pierre, Arthur, Charlotte, and
Christiane were not even ordered to present their identification cards.
They were simply allowed to board.

The bus plodded between tram lines and through dense traffic
composed mainly of other buses and military vehicles and lumbered
south to the sprawling Bordeaux suburb of Talence. Jean-Pierre rose
as the bus stopped at the entrance to a narrow, cobblestone "close," a
dead-end street where Old Bordeaux's three-story, stone-walled apartment houses and homes were separated only by tiny alleys.

Inside one of the single homes, Number 19 rue Félix-Goulet, Mrs.
Dupin, petite and blond with a vivacious smile, greeted them. She
hugged Arthur and, as he was now becoming accustomed to, kissed
him gently on both cheeks. She immediately made him feel like he was
a welcome guest, not a dangerous burden.

A tall, lean man with wiry salt-and-pepper hair and a friendly but
guarded visage extended his hand to Arthur and introduced himself
as Robert Ardichen as they shook.

Jean-Pierre explained that since Arthur would be spending only
three or four days in Bordeaux, it was better for everyone if he did not
leave the house. The time for hiding in plain sight would come soon
enough. Jean-Pierre and his wife apologized to their guest for having
to conceal him in the attic annex until the Michels, who would leave
shortly for Lesparre, returned to take him to his next destination.

"Once you are on the move," Jean-Pierre added, "you will frequently have to go out in the open as Lambert to receive your food rations from the Germans. You must also go out so that people will not get suspicious about you."

In one way, Arthur was relieved that he would have a few days' respite from pretending to be Georges Lambert, but the sight of so many Germans everywhere in Bordeaux was not just unsettling, but frightening. Jean-Pierre said, "You must climb out of the annex and onto the roof if the Gestapo or the police come into the house."

The warning heightened Arthur's uneasiness. The Dupins promised to check in on him and to bring him a valise with several changes of clothes, underwear, and socks for the days ahead. Shaking the American's hand, Jean-Pierre assured him that his French friends knew what they were doing; Charlotte embraced him, kissing him on each cheek as Gisèle and Mrs. Dupin had done and arousing new pangs of loneliness in him. Christiane smiled and gave him a little wave.

Before she left, Charlotte promised Arthur that she would be back in a few days and urged him not to worry. He never even considered asking where she would take him next; it would just be another unfamiliar spot on a map.

Jean-Pierre took Arthur up several flights of stairs to a cramped, musty annex that contained an old French Army bedroll and blanket. That was all—no chair, no desk, and no room for anything except the bedroll and what looked like a covered wooden box and a porcelain vase in a corner. Arthur had to stoop, as the space was no more than five and a half feet high. There were no books or anything else to read and even if there had been, he knew only a handful of French words.

It was then that he suddenly realized that the large porcelain vase was actually a chamber pot and the box was a portable toilet of some sort. Hunched over, he opened the box, which had a funnel that obviously sent waste to a container somewhere downstairs. A roll of toilet paper he had not noticed before sat behind the box. Bad, but not as bad as trying to go to the bathroom in one of a B-24's waste units.

Jean-Pierre said, "I must apologize for the accommodations."

Arthur grinned and shrugged. Compared to where the Gestapo might house a Jewish airman, the annex was as good as the Waldorf Astoria.

After Jean-Pierre closed the door, the unmistakable ring of a metal latch on the other side caused Arthur to look at the grimy window, just large enough for a man to wriggle through and pull himself up onto the flat roof.

On his knees, he unfurled the bedroll and its thin, shapeless pillow and eased himself onto it. He might as well have been lying on the floor itself, as the first stabs of pain from his back reminded him.

Arthur languished in the annex for three days and nights, constantly shifting his position on the bedroll to relieve not only his back, but seemingly every other cramped muscle in the tight space. The wails of air-raid sirens and the thumps of flak and bombs in the distance every night made him wonder if his squadron, the 715th, was up there. The annex shook every time the unmistakable grind of half-tracks' treads or the sudden squeals of tires rose from the surrounding streets.

Three times a day, Mrs. Dupin unlatched the door to bring Arthur a tray with a meager ration of bread, a few vegetables, thin soup, and water. Twice a day, she gave him a basin of water, fresh towels, and soap, but no razor.

Pierre would visit him in the morning before he left on Brutus business and in the late afternoon when he returned. When Mrs. Dupin carried up Arthur's meals, she always sat with him, eager to learn about New York, his family, and his dreams for after the war. Grateful for the company and charmed by her laugh and gentle teasing, Arthur again felt like he had suddenly found an older sister, one who would do anything to help him.

Early on the morning of the fourth day, urgent footsteps yanked Arthur from a restless sleep. He recoiled as the latch grated and the door opened. He feared that the Germans had found him. Then, as Jean-Pierre smiled at him, Arthur unclenched his fists. Jean-Pierre beckoned him to crawl out of the space and follow him downstairs. The Frenchman helped Arthur to his feet outside the annex, Arthur gasping from the pain in his cramped muscles. He would have fallen if not for his new friend.

Steadying himself on Jean-Pierre's arm, Arthur carefully navigated the stairs to the first floor, where his host offered him a razor, cup, and brush and showed him to a bathroom. The sink and a four-legged stand-up bathtub were filled with steaming water. Arthur scraped four days' worth of stubble from his face and then sank into the tub for what he would remember as one of the best soakings of his life. Although he would have loved to stay there for an hour, he was soon out and dressed in a clean shirt and pants provided by Jean-Pierre.

When he went downstairs, he walked straight into a meeting of Brutus operatives. Jean-Pierre introduced him to a man named Georges Tissot, and Ardichen was also seated in the room. Arthur sat, and for the next hour listened to an animated conversation among the men. He could make out a few words, such as "Gestapo," and even though he could not speak French, he had no doubt that a crisis of some sort was being discussed. That crisis was the grim fact that the Nazis had been infiltrating Brutus since the early fall and arresting some of the network's key leaders.

As Arthur listened, Jean-Pierre gestured to a suitcase near Arthur's chair. It was a valise for the airman with more clothing and a shaving kit. The suitcase was dilapidated and ripped in one corner, but an "agricultural worker" carrying stylish, expensive luggage would immediately evoke unwanted attention from the authorities.

Arthur's head swiveled toward the front door at the sound of knocking, but he relaxed as soon as Charlotte and Christiane entered, beaming at him. Madame Dupin handed him a little paper bag holding an apple, a pear, and a small wedge of cheese. Clasping his hand, Jean-Pierre said that Arthur was going to the city of Moissac and that while Jean-Pierre would not be going with the Michels, he would see Arthur soon. Seconds later, Arthur, in his beret and Pierre Chauvin's overcoat, was walking back with the Michels to catch the city bus to the Esplanade des Quinconces. To his surprise, their identification cards were not checked.

Shortly after they reached the busy terminal and disembarked from the city bus, a man in an elegantly cut cashmere coat and a dark beret appeared beside them. Arthur tensed up, but Charlotte gave his arm a squeeze and nodded at him—she did not dare whisper to the "mute" that the stranger was "a friend," but Arthur read her gesture as she intended. The man was carrying what looked like a black doctor's bag, and his clothes were indeed expensive but obviously a few years old, the coat patched at the right elbow.

Moving into the line for the Bordeaux-to-Moissac autobus with the Michels and the newcomer, Arthur noticed that only one man, a police officer, was checking identification cards and documents. With a bored, almost pained expression, the man barely seemed to glance at passengers' papers and allowed them to board quickly. Maybe the bitter wind blowing in from the Garonne and raking the plaza had something to do with the man's indifference, Arthur thought.

When Arthur stood in front of him, the officer gave the photo card and papers a cursory look and sent Arthur onto the autobus. This time he sat between Charlotte and Christiane, not behind them as on the trip to Bordeaux. The man with the bag sat directly across the aisle from them, but did not look their way. Charlotte patted Arthur's hand and smiled reassuringly as the door closed and the bus creaked out of the plaza for the ninety-seven-mile drive southeast to Moissac. He welcomed the motherly touch of Charlotte's fingers, gentle and surprisingly soft despite the calluses raised by the toil and privations of war.

As on the highway from Lesparre to Bordeaux, snow-covered vineyards, farms, and châteaus, as well as villages and market towns, stretched along the entire route to Moissac. Thankfully for Arthur, this autobus was in far better shape than the previous one, giving his back a bit of a rest.

They pulled into the town square of Moissac a little over two hours after leaving Bordeaux and stopped near the twelfth-century Abbey Church of Saint-Pierre, with its graceful portico and world-famous exterior carvings. Another sight shattered any momentary sightseeing for Arthur. Two Gestapo agents, both in the blood-chilling black uniform and jackboots he had already come to loathe and fear, strode up to the autobus.

Charlotte and Christiane went ahead of Arthur into the line, and when he started to move behind them, the man with the medical bag slipped directly behind him.

After Charlotte's and Christiane's papers passed inspection and one of the men brusquely told them to move on, Arthur stepped in front of the Germans. His heart was throbbing, and despite the cold, his palms turned moist. When the German snarled for the "French-man" to produce his papers, Arthur hoped that his face showed no tinge of anything more than the natural fear anyone would have for the Germans at that time. This time, however, he was more frightened than in his first few encounters with the Gestapo.

Following the Chauvins' lessons precisely, he stared at the Nazis as if confused, then nodded in sudden understanding, and reached into his jacket pocket for his identification card and the letter embossed with the signature and official seal of the mayor of Soulac-sur-Mer and attesting to the fact that the bearer was town resident Georges Lambert.

The agent scowled at the photo card and the letter and grunted something to his comrade. He leaned over the card, studying it. He glared at Arthur.

In French, he asked Arthur if he was Georges Lambert. Arthur stared back blankly. A beefy man, the German screamed at him to answer.

Again, he looked without expression at the man.

His face scarlet, the Gestapo agent slapped him hard across the face. The crack of the German's leather glove against his cheek echoed across the chilly plaza.

Arthur winced from the sting, a welt already rising from his cheek to his eye. Still, he said nothing.

From behind him, a man's courtly voice said in French, "Do you not realize that this man is a deaf mute? He cannot *hear* you."

The Nazi who had struck Arthur snapped back, "Who the hell are you?"

The Frenchman stepped between Arthur and the two Germans and carefully produced his photo identification card. "I am Dr. Pierre Auriac. I live here in Moissac."

"Open your bag, and we'll see if you really are a doctor."

Pierre cautiously opened the bag and showed its contents to the pair. The silvery glint of a stethoscope and other medical instruments brought disappointed frowns to both Nazis' faces.

"May I close it?" Pierre asked. "This man, Georges Lambert, has come to work for a friend of mine on his farm. Since I was in Bordeaux, I was asked to help escort him to the farm. It's a few miles outside of town. He will spend the night at my home, and I will take him to my friend tomorrow."[1]

The Germans appeared skeptical, but then Pierre provided them the farmer's name, Jacques Garric, and proceeded to launch into a discourse about the extent of Lambert's condition. The agents' skepticism faded to irritation, and as their eyes started to glaze at the flood of medical terms they were hearing, they flung the identification cards and papers at Arthur and Dr. Auriac and ordered them to be on their way.

Both retrieved their documents from the wet cobblestones and walked across the square to Charlotte and Christiane. In silence, the two women and Arthur trailed Pierre through a cold mist to the outskirts of Moissac.

CHAPTER 12

||||||||||||||||||||||||||||||||||||||||||||||||||||

A NARROW ESCAPE

Arthur, Charlotte, and Christiane followed Dr. Pierre Auriac through the backstreets of Moissac, passing rows of half-timber, half-stone medieval homes. The doctor stopped in front of one of the houses near the walled bank of the Tarn River and a marina where several hulking barges thudded against their docks in the current. Atop a brick riverside warehouse, a large sign with blue lettering read *Canal des Deux Mers*, the canal between the Atlantic Ocean and the Mediterranean Sea.

Pierre unlocked the ancient wooden door, held it open, and beckoned to the others to step inside. With its whitewashed interior walls and wooden beams so old they appeared almost black, Pierre's house seemed frozen in the Middle Ages. Then Arthur noticed the collection of antiques and chic furniture that made the open foyer and high-ceilinged living room a blend of modern and medieval.

Walking toward them from the kitchen was a woman with lush,

dark hair flowing past her shoulders. She fixed her golden-flecked brown eyes and a welcoming smile on Arthur.

She introduced herself to Arthur as Louisita Chango, Pierre's fiancée, and gave the airman the now-customary embrace and kiss of each cheek. Instead of another confined hiding place like the Dupins' annex, she and Pierre led him to a second-floor bedroom with the same style beams as downstairs. Louisita smiled at Arthur again and told him that his stay in Moissac would be brief, just one day and night.

Pierre had told the Gestapo the truth when he said he was bringing "Georges" to the farm of Jacques Garric the next day. Chuckling, Pierre asked Arthur if he had ever worked on a farm.

Arthur replied, "I'm not sure I've ever even been on a real farm."

"Monsieur Garric is happy to host our friends such as you," Pierre said, "but he will expect you to help out."

That evening at dinner, Pierre carved a fragrantly spiced roast chicken—"Basque style," Louisita said—into equal portions for Arthur, Charlotte, Christiane, Louisita, and himself.[1] Louisita spooned generous portions of seasoned vegetables onto everyone's gleaming china plates, which were decorated with a delicate floral pattern and looked to be centuries old. Reading Arthur's thoughts as he tried not to wolf down his meal, she told him that it was possible sometimes to get a chicken or a bit of beef and fresher vegetables and fruit. There was no way, Pierre added, that tonight's meal could have come from their ration cards. One could wait in the ration lines for hours, only to reach the front and be brusquely told that there was nothing left.

It was the same for the two bottles of Bordeaux they savored. Without the black market and vintners' stashes, the Germans would have seized every bottle in southern France.

For dessert, they shared a few bowls of delicious, gold-hued grapes, Arthur's hosts laughingly telling him that Moissac was one of the region's few areas that did not cultivate grapes for wine. Instead, the local farmers grew the *chasselas de Moissac* grape, famed as a delicacy for all seasons.

The scene was almost dreamlike. With Pierre in a starched shirt, tie, and tweed jacket and Louisita in a lacy white blouse and a small, shimmering strand of pearls, the couple's refinement was faintly exotic. Both Pierre's and Louisita's fluent English reflected their cultured background. That dinner in Moissac belied for a few welcome hours the danger just a harsh knock on the door away.

The distant drone of Allied bombers and the crack of 88 antiaircraft cannons brought everyone at the table back to the reality of war and occupation. Pierre announced that they had to obey the German blackout regulations and turn off the lights. As the unmistakable thumps of five-hundred-pound bombs striking Nazi targets intensified, the others looked at him with silent respect and something else, something between admiration and a form of appreciation. Later, Charlotte Michel would tell Arthur: "One day, aeroplanes [sic] fell down. In the aeroplanes there were men who were fighting for us and who were coming from free countries. You have been the first to bring us this breath of liberty which we missed for ever so long."[2]

His stomach full, and stretched out in a canopied bed with down pillows, Arthur slept better than he had since he jumped into France. When Pierre's firm knock on the door awakened him at 5 a.m., the last thing he wanted was to climb out of that bed and leave Moissac. He knew he had no choice and pushed himself out of the covers and dressed. For once, his back did not protest.

As Arthur, holding his tattered valise, joined Pierre and the Michels in the kitchen, Louisita was frying eggs in a skillet, and Arthur took a seat at the table. A slab of warm, coarse bread sat on each plate, and Louisita slipped two eggs on Arthur's plate first. They finished breakfast, and Pierre stood up and nodded at Arthur. Christiane sprang from her seat and hugged him tightly. Charlotte also came over and did the same, tears glistening on the faces of both women.

Arthur reassured mother and daughter that they would see each other again.

Breaking the embrace, Arthur picked up his suitcase. The scent of Louisita's perfume again wafted around him. She leaned up, kissed his cheeks, and wiped off the traces of her lipstick with her finger.

Arthur felt a hand on his shoulder. It was Pierre. It was time to go.

‖‖‖‖‖‖‖‖‖‖‖‖‖‖‖‖‖‖‖

Like Pierre Chauvin and Marcel Taillandier, Pierre Auriac owned a motorcycle, though nothing as powerful as Marcel Taillandier's Gnome. Perched behind Pierre on the 1929 Alcyon 250-cc bike, Arthur hung on tightly as the doctor skimmed across ice-slicked country roads south of Moissac. He slowed down and stopped at a slope-roofed, dull yellow stone farmhouse indistinguishable from dozens of others the pair had passed. A long barn of the same colored stone stood some thirty yards behind the house.

Jacques Garric, a short, thin man in a wool cap, a drab, patched coat, and trousers tucked into ripped knee-high boots, emerged from the barn, waved, and trudged through a mix of snow and mud to the motorcycle. He and Pierre chatted in French for a few minutes before Pierre told Arthur that Garric understood some English, but spoke it poorly. Around Moissac, few people had any English.

Arthur got off the Alcyon. As he shook the farmer's hand, he had no way of knowing that behind Pierre Auriac's polished, calm demeanor lay a man consumed by his rage at the Nazis. In July 1941, his brother, Jean, a professor of medical physics and as patriotic as Pierre, was also a high-ranking member of the Resistance. Arrested by the Gestapo that month, Jean had committed suicide by slashing his wrists before the Germans could torture him. He would not risk being forced to give up his comrades.

Before he left, Pierre explained to Arthur that Jacques would shelter him in the basement, but not because the Garrics did not want him upstairs. It was common practice for local farmers to let field hands sleep in the barn during the warmer months and in the cellar when the weather turned cold. Any other arrangement might cause neighbors to wonder. If the Germans suddenly showed up at the farmhouse, Arthur would have to play his part as Lambert and hope for the best. Garric would say that he had hired Georges Lambert as a temporary field hand but had no idea of his background except that, as his identification card read, he was an experienced agricultural worker.

Arthur's new cellar lodgings were not as rough as they could have been. As with many farmers of the region, Jacques Garric had placed a cot, a night table, and a small lantern in a corner of the basement. Although it was cold and damp, the space was far better than the woodcutter's shed near the Barbots' farm.

Arthur was awakened by Jacques before sunrise, trudged up to the kitchen, and was given several slices of bread, a dried apple, and weak tea by the farmer's wife. He did not see any children. After they ate, Jacques went to the small living room and returned with a small hunting rifle; in rural areas, the Nazis allowed locals to possess one old rifle or shotgun for hunting. Since no one was allowed to purchase bullets or shells, Garric was limited to any he had on hand or managed to scrounge from neighbors.

Cradling the rifle, Jacques led him into the barn, empty except for straw on the earthen floor and perhaps the largest pile of wood Arthur had ever seen. The farmer pointed to a long handsaw leaning against the pile, which stood nearly six feet high. He handed Arthur the rifle and pulled a long, knotted piece of timber from the stack. He laid it on the floor, picked up the saw, knelt, and spent the next twenty minutes cutting the wood into four pieces. Then he picked them up one at a time and started to build a neat stack opposite the pile. He handed the saw to Arthur, pointed to a thick pair of leather work gloves on a shelf next to the heap, took back the rifle, and left wordlessly.

Arthur jammed his hands into the gloves, dragged a four-foot limb from the top of the stockpile, rolled it onto the floor, got on his knees, and began to saw. In seconds his back was on fire. Gritting his teeth, he kept sawing. Thankfully, he still had a stash of painkillers that Gisèle had given him.

It took him over an hour to do what Garric had completed in some twenty minutes, but Arthur did not stop. Despite the wintry air in the barn, his lungs were burning. His hands began to blister beneath the cracked leather gloves. Still, he continued to saw. At noon, Madame Garric brought him several more heavy slices of dark bread with a light covering of salt and two more dried apples, as well as a chipped pitcher of water and a tin cup.

Arthur lost all sense of time in the dim barn. A shot rang out in the distance sometime after his lunch, and he froze. No others followed. A few minutes went by, and he grasped the saw tight again. The rasps of steel against wood filled the barn.

As dusk began to chase what little light remained, Arthur whipped his head around at the sound of heavy steps against the straw behind him. Garric stood in front of him, grinning, the rifle in one hand, a dead rabbit in the other. He gestured for Arthur to lay down the saw and come into the house.

For the next nine days, Arthur's routine remained the same. The pile actually began to dwindle. The growls of Nazi armor and trucks from time to time made him pause from his task inside the barn. Each time, however, the ominous noise faded as the vehicles ground past the Garric farm. Few, if any, visitors came to the house.

By the time Garric summoned him from the barn late each afternoon, Arthur was exhausted. His back was adapting to the grueling labor in one way: instead of the near-blinding pain of his first day with the saw, Arthur now felt something between an insistent throb and a dull ache. He passed out from exhaustion by 8 p.m. each night within a few instants of settling atop his cot, the pleasant smell of drying fruit, vegetables, and roots drifting toward him.

On January 16, 1944, Arthur was sawing wood when Garric came into the barn with another man, who was wearing a black turtleneck, a baggy belted overcoat, and a beret. Arthur rose from his knees. Garric nodded, and Arthur followed them to the house, grabbed his valise, counted out several hundred francs that he handed to Garric, and said a quick good-bye to the farmer and his wife.

The stranger warned Arthur in thickly accented English that a neighboring farmer had told the Gestapo that a new and suspicious-looking man was working for the Garrics. The Germans could arrive in minutes or within a few hours. The pair set out on foot, and Arthur followed the man at a near run into the woods and down an overgrown, twisting path deeper into the forest.

Behind them, in the direction of the farm, the slams of car doors, guttural voices, and snarling, barking dogs echoed. Arthur and his guide broke into a full sprint, fighting to stay upright on the gnarled track. They had to keep moving. There was nowhere they could hide if the Gestapo turned their dogs loose in the woods.

Arthur had no idea how long or how far they had gone when the Frenchman suddenly stopped, put up his hand to halt Arthur, and listened for several seconds. Except for their heavy breathing, there was no sound in the woods.

The man turned to Arthur and motioned for him to lean against a tree to catch his breath while he did the same. Suddenly Arthur reached into his coat pocket to make sure he had not left his papers in the cellar or that they had somehow slipped out in the frantic sprint through the woods. His fingers brushed against the stiff identification card and his other documents.

His companion produced a small silver flask, uncapped it, and held it out to Arthur. He grasped it and drank; the warmth of brandy in his throat was welcome. The Resistance fighter took it back, sipped, and returned it to his overcoat. Then he pulled out a .45 pistol, the same as American officers carried.

Hours dragged by as they slogged past the forest's hulking trunks. He said nothing to Arthur. Arthur just made sure that he never lost sight of the Frenchman's back.

Dusk gave way to twilight and then nightfall, and still the airman and the Resistance fighter tramped through the snow and brush. His fingers and feet numb from the cold, Arthur concentrated on keeping one foot in front of the other. Neither man could waste a moment thinking about fatigue, fear and adrenaline pushing them forward.

Suddenly the Frenchman halted. Ahead of them was an opening in the trees, and a large, snow-covered field stretched toward the outlines of a town whose medieval shapes loomed even in the darkness.

The Resistance man pointed to the right-hand edge of the town's outskirts and broke into a run across the field. Clutching his suitcase, Arthur stumbled behind him out of the woods. It was after curfew, and if they were spotted by the enemy, they would be shot down in the snow or dragged off for a worse ending in the hands of the Gestapo.

Tripping and sliding countless times on the slick field, they neared a four-foot-high stone wall marking the boundary between the farmland and the town's fringes. The Resistance fighter hit the ground and crawled the final few yards to the wall, sixteen miles from Garric's home. Arthur followed him. Slowly, the Frenchman lifted his head just high enough to study the door of a stone-and-timber house similar to that of Dr. Pierre Auriac. The door stood slightly ajar.

Quickly and quietly he vaulted the wall, and Arthur followed immediately. They slid across the frozen cobblestones and into the house. The door closed behind them, and Arthur turned to find two women. One was plump and middle-aged, her kindly features creased with concern and relief in the light of the small candle she was holding. The second woman, bathed in the same glow of the candle, was younger, attractive but somehow hard-looking.

The older woman introduced herself to Arthur as Madame Rigal and her friend as Mimi Dumas.

With a smile, she told him he was with friends who would provide him all the comfort and safety they could.

"Welcome to Beaumont-de-Lomagne," she said.[3]

Without a word, Arthur's guide slipped back out the door and disappeared into the dark.

CHAPTER 13

TROUBLE IN BEAUMONT-DE-LOMAGNE

As Arthur settled into the annex of Mimi Dumas's house in Beaumont-de-Lomagne, Mimi and Madame Rigal told him that for the time being, he would remain hidden in the attic. The town was too close to Moissac for him to comfortably go outside. Perhaps Garric had talked his way out of trouble with the Gestapo by convincing them that all he knew about his temporary farmhand was that his name was Georges Lambert, he was deaf and unable to speak, and he had done a good job that he had finished that very day. Even so, the Brutus Network could not take the chance that the authorities might investigate further. Until the Resistance band was certain that no one was looking for the farmhand, Arthur would remain housebound.

Arthur bore his isolation stoically, keeping all anxieties and fear hidden from his helpers. The relative comfort of the annex, which was a finished bedroom and large enough for a chair, a dresser, and mirror, made his situation a little easier to bear. He was also allowed to use the second-floor bathroom to bathe each day. As had been the case in the other homes where he had stayed—with the exception of those two special dinners at the Chauvins' and Pierre Auriac's—the food was sparse, mainly the familiar coarse bread, the occasional egg, some vegetables and fruits, and gruel-like soups. Occasionally, there was a bit of chicken or beef.

Once again, the worst part of hiding was listening to the passage of every car, truck, or military vehicle in the street below; he prayed silently that they would not stop outside Mimi's home. He tensed every time he heard unfamiliar voices downstairs. At night, he could sleep a little better, having become accustomed to the bombing raids in the distance, but a little better still meant fitful rest when he was alone with his thoughts in the darkness of the annex.

During the day, both Mimi and Madame Rigal visited him and talked for hours. Rigal was especially interested in hearing about his mother, his father, and his brother. At first, he was reluctant to speak much about them because it intensified his loneliness, but the woman's maternal manner won him over. He found himself comforted by talking with her, her warmth conjuring images of his own mother. Rigal even understood his life as an airman, as her late husband had served in the French Air Force in World War I.

In a letter to Rose Meyerowitz after the war, Rigal would recall: "Poor dear [Arthur], we were obliged to hide him and I did my best so he could have the most comfort we could offer him. It has been a great trial for him but he was so courageous and a real soldier. I admired him so much . . ."

She later confided that she "considered him as my son."[1]

Madame Rigal certainly did watch out for Arthur as if he were her own child. Several times, when Mimi planned to have over guests whose loyalties lay with the Vichy regime, Madame Rigal insisted that Arthur be sneaked over to the nearby house of another Brutus supporter, whom Arthur later identified only as "Dr. Rey." She had no qualms about Arthur's treatment in the Dumas home. Mimi took good care of him.

Still, as Arthur's stay in Beaumont lengthened and no word to move him arrived from Dr. Auriac, Madame Rigal began to suspect that Mimi, though not a collaborator, had a loose tongue and could inadvertently tip off a Vichy or Nazi sympathizer about the Allied airman in her home.

By mid-February, Madame Rigal refused to take any more chances that Mimi might compromise Arthur, as well as herself and Dr. Rey. The older woman decided to send a message for help—not to Dr. Auriac in Moissac, but to Toulouse. This urgent request demanded not the measured attention of the genteel doctor, but the intervention of a different sort of man—Marcel Taillandier.

Madame Rigal, Taillandier, and anyone even remotely associated with helping Arthur understood that, through no fault of his own, he had parachuted into Occupied France at the worst moment for an Allied airman, between late December 1943 and June 1944. This was especially true for a Jewish airman.

Most of the time, the German Army treated Jewish prisoners of war according to the rules laid down by the Geneva Conventions. Such notable historians as Joseph Robert White, however, have chronicled how the Nazis decided for those six to seven months to "make an example of *Terrorflieger* ('terrorist aviators'), pilots and crewmen whom the Gestapo classified as spies, because they had been disguised as civilians or enemy soldiers when they were apprehended."[2] With his forged identification card and papers, Arthur was likely marked for the horrors of Fresnes Prison if captured.

Built in the 1890s just south of Paris, Fresnes Prison, a grim, six-story gray edifice, was the nation's second largest jail and was generally used by the Nazis to incarcerate British spies and captured men and women of the Resistance. The jail posed a special problem for Allied airmen.

In the first six months of 1944, the Nazis imprisoned 168 Allied pilots and airmen whom they had captured, with members of the Resistance in Fresnes. The Gestapo tortured many of these captives in order to obtain information about the French men and women who had aided them. Those who survived the brutal interrogations were shipped to Buchenwald Concentration Camp near Weimar, Germany. A number of Jewish airmen who survived Fresnes would never make it out of Buchenwald alive.

White points out that prisoners were sent to concentration camps "for a variety of reasons, including being Jewish." He goes on to mention what he calls a "sub-camp for U.S. POWs at Berga an der Elster, officially called *Arbeitskommando 625*" and also known as Stalag IX-B. Berga, he writes, "was the deadliest work detachment for American captives in Germany. 73 men who participated, or 21 percent of the detachment, perished in two months. 80 of the 350 POWs were Jews."[3]

Madame Rigal was determined to spare Arthur that terrifying fate. In contacting Taillandier, she was guessing that the ruthless leader of Morhange would feel the same and would also ensure that Mimi would control her mouth or face the consequences.

Madame Rigal could not have picked a more fortuitous moment to contact Taillandier rather than Pierre Auriac or another Brutus leader about her concerns over Mimi. In early February 1944, Dr. Auriac, Jean-Pierre Dupin, and other Brutus operatives began to worry, with good reason. Since the arrest of the network's chief, Andre Boyer, in December 1943, the Germans had been arresting rising numbers of the group's operatives.

|||||||||||||||||||||||||

On the afternoon of February 12, 1944, two and a half weeks since his arrival at the house, Arthur was sitting in the annex's worn but comfortable reading chair, leafing through old French magazines whose articles he could not understand but whose photos, illustrations, and ads provided a little diversion, when several voices—men's voices— suddenly drifted upstairs. Then he recognized Mimi's voice, but could not make out what she was saying. His fingers clenching the magazine, he strained to listen, a coldness creeping through him at the low, deep tone of the male voices, but he did not move.

Although the voices were muted, the words simmered with some sort of tension. His breath quickening, Arthur moved softly and slowly the few feet from his chair to the closed door in hopes he might hear a little bit more. The people downstairs were speaking French, but that meant little—the police would certainly speak that language, and he had learned firsthand that Gestapo agents also spoke it. Although the annex was chilly, a few beads of sweat dripped down his brow.

As footsteps echoed up the first flight of stairs and grew louder, Arthur backed away from the door toward the sole, shuttered window. He started to open the shutters when he recognized the click of Madame Rigal's thick-heeled shoes. She knocked gently, opened the door, and saw Arthur at the window. She assured him he was safe and asked her "darling boy" to close the shutters and come downstairs with her.[4] Then she paused, blinking back tears, and told him to bring his suitcase.

He grabbed his bag, his overcoat, and his beret and followed her down the three flights of stairs without a word or a look back.

When they stepped into the dining room, Mimi was slumped in a chair at the table, her head in her hands, her elbows resting on a tablecloth soiled by smoke from one of the house's two wood stoves.

There were several other people in the dining room, and Arthur's eyes widened at the sight of one, Marcel Taillandier, whose dark, unsettling eyes, beneath the same fedora he had worn at their first meeting, seemed to bore into him.

Glancing from Taillandier and the disconsolate Mimi to the five other men, Arthur found three of the scarred faces sullen, with eyes that seemed cold and cruel. The trio, who wore workers' caps and belted leather jackets over thick sweaters, resembled the menacing types who used to shake down Bronx store owners. Madame Rigal, who had nothing but praise for Taillandier, once said, "You know that he [Taillandier] had always with him several men he had been obliged to take [by order of Colonel Paillole] . . . because he wanted men able to kill. Well, they were gangsters."[5]

One of the men held Arthur's attention longer than the others. This Frenchman appeared even more sinister than his comrades, but there was still something about his demeanor that was more refined than that of a common thug or gangster. Square-jawed and tall, the broad-shouldered man fixed his narrowed, dusky eyes on Arthur. Deep, almost black hollows framed his eyes, and his shock of black hair rose up and back from a pronounced widow's peak. Arthur forced himself not to lower his gaze.

The man's lips curled back slightly toward his large nose, which had obviously been broken more than once. It was impossible to tell if the man's expression was a sneer or some semblance of a smile.

"Fontes," the Frenchman said in a strangely even tone.[6]

From a brutal and murky upbringing in Toulouse, Andrés Fontes had earned a reputation as a ferocious fighter. He had also paid attention in school and won a spot among some of France's sons of privilege at Saint-Cyr, the nation's equivalent of West Point or Sandhurst. Now thirty-two, Fontes had served as an infantry lieutenant until the fall of France, in 1940. Like Taillandier, he seethed with hatred for the Nazis and French collaborators. Also like Taillandier, Fontes had caught the attention of Colonel Paillole and proved himself in several counterintelligence missions in northern France as a man with no qualms about killing Germans and traitors face-to-face. Paillole described Fontes as a "smart and perceptive officer" and as the perfect top aide to Marcel Taillandier.[7]

Madame Rigal walked over to Arthur and clutched him tightly. She told him that she and Taillandier believed that "Mimi Dumas talked too much."[8]

Taillandier leaned down to Mimi and whispered. She lifted her head from her hands, her face pallid. Then Taillandier nodded at Arthur and led him, Fontes, and the four other men out the door. Arthur glanced back at the house. Through the window, Madame Rigal stood above the still-seated Mimi Dumas, shaking her finger at the younger woman.

Outside, no motorcycles or cars waited. As Fontes and two comrades walked down the street and turned a corner, Taillandier, Arthur, and the other two men waited. After five minutes passed, the two men headed in the same direction as Fontes's group. Only Taillandier and Arthur remained.

Checking his watch several times, Taillandier scanned the street in both directions. Then he tapped Arthur's shoulder and began to stride down the street. Arthur caught up to him, and as they rounded the corner onto a winding cobblestoned road in the shadow of a well-preserved thirteenth-century defense wall and roofed tower, a train whistle shrieked somewhere behind them; Taillandier quickened the pace.

Although traveling by train was risky for the Resistance, Taillandier knew that he could use the local railways for a few more weeks without worries of Allied planes attacking the tracks. Coded radio transmissions from London had alerted Resistance leaders to the fact that in March 1944, the Allies would put the long-debated and controversial "Transportation Plan" into effect. The purpose of this plan was to conduct large-scale bombings to destroy any French rail centers and lines that the Germans could use to send reinforcements from anywhere in France when Operation Overlord, D-Day, began.

Arthur followed Taillandier to a wider street named rue Fermat-Maison. At the far end, perhaps a hundred yards away, an elevated concrete platform rose from the street covered by a hulking, sharply sloped red-tiled roof. A sign hanging above the platform read *Matabiau-Toulouse*. The waiting area was not enclosed, and as they neared the steps to the platform, Taillandier's comrades separated and spread out among a dozen or so people awaiting the midafternoon train to Toulouse. Smoking cigarettes, the Morhange men all appeared to be alone and have no connection to each other.

Taillandier and Arthur, holding his suitcase, climbed onto the platform just as the train pulled up. The passengers lined up in front of the second car and waited. A police officer in a dark blue greatcoat and *képi* stepped from the train. Neither a uniformed nor a plainclothes Gestapo agent appeared behind him. As the official began to check identification cards, Taillandier pressed something into Arthur's free hand. It was a one-way ticket to Toulouse.

Four of Taillandier's men stood in the line ahead of Arthur. Turning his head almost imperceptibly, Arthur spotted Fontes near the group's rear. Fontes's right hand was buried in his coat pocket.

When Taillandier reached the police officer and carefully produced the identification card, the man did not even view it. Arthur was next, again staring woodenly at the officer's request and then acting in sudden understanding. "Georges" handed over his card and papers. As with Taillandier, the policeman did not even look at them or at Arthur, gave them back, and waved him onto the train. The gendarme must have been paid off by Taillandier or been one of his operatives.

Arthur was now traveling with a far different type of Resistance group than those he had met while in the care of Dr. Pierre Auriac, Dr. Pierre Chauvin, and pharmacist Gisèle Chauvin. While all of them were valiant and could certainly kill if they had to, Taillandier's men looked as though they *liked* to kill.

Colonel Paillole's orders to Taillandier were brutally simple: "Paralyze the enemy and destroy the traitors."[9] Men such as the late Alphonse Alsfasser were necessary for that mission. Throughout southern France, a half-dozen "repentant gangsters" who, despite their crimes, loved their nation and despised the Nazis and collaborators, had been recruited by Paillole's agents and assigned to Morhange for one simple reason.[10] They had no qualms about killing any German or any man or woman who was a traitor to France. They would shoot, stab, strangle, run over, or blow up anyone on Taillandier's command.

Paillole did not condone unwarranted executions, ordering that "the use of 'D' [the death lists] measures was to be systematic but in accordance with our rules."[11] For Taillandier, the phrase "in accordance with our rules" was key. It gave him latitude to "remove" any Nazi or collaborator whom he believed it necessary to kill on his own initiative. In short, Paillole gave Taillandier close to a free hand in deciding who was to die anywhere in the region. The men escorting Arthur to Toulouse served as Morhange's hit team—and they did their jobs with savage efficiency.

Arthur was seated beside Taillandier and next to a window from which he could watch the wooded foothills and ridges and ancient, walled market towns of the Midi-Pyrénées quickly slide by; the American shifted his position to find Fontes glancing at him across the aisle, measuring him, probing for any hint of fear or weakness. Arthur did not look away.

Once again, Fontes's lips curled up in that unreadable expression. He leaned back in his seat and closed his eyes. His right hand was still thrust deep into his coat pocket. Next to Arthur, Taillandier, who had obviously caught the silent exchange between his lieutenant and the airman, was wearing a hint of an approving smile. Most men averted their eyes instantly if Fontes looked at them. Staff Sergeant Meyerowitz had not lowered his gaze—even if he had wanted to do so.

As the train steamed along the tracks, the Gestapo was poised to unleash a catastrophe for the Resistance from Toulouse and Bordeaux to Lesparre.

CHAPTER 14

||||||||||||||||||||||||||||||||||||||||||||||

DEATH IN THE PINK CITY

When the train chugged into Toulouse about an hour and a half after departing Beaumont-de-Lomagne, the sprawling city was bathed in the day's last shreds of twilight. Countless brick buildings gave off a pale, roseate glow that over the centuries had earned Toulouse the nickname "the pink city."

The train slowed and inched its way into the giant station of Matabiau among dozens of other trains from which passengers streamed onto broad platforms. Pairs of Nazi soldiers patrolled everywhere, many of them with German shepherds or Dobermans ready to chase and pounce and tear apart anyone on their masters' command. As soon as Taillandier stepped into the aisle, Arthur followed. They stepped off the train and into the crowd filing into the station's concourse and forming lines in front of Gestapo agents.

Arthur had caught a break on the platform at Beaumont-de-Lomagne, thanks to Taillandier; however, the two Nazis checking the papers of the people ahead of him were taking their time with each passenger.

Shouts suddenly erupted at the front of an identification-inspection line. Taillandier and everyone around Arthur instantly flung themselves onto the floor as the concourse rang with commands of "Halt! Halt!" The Morhange men hugged the tiles, and Arthur did the same.

A young man in a tan coat desperately raced for the row of exit doors, a German shepherd closing fast behind him. He slipped on the tiles and crashed to the floor beneath one of the many bloodred, white, and black swastika banners hanging from the steel ceiling beams. An instant later the dog leaped onto him and began to tear at his face and neck.

As he screamed and tried to cover his face, Gestapo agents stood by and watched, grinning and pointing, and let the dog rip away part of an ear and the man's nose. Several soldiers ran up, and one called off the dog, who immediately stopped biting but stood growling over the shrieking man. One of the agents then slammed his jackbooted foot several times into the man's face.

As the Germans dragged the unconscious man away, people pushed themselves off the floor and re-formed their lines, no one uttering a word. The concourse stayed eerily quiet for a minute. Then commands of "I have *papieren*" (your papers) filled the terminal again. Several pools of blood seeped across the tiles where the man had fallen.[1]

Now, as Taillandier and Arthur reached the head of the line, Arthur's first personal encounter with the Toulouse Gestapo was at hand. The routine at the station always began the same way. At the agents' order, Taillandier reached into his coat and presented his identification card and papers. The Germans examined them and returned them promptly. He moved out of the line and kept walking.

Once again, the Nazis had no idea that "Ricardo" had walked right past them.

Arthur waited as one of the Nazis demanded his identification card and papers. The German cocked his head, scowled at Arthur, and shouted a second time for the papers as heads turned toward them. Waving the clipboard while pointing to a piece of paper, the Gestapo agent pointed at Arthur until he showed a sudden understanding. Carefully, he opened his coat, reached into the lining pocket, slowly took out his card and papers, and handed them over.

The Germans pored over his photo and documents, staring back at him and then to the photo several times. Arthur did not stir, keeping his hands in plain sight and straining to keep his face blank. Then, finally, one of the agents handed him back the papers.

Arthur stepped past the Nazis cautiously—again, hurried movements could attract unwanted scrutiny—and headed toward the long line of doors at the terminal's exit as one of the Germans bellowed for the next person in line.

Outside the station, people filed toward city buses or down the broad boulevard de Marengo on their way home before curfew. Taillandier, in his black fedora and expensive black coat, met Arthur in front of the station, whose lofty Romanesque facade was decorated with twenty-six colorful coats of arms cut into the stone and representing each town the original station had served in 1856. Near the mammoth clock, another gargantuan red banner with a swastika was hung, flapping in the wind. Taillandier glowered for an instant at the flag.

After about a forty-minute walk from Matabiau, Taillandier led Arthur onto another expansive street, the boulevard Deltour, crowded on both sides by three-story brick town houses and apartment buildings, many of them with ground-floor storefronts, cafés, and restaurants. Several of the buildings were mansions that had been passed down from one generation to the next.

The two men picked their way along the crowded sidewalks past a stunning granite hotel with gilded doors and giant arched windows. Somewhere behind them, Taillandier's men followed. Taillandier turned up the steps of a town house at 96, boulevard Deltour and rapped the brass door knocker. A young woman in a mauve blouse and dark skirt answered, smiled at Taillandier and Arthur, and let them inside. Before she closed the door, she looked up and down the street to make sure the men had not been tailed.

She introduced herself as Mademoiselle Thoulouse, daughter of the house's owner, M. E. Thoulouse, who owned a paint store in the city center and would be home soon to meet Arthur and Taillandier. She was Taillandier's chief supplier of stolen ration books, a wizard in the murky, dangerous black market.

Unlike most of his previous stops, the American airman would not be concealed in an attic or a shed, but would be hiding in plain sight as Georges Lambert, M. E. Thoulouse's new assistant at the paint store. Although the Resistance preferred to arrange escapes for downed Allied pilots and airmen as quickly as possible, the snow and ice choking the trails from October to late May created virtually impassable conditions even for a man in top shape. With his back injury, Arthur was not yet ready for the rigors posed by a trek across treacherous mountain passes even if it were summer. Taillandier not only needed to protect him by hiding him longer than usual, but also could not afford to put other escapees across the mountain routes in additional danger of being slowed down by an injured comrade. Arthur would have to stay in Toulouse until his back had healed or until the Germans got too close.

Every day, Arthur would have to leave the house to sweep the business's floors, dust the shelves, stock and restock the shelves, and run any number of errands for his "boss." He would have a comfortable bedroom on the second floor, an arrangement that would raise few suspicions, as Toulouse store owners often provided room and board for employees. He would take his meals with the family, and

Morhange would provide him with a ration card so that he would not deplete the family's own meager stores of rationed food. Like every other citizen, he was to stand and wait in long lines at nearby grocery markets and hope that the merchants did not run out of food before he got his allotted share.

The ruse Arthur was expected to play was daunting. One misstep, and he jeopardized everyone. Taillandier was placing enormous trust in him.

He was told to rest for a day or two before starting his job. Meanwhile, the Thoulouses began telling neighbors that they had hired a deaf mute named Georges, who came from Algiers and was a Soulac-sur-Mer resident seeking work in Toulouse. His limp came from a "farm accident" that prevented him from doing agricultural work for a while. No one outside his Resistance friends could ever suspect that his chronic limp was actually the result of a parachute jump from a burning B-24.

||||||||||||||||||||||||

While Arthur prepared for his new role, events that would place him in severe peril were taking shape in Bordeaux. The Gestapo, tipped off by informers and double agents, was closing in on Dr. Robert Neel—the head of Brutus in the Bordeaux region—and Jean-Pierre Dupin, and were searching for Dr. Pierre Auriac, Georges Tissot, and other operatives of the network. The Nazis had also gotten their hands on a Brutus courier who had documents with names of several network leaders and regional chiefs. Prominent on those lists were Pierre and Gisèle Chauvin.

At a little before 11 a.m. on February 20, 1944, Neel strolled into the Café des Arts in Bordeaux, found a small, white-clothed table near the front window, and tried not to appear too anxious as he peered at the entrance. He was supposed to meet with a courier and another Brutus agent, a young French naval officer. The brasserie was

Arthur Meyerowitz in New York
before World War II.
Courtesy of Meyerowitz Family

David Meyerowitz, Arthur's father.
Courtesy of Meyerowitz Family

Sergeant Arthur Meyerowitz,
aviation cadet, 1942.
Courtesy of Meyerowitz Family

B-24 *Harmful Lil' Armful*,
shot down over France on December 31, 1943.
National Archives

The 448th Bomb Group's commander,
Colonel James M. Thompson.
Arthur Meyerowitz served in the unit's 715th Bomb Squad.
National Archives

A crippled B-24 that made it back to Seething Airfield, England.
National Archives

Gisèle and Dr. Pierre Chauvin trained
Arthur Meyerowitz to portray
deaf-mute Georges Lambert
to fool the Gestapo.
Courtesy of Archives Nationales de France

Forged French I.D. depicting Arthur Meyerowitz as deaf-mute Georges Lambert.
Courtesy of Meyerowitz Family

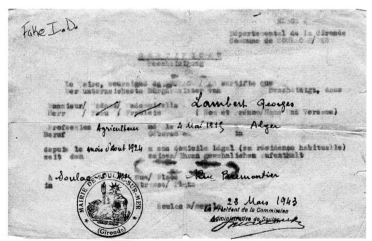

Forged letter presenting Arthur Meyerowitz as Georges Lambert,
a French-Algerian resident of Soulac-sur-Mer.
Courtesy of Meyerowitz Family

Marcel Taillandier, founder of Resistance network Morhange,
planned the escape of Arthur Meyerowitz and Lieutenant R.F.W. Cleaver. 1940.
Conseil départemental de la Haute-Garonne Musée de la Resistance et de la Déportation

Identity-card photo of Marcel Taillandier, 1942.
Conseil départemental de la Haute-Garonne Musée de la Resistance et de la Déportation

Andrés Fontes, a tough, trusted Morhange operative
who helped save Arthur Meyerowitz.
Conseil départemental de la Haute-Garonne Musée de la Resistance et de la Déportation

Lilli Camboville, Morhange agent and close friend of Marcel Taillandier.
Conseil départemental de la Haute-Garonne Musée de la Resistance et de la Déportation

A Nazi stop and search, July 1944. Arthur Meyerowitz faced searches such as these numerous times in occupied France.
Courtesy of Bundesarchiv, Berlin

German tanks rolling through Toulouse, a familiar sight for Arthur Meyerowitz.
Conseil départemental de la Haute-Garonne Musée de la Resistance et de la Déportation

Chateau de Brax, outside Toulouse.
Morhange Resistance held secret trials and executions of Nazi collaborators here.
Conseil départemental de la Haute-Garonne Musée de la Resistance et de la Déportation

Near Bordeaux, a maquis, a Resistance hideout similar to the one
where Arthur was hidden from the Gestapo.
Photo by Seth Meyerowitz

Interior of maquis, with inscription by a Resistance fighter on the wall.
Photo by Seth Meyerowitz

One of the Gestapo's torture chambers in Toulouse.

Conseil départemental de la Haute-Garonne Musée de la Resistance et de la Déportation

Highly decorated RAF pilot Lieutenant R.F.W. Cleaver
escaped the Nazis with Arthur Meyerowitz.

Courtesy of National Archives, UK

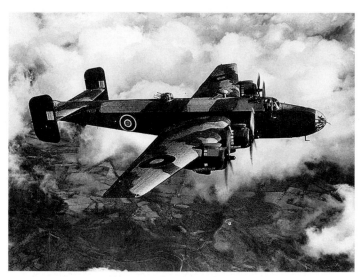

Halifax Bomber like the one Lieutenant R.F.W. Cleaver used
to drop supplies to the French Resistance in 1944.
Courtesy of National Archives, UK

Halifax Bomber shot down over France,
like that of Lieutenant R.F.W. Cleaver in April 1944.
Courtesy of National Archives, UK

A Resistance fighter facing a Nazi firing squad.
Courtesy of Archives Nationales de France

Marie-Louise Dissard,
second from left,
ran an escape network
for downed Allied airmen.
Photo by Francoise Jean Dieuzaide, 1944. Courtesy of Archives Nationales de France

The Pyrénées—Le Chemin de la Liberté—the road to liberty
for some three to five thousand Allied airmen.
Many others died or were captured in the attempt (figures vary).
National Archives, U.S., World War II Escape and Evasion File

The towering Pyrénées. The dangerous passes took four days
for Arthur and his companions to cross from France into Spain.
National Archives, U.S., World War II Escape and Evasion File

Arthur Meyerowitz shortly after the war.
Courtesy of Meyerowitz Family

Gisèle Chauvin survived torture by the Gestapo and Nazi concentration camps
to return to her family in Lesparre, France.
Photo courtesy of Patrick Chauvin

Pierre Delude, Resistance fighter and friend of Arthur Meyerowitz,
with Mark Meyerowitz, Arthur's son.
Photo by Seth Meyerowitz

already packed with people taking an early lunch. Many sipped coffee, as the café, frequented by Germans and locals alike, was one of the few spots in the city where the brew at least tasted better than the watery mess that passed for coffee anywhere else in Bordeaux.

As the minutes passed, neither man came through the door. Neel remained outwardly calm, but tension seeped through him. Something was wrong. Finally, he rose from the table and left the café. Historian Bernard Boyer writes, "He [the naval officer] would not come to the appointment given to him by his superior, Dr. Robert Neel, at the Café des Arts."[2] Earlier that morning, the Gestapo had tried to arrest the officer, but he had put up a fight, taking down two agents with his revolver before dying at a military hospital from his wounds. He had been dead for hours before Neel went to the café.

Neel headed down the street toward the small office where he and his operatives met in secret. Boyer relates, "The head of the Bordeaux region, wanting to do too much, then made a mistake: he rushes to the [office] at Tondu Street . . ."[3]

Waiting there for Neel were four French police officers who were collaborators and part of a special antiterror unit. They seized him and turned him over to the Gestapo.

The search for his colleagues Jean-Pierre Dupin, Dr. Pierre Auriac, and Georges Tissot was under way. The Gestapo was also about to pounce on Pierre and Gisèle Chauvin.

CHAPTER 15

‖‖‖‖‖‖‖‖‖‖‖‖‖‖‖‖‖‖‖‖‖‖‖‖‖‖‖‖‖‖‖‖‖‖‖‖‖‖

THE GESTAPO AT THE DOOR

At 7 a.m. on February 27, 1944, in Lesparre, the ringing doorbell and sharp knocks brought Simone Blanchard, the Chauvins' maid, to the front door of the house. Upstairs in the dining room near the wood stove and still clad in her dressing gown, Gisèle wondered who was on her stoop so early. The pharmacy was not yet open, as almost anyone in Lesparre would have known, and she and Pierre were not expecting any new "guests." Pierre, who was planning to visit several patients on his motorcycle, was in the children's bedroom talking with his mother-in-law and helping the children to get dressed.

Simone opened the door to find three well-dressed men. Sneering, one introduced himself and his companions as "Dupont, Durand, and Dubois." Despite their French names, something seemed off about them, and Simone hesitated. In that instant they pulled out pistols, pushed into the house, and grabbed her. She screamed to alert Pierre and Gisèle and struggled for a moment to try to break their grip, but quickly stopped, realizing that they were Gestapo and that resistance was useless.

As the clamor moved up the stairs toward the dining room, Pierre instinctively took a step to join his wife there, but stopped. He and Gisèle had discussed what they might do in a situation like this and had agreed that if one of them could escape capture and alert the rest of the Brutus Network that the Gestapo was onto them, that's what they had to do. As hard as it would be, they had to do it.

Though he despised leaving the house, he realized he had no choice. He climbed out the children's bedroom window and onto the roof above the vacant pigsty and jumped to the backyard.

As more Gestapo arrived in dark sedans and poured into the house, several Germans emerged through the back door and fanned out across the small yard. It did not take long to find the doctor's hiding spot, haul him to his feet, and begin a harsh interrogation on the spot.

Inside, the three agents shoved the ashen-faced Simone upstairs and into the dining room, where Gisèle waited. One of the Nazis pointed his pistol at her and growled, "You will come with us!"

Upstairs from Gisèle, the Germans had rounded up the rest of the family. The three children and Gisèle's mother, fifty-eight-year-old Mercédes Lacombe, who lived with them, were in the master bedroom. Gisèle, knowing there was no chance of escape, was determined to delay the Nazis long enough for her mother to destroy the Brutus paperwork, fake ID cards, communiqués, codes, and other damning evidence hidden in an armoire conveniently placed close to the bedroom's fireplace for just such a moment.

Gisèle forced a slight smile at them. She insisted that if they were to take her away for questioning, proper German gentlemen would first allow her to bathe and change.

After a brief discussion, the head agent nodded brusquely to her and told her to make it fast. Gisèle had other ideas. The moment she saw the young agent assigned to stand guard between the open doors of the bathroom and the bedroom, she improvised a plan. The other men pounded down the stairs to join the rough interrogation of Pierre. Gisèle tried to ignore the shouts from below.

Mercédes Lacombe watched the guard, anticipating that her daughter would try to divert his attention. Mercédes, a patriot like her daughter and Pierre, knew the drill—whoever was closest to the papers at such a moment was responsible for destroying them. If the Gestapo found the Brutus documents, torture and possible execution awaited Gisèle, Pierre, and herself. The fate of the children would be anyone's guess. Seizure of the papers would also doom Arthur Meyerowitz and the other airmen Brutus was helping.

As soon as she felt the young Nazi's eyes on her, Gisèle began filling the tub, slowly unbuttoned her blouse, then slipped out of her skirt. She knew that it would be enough to hold his attention. Turning her back to him, she finished undressing and stepped into the tub. Leaning against the doorframe, mesmerized, the agent watched her clean herself with the warm, soapy water.

Mercédes, less than six feet from the guard peering into the bathroom, called out to the agent and asked if she could light a fire because the children were cold. He did not even turn from the bathroom, staring at Gisèle, and snapped, *"Oui."*[1]

Mercédes hastily lit the bedroom's fireplace, removed the papers from the armoire, and tossed them into the blaze as fast as she could. Sensing that her daughter would step from the tub shortly and that the Nazi agent might turn and see what the grandmother was doing at the fireplace, she slipped over to Patrick's crib, picked him up, cradled him in one arm, and used her free hand to stuff the last few papers into his diaper.

When Gisèle finished dressing, Mercédes, who was crying, came over to her and held up Patrick for his mother to kiss for what both women believed was the final time. Nine-year-old Jean-Claude and six-year-old Monique rushed up to hug their mother, who blinked back tears. The German who had watched her in the bathroom tore Gisèle from her children and escorted her down the stairs and outside to the waiting Gestapo sedans.

Although she could not see her neighbors looking through shutters at the scene, she felt their eyes on her. Most, she knew, were terrified for the Chauvins. She did not dare glance in the direction of Pierre and Mimi Delude's house, just across the street from the Chauvins and in the same block of buildings as Gestapo headquarters. She prayed that they were not next.

As the agents opened the rear passenger door of a sedan and ordered her inside, she stiffened at the sight of Pierre, whose face was battered, being shoved into another car. She suspected that it was likely her last glimpse of her husband and that she would never see her mother, her children, or her home again.

Having found no evidence in the house, the Gestapo left Gisèle's mother, the three children, and Simone behind and sped off to the Villa Calypso with Gisèle, who knew what awaited her there. It is uncertain whether the Gestapo took Pierre just across the street to their Lesparre headquarters or elsewhere, but he was not brought to the same spot as his wife. The fate of Arthur, Brutus, and the other Allied fighters helped by the Chauvins lay in how the couple stood up to their coming ordeal.

CHAPTER 16

HIDING IN PLAIN SIGHT

The news that the Gestapo and the police had shattered Brutus and arrested its leaders spread throughout southern France. In London and in Algiers, where Free French and British intelligence units had set up shop after the Allied invasion of North Africa, the fallout from the February 1944 ambushes in Toulouse and Bordeaux was alarming. If Jean-Pierre Dupin, Gisèle Chauvin, and other captured Brutus agents cracked under torture, the Nazis would surely show up at the homes of the network's other associates.

By early March 1944, Arthur had learned to play his part well. He turned into Georges Lambert every time he left M. E. Thoulouse's old, three-story stone house at 96, boulevard Deltour. Neighbors usually greeted the handsome young man with a wave or a smile, but not with words. As far as they knew, Georges was a deaf mute from Algiers and a Soulac-sur-Mer resident who was visiting Toulouse from the coastal town.

As Arthur's confidence and ability to feign deafness and a complete lack of speech grew, he started to explore Toulouse. He wasn't sightseeing, however, but instead doing reconnaissance. In briefings on how pilots and airmen were to seek help and conduct themselves if shot down, lecturers had told crewmen that if they were presented with any opportunity to reconnoiter enemy positions/movements or to gather potentially useful information about the German forces and targets for Allied bombers, they were to take it. Later, if they escaped from France, they were expected to write down their observations for American and British intelligence officers.

When he was not helping out at Thoulouse's paint store during his first few Sundays in the city, the American walked among the crowds of the grand Place du Capitole. Passing chapels, churches, Gothic cathedrals, and splendid old mansions such as the sprawling Hôtel d'Assézat, he noted the faces and morale of the thousands of German troops occupying Toulouse. He strolled along the Canal du Midi, which connected the Garonne River to the Mediterranean, and made a mental note that the Pont Neuf and other railway bridges across the river offered inviting targets for bombers. He did the same every time he spotted German supply depots and barracks.

He was somewhat surprised at either how young or how old many of the soldiers were. To Arthur, many of the Germans looked as though they had served in World War I. He was right. Nazi casualties on the Eastern Front against the Soviets were staggering, forcing the Germans to press teenagers and old veterans into service.

Arthur found a city swarming with Germans always looking over their shoulders for any hint of Resistance operatives about to launch an ambush or peering skyward for any sign of Allied bombers. For the first few weeks of March 1944, the Allies bombed targets outside the city, but not Toulouse itself. All of that was about to change as the countdown to the invasion of Fortress Europe began in earnest.

Plastered on the walls of buildings all over Toulouse were posters urging citizens to turn in Jewish neighbors to the authorities and depicting them as half rat, half human. Arthur did not have to read French to understand the savage messages on those placards. No matter how many times he viewed them, anger simmered inside him. Even worse, many times he stopped in his tracks as the Gestapo dragged men, women, and children from apartment buildings and shops or simply grabbed them on the streets. The Germans' shouts of *"Juden!"* pealed through the air, and Arthur could do nothing except watch as the Nazis pummeled the men and sometimes the women with fists, jackboots, and batons. The beatings stopped only when a truck rolled up and the Gestapo tossed the Jews into the back. Their next stop was the train station and a long, hopeless journey northeast to the concentration camps. His head throbbing from the scenes, Arthur yearned to get back into the fight.

Wherever he went in the city, swastikas surrounded him. Not only were Nazi flags draped above the doorways of every public building, but they also fluttered from every flagpole. Banners with the loathsome symbol were affixed to streetlamps and trees. Giant gilded brass eagles whose talons grasped lightning bolts and swastikas were attached to walls throughout Toulouse. In every corner of the city, there was no escaping the Nazis' emblems of occupation.

Arthur learned that life in occupied Toulouse meant shortages of food and virtually every consumer good. For all but well-connected citizens or those with access to the black market, rationed food was poorly or indifferently distributed. Malnourishment, especially among children and the elderly, was rampant. The Germans seized 20 percent of all crops, meat, and dairy products from the farmland outside the city. Making matters worse, fertilizer and gas for farm vehicles were in short supply, hampering production because farmers had to use their own muscle or spindly old horses to work the fields. Near-empty shelves were common in every food store Arthur entered.

With German officials setting the policies, hunger prevailed. Arthur stood for hours in the long queues in front of food shops and

was grateful that his diet was augmented by the black-market deal-
ings of Taillandier and his Morhange operatives. In the rural safe
houses outside Toulouse, however, he had found food more plentiful.
Farmers who were not always under the scrutiny of the Germans and
the Vichy police secretly slaughtered livestock, planted hidden vege-
table gardens, and hid milk and cheese.

Through Mademoiselle Thoulouse's skills in amassing counterfeit and stolen ration books and coupons, Taillandier had access to
additional sources of food and also dealt them on the black market to
help fund Morhange's lethal operations. He also garnered a sizable
stash of francs and Reichsmarks (Nazi currency) by trading ration
books, food, liquor, and cigarettes for weapons. Many of those arms
were smuggled in from Algiers or dropped for the Resistance at night
by Allied planes. Much of Taillandier's illicit money went to purchase
one of the region's scarcest commodities—gasoline. Taillandier
hoarded the precious fuel for Morhange's hit-and-run operations such
as the Courier de Nice ambush in January 1944.

At 96, boulevard Deltour, Taillandier visited Arthur often and
also met there with key Morhange members. Taillandier included
Arthur in nearly all of the gatherings, and because the operatives,
several women among them, conversed only in hushed French, Taillandier would turn to Arthur and explain much of what the agents
were discussing. Because the Morhange leaders obviously trusted the
American airman, the others quickly accepted him as one of them, at
least in some ways.

Arthur came to know several of the Morhange leadership well,
but only by their first names. They made certain that they never mentioned their surnames in front of him, but not because they did not
trust him. It was far safer for him not to know their complete names
in case he fell into Gestapo hands. He sat down on numerous occasions with Taillandier and Andrés Fontes, who had "four fingers off
his left hand" from an injury he suffered during the Fall of France in

1940.[1] A crafty Morhange agent named Jeno had infiltrated and worked with the Toulouse Gestapo and had full access to their operations and documents. Additionally, he and Taillandier had five other plants inside the local Gestapo. The man whom Arthur knew only as "Leo" was one of Morhange's bravest and most cunning leaders under Taillandier's command. Henri was a Vichy police officer and one of Taillandier's most trusted operatives. At the wheel of a Citroën sedan for scores of Morhange hits of Nazis and collaborators was Robert, a gifted "chauffeur."

Arthur came to know all of them, as well as Yvonne, a young operative who came often to Thoulouse's house for the meetings.

On numerous occasions, Taillandier took Arthur for lunch or dinner at the Frascati, the downtown Toulouse café that was always crammed not just by the locals, but also by Vichy police, German soldiers, and Gestapo. Arthur realized that the attractive women who worked at the café were actually prostitutes who used the bedrooms upstairs to service clients, and also to pry useful intelligence from Nazis and collaborators and pass it on to Taillandier. In meetings at Thoulouse's house, Taillandier had told Arthur, several times, that he and "his girls" blackmailed French police and collaborators to provide information to Morhange. Often, Taillandier's operatives forced them to pass sensitive intelligence to Morhange or be tried and executed at Chateau de Brax. None of them ever saw Taillandier unless they refused to cooperate, in which case his face was among the last the collaborators ever saw. He made certain that no one could connect him in any way to the unit.

To the patrons of the Frascati, Taillandier appeared the very picture of a dapper, French professional. His neat, pencil-thin mustache, dark, slicked-back hair, and well-tailored suit made him fit in perfectly. Arthur sipped his wine, admiring how Taillandier practiced what he preached about hiding in plain sight. The often ruthless Morhange chief moved seamlessly among his enemies.

Once, when a known collaborator confronted Taillandier at the café and demanded proof that he was not a member of the Resistance, Taillandier sprang from his chair and knocked out the accuser with one swift punch. Standing over him, he shouted that no one could accuse him of being a member of the Resistance and get away with such a lie. His "outrage" duped the Gestapo agents watching with both amusement and alertness as several of his "associates" dragged the man out the back door. The man's fate is unknown, but it seems reasonable to assume he "disappeared."

Arthur did not want to be taken alive by the Nazis and wanted a pistol so that he could go out fighting if the Gestapo tried to seize him. Again and again, he asked Marcel for one. Taillandier was reluctant to comply, knowing that if the American—a Jewish American no less—was ever discovered to be concealing a weapon, it would be all over for him.

Arthur was subjected to increasing stop-and-checks by the Gestapo and police in mid-March. The American and British Air Forces were launching the Transportation Plan to soften up the Nazis for the imminent invasion. By day, American bombers pounded targets on the city's outskirts, where Nazi munitions dumps were camouflaged but identified by the Resistance for Allied airpower; by night, it was the Royal Air Force's turn. The bombers left the city's center, which was devoid of bona fide military targets, alone. Even though Allied intelligence, thanks to the Resistance, knew where Gestapo headquarters and outposts in the heart of Toulouse were located, they did not strike the city center, believing that civilian casualties among the patriotic French would far surpass any damage to the Nazis.

Though Taillandier had insisted several weeks earlier that the American go outside every day and Arthur was not afraid to do so, he did wonder if the escalating searches by the Gestapo and heightened fears among neighbors who collaborated with the Nazis might make some question the identity of Monsieur Thoulouse's guest.

During one of Taillandier's frequent visits to the house on the boulevard Deltour, Arthur asked him, "Wouldn't it be safer for all of you if I were to stay inside more?"[2]

Marcel, knowing that Arthur now relished his cautious forays into the city, leaned back on a battered divan, lit a cigarette, and took a drag. Smiling, he explained that with the Nazis and the police growing more anxious by the day, anything out of the ordinary attracted attention. If a suspicious neighbor noticed that Georges Lambert was suddenly absent, the Gestapo would show up at Monsieur Thoulouse's door.

Arthur was confronted the very next day. He left the house and walked to an open-air market to buy bread and fruit. Suddenly a Gestapo agent in the blood-chilling black uniform and jackboots emerged from behind a produce stall, munching an apple. He peered at Arthur, took a bite of the apple, and hurled it at Arthur's shoes.

The German strode up to him, Arthur's heart racing. When the German snarled for the "Frenchman" to produce his papers, Arthur hoped that his face showed no tinge of anything more than the natural fear anyone would have for the Germans at that time.

Arthur stared at him as if confused, then nodded in sudden understanding, and reached into his jacket pocket for his identification card and the letter embossed with the signature and official seal of the mayor of Soulac-sur-Mer and attesting that the bearer was town resident Georges Lambert.

The agent glared at the photo identification card and letter, grunted something, flung them at Arthur, and stomped away to stop another passerby.

The people of Toulouse were subjected to daily stop-and-checks. Even though the risk of discovery threatened him every time he went out, his practiced self-discipline and dread of capture had turned him into Georges Lambert to the outside world. In public, Arthur never reacted to loud noises, never reacted to voices, and never spoke. He communicated only through hand gestures. Although he had picked up some French in the weeks since *Harmful Lil Armful* had gone down, he never spoke a word of it outside the safe house.

In late March 1944, Arthur took a bus to the city center of Toulouse to bring Monsieur Thoulouse his lunch: a baguette, cold chicken, and fruit. As always, when Arthur stepped off the bus in front of the store, he fought a cold flush of fear raised by the giant swastika flag that was draped above the entrance of the adjacent building—the local Gestapo headquarters. Agents in black uniforms with skull-and-crossbones-adorned caps or dark suits with low-brimmed black fedoras bustled in and out of the building. It was a medieval structure with narrow-slit windows, parapets, and two steel front doors. To Arthur, it reeked of the horrors of the Inquisition and now those of the Gestapo.

He shivered slightly and headed from the bus stop toward the store. A tall man in a black uniform strode down the steps of the headquarters, folded his arms, and fixed his light blue eyes beneath his visor on Arthur. Arthur walked by him as casually as he could.

"Halt!"

The harsh command exploded in Arthur's ears, but he kept walking as he had been trained to do.

"*Halt!*" the agent barked a second time.

As Arthur approached Thoulouse's door and reached for the knob, a huge hand clamped down on his forearm and spun him around. The Gestapo agent released his grip and leaned so close to Arthur that he could smell beer and onion on the man's breath.

"*Papieren!*" the German snarled. Every Frenchman and woman knew the word now—*papers*. Arthur stared with practiced confusion at him, saying nothing.

Glaring, the Nazi shouted again at Arthur to show his papers. The agent took a step back, sizing up the "Frenchman" in his patched overcoat and neat but old brown woolen suit and worn shoes.

Arthur widened his eyes, raised his hands slowly with his palms up as if in supplication, and shook his head.

The German cocked his head, appraised Arthur for several seconds, and then reached into his pocket. He produced his Gestapo identification card and pointed to it. For a few more moments, Arthur feigned confusion. Suddenly he nodded and reached carefully into his coat. He pulled out his ID card and documents.

The Gestapo agent studied the photo and looked up at Arthur at least a half-dozen times. Frowning, he handed the papers back, and as Arthur tucked them back in his overcoat, the German stepped quietly behind him. Arthur noticed the movement, steeling himself not to flinch no matter what the Nazi did. Still, Arthur would not have been surprised if his face somehow reflected the sudden dryness in his throat and tightness in his chest.

CLAP! CLAP!

Arthur felt every muscle constrict at the sound of those two giant hands slamming into each other, but did not react. He remained still.

Finally, the German stepped back in front of him and thrust a thick forefinger in his face. As the man's lips twisted into a sneer, he fixed his cold, pale blue eyes on the American.

Arthur's jaw tightened, but he did not flinch, not a muscle quivering with any hint that he understood. The German wagged his finger several times in Arthur's face, still sneering. The German demanded an answer in English, waiting for any flicker of a response. To trip up Allied airmen posing as civilians, the Nazis routinely snapped questions in English during stop-and-checks.

Arthur looked back at him vacantly.

The German stepped back, grinned maliciously, and backed away a few steps. He turned, laughed, and stomped away.

Arthur did not budge until the German vanished around a corner.

As Arthur finally returned to the paint shop, Monsieur Thoulouse opened the glass door. Arthur, his face pale, hoped he would not run into the Gestapo agent again, although he would now watch for him every second.

It became obvious over the next few days that the man was also watching for Arthur. Whenever he got off the bus to walk over to the paint store, the agent was always standing on the sidewalk nearby, smoking and staring at him with a tight smile. Arthur tried to vary the times of his trips back and forth from Thoulouse's shop, but it did not matter. The Nazi was always lurking, always watching for Georges Lambert. Although Arthur feared that the Gestapo agent would one day follow him to 96, boulevard Deltour, the man seemed content for the moment with tracking him from the bus to the store.

⫿⫿⫿⫿⫿⫿⫿⫿⫿⫿⫿⫿

A week after his first brush with the suspicious German, Arthur was sitting with Taillandier and another Morhange agent over lunch at a white-clothed table near the Frascati's gleaming marble-topped bar. As Taillandier and the other man chatted in a low tone, Arthur played his usual role of Georges, unable to hear a sound. Taillandier rose from his seat and walked over to the bar, where he began speaking to the bartender.

The door to the café swung open. Three uniformed Gestapo agents strutted into the restaurant, scanned the crowded room, and walked up to a table near Arthur's, their hobnailed boots clattering against the floorboards.

Arthur's eyes widened. There was no mistaking it. The massive Gestapo agent who was so suspicious of him just a week prior now loomed a few feet from his table and was looking right at him. From the bar, Taillandier caught the look that the German shot at the American, and edged subtly to the end of the bar, out of the Germans' line of vision.

The trio stopped. A portly agent wearing a major's insignia pointed at the other table's two middle-aged Frenchmen and their female companions, two young women in low-cut dresses and slit skirts, unquestionably expensive prostitutes. The major ordered the two men to disappear and the women to remain with the snap of his fingers. The men sprang from their chairs and startled a busboy right behind Arthur's table. The youth stumbled and dropped his overloaded bin of dishes, glasses, and utensils.

Heads turned to the crash of ceramic, glass, and metal—Arthur and his two companions leaped from their chairs. The giant Gestapo agent smiled at Arthur and then lunged at him with frightening speed. Before he could pin Arthur's arms, Arthur slipped his identification card and paper out of his jacket and under the table too quickly for the German to detect. Taillandier saw Arthur's move, eased behind the bar, and waited.

An instant later the Nazi grabbed Arthur. "Georges Lambert" could obviously hear something.

Another Gestapo man handcuffed Arthur, and the three dragged him out the door. Arthur knew where they were headed. He knew he was a dead man.

Taillandier had vanished out the back door of the café but not before waiting for the Gestapo to leave and deftly scooping up Arthur's identification card and papers. By the time that one of the three Gestapo agents thought to race back into the Frascati to look for anyone who had been with Arthur, both Taillandier and the other agent were long gone.

Arthur was tossed into a dank, windowless cell in the Gestapo headquarters next to the paint store.

In an hour, two Gestapo agents in plain clothes stepped into his cell and closed the door. They removed their jackets and rolled up their white shirtsleeves. One pulled Arthur to his feet, twisted his arms behind his back, and held him so that he faced the other German.

The man in front of Arthur said something to him in French.

Arthur remained silent. Then, in English, the agent said, "Tell us the names of your friends at the restaurant, and we might let you live."

Arthur stared blankly.

Again, the Gestapo agent asked something in French, and then in English: "Why don't you have an ID and photo? Who are you?"

He waited a few seconds for an answer.

When none came, the German suddenly slammed his fist into Arthur's stomach. The breath rushed from him, the hammerlock on his arms preventing him from doubling over. Again and again the Nazi's fist thudded against Arthur's stomach. Still, he said nothing.

A swift, savage kick to Arthur's groin caused him to pass out. The German behind him released his grip and shoved the airman to the floor. Slowly, he came to, pain rippling through him. Kicks now rained on him from every angle, to his face, his torso, his arms, and legs. Drifting in and out of consciousness, he lost track of time. All he sensed was the pain everywhere.

At some point, the agents pulled him from the floor and tied him to the cell's sole piece of furniture, a cracked, sagging wooden chair. One of them tossed a pail of frigid water in his face.

Grinning, the Nazi said in French, "Wake up."

His comrade grabbed Arthur's chin, squeezed hard, and turned his face upward.

"Now, your name," he hissed, again in French.

Arthur said nothing.

The German's fist smashed against Arthur's left ear and sent the chair careening at a wall. Arthur crashed against the stone and grunted as he and the chair toppled to the floor.

Both Germans loomed over him. The kicks thudded into him again for several minutes before the pair picked him up and drove the chair upright against the floor.

His eyes were nearly closed from the swelling tissue around

them, and the Germans' faces were hazy. Arthur gagged from the blood pouring from his mouth to his throat.

"Your name?" exploded in French again in his ears—and then in English.[3]

Arthur did not answer. The two men kicked the chair back to the floor and rained kicks on Arthur's ribs, back, and stomach.

Finally, the blows ceased. Arthur was barely aware of the Gestapo agents untying him, flinging him into a corner, and leaving him alone in the cell to await their return.

CHAPTER 17

NOT A MOMENT TOO SOON

Taillandier did not flee the city. Despite de Gaulle's directive not to become too involved in escape and rescue of Allied airmen, Taillandier had no intention of abandoning Arthur to the Gestapo. However, he had to move fast before the torture began. Mere hours were all that he had, but he knew someone who just might be able to stroll into Gestapo headquarters and emerge unchallenged with Arthur. Even though it could jeopardize the survival of Morhange, Taillandier had made up his mind. He could not let the Germans go to work on the brave airman.

Taillandier circled back to the town center, skirting the Gestapo headquarters. He strolled into another medieval-era structure with damp, grimy stone walls—the local police station. There, the Vichy police decided whether to rough up locals before turning them over to the Gestapo, or to simply bring them to the Germans. In Toulouse, the police killed only one member of the Resistance. The Gestapo did the rest, torturing and executing many French men and women first arrested by the police. As far as Taillandier and Morhange were concerned, the police were collaborators and traitors. Scores of policemen were gunned down in Toulouse by Morhange or tried, executed, and buried at the Château de Brax.

Taillandier slipped the desk clerk an envelope with the usual amount of francs and asked him to tell Henri that a friend needed to speak with him immediately in the usual place.

Taillandier walked out of the station and darted through a boulevard teeming with cars, trucks, and military vehicles to a small brasserie. He stepped inside, his eyes adjusting to the low-wattage lamps that did little to illuminate the dark-walled, dark-draped interior. Nodding to the elderly man sipping coffee and reading a paper behind the scarred bar, Taillandier slid into a booth near the rear exit, pulled the threadbare curtains closed, and waited for Henri.

Fifteen minutes later, the curtains parted to reveal a short, wiry middle-aged man in the Legionnaire cap and dark blue uniform of the reviled Vichy police. He sat in the frayed leather seat opposite Taillandier, pulled the curtains shut, and peered through his tight-fitting pince-nez glasses at him. Taillandier took out a gold case and offered the policeman a cigarette, which he accepted and lit.

Henri, a captain in the Vichy police, was one of Taillandier's most trusted and cunning agents and had met Arthur a number of times at Thoulouse's house. Taillandier relied on Henri and other Morhange operatives who had infiltrated the Vichy police and even the Gestapo, spying on the enemy's movements and passing the intelligence quickly and efficiently to Taillandier.

Taillandier lit up a cigarette, took a deep drag, and said in a near whisper that he needed Henri to deliver an order to someone named Jeno about the American immediately and warned the officer that the Gestapo may have "made" Taillandier at the Frascati.

As always, Henri followed Taillandier's orders to the letter.

Less than an hour later, Jeno, wearing the black Gestapo uniform, embarked upon his mission. Taillandier's best and most fearsome "inside man," he terrified even the most vicious Gestapo agents with his huge shoulders and chest, his jutting-jawed, deeply creased visage, and feral amber eyes. No one in Toulouse even knew where he had come from. The simple fact was that people feared him, and that allowed him to convince the Gestapo of his high value.

A trusted Nazi sympathizer, the giant Frenchman had risen to second in command of the Toulouse Gestapo, and none of the Germans questioned his loyalty. No one suspected that Jeno was a Morhange agent who had been passing intelligence to Taillandier for months. Further, no one suspected that Taillandier had five other men working for the Gestapo as clerks with access to sensitive documents.

Time after time, Jeno had helped Taillandier and other Resistance men and women elude capture or betrayal. The task Taillandier had just relayed to the operative, however, was the riskiest that Taillandier had ever given him. Although Jeno knew that one misstep on his part could ruin Taillandier and Morhange, he understood that Taillandier would not relent.

With Taillandier commanding that the matter be resolved immediately, Jeno knew what he had to do, even if it meant blowing his cover.

Jeno took a deep breath, walked up the steps of the Gestapo headquarters, opened the heavy steel doors with little effort, and entered. He glowered at a young Gestapo agent manning the front desk. At the sight of Jeno in his black hat, emblazoned with the skull-and-crossbones emblem, the agent nearly fell as he scrambled from his chair to salute him.

Jeno demanded to know where the prisoner from the Frascati was being held and whether he had confessed to anything or had revealed any names of his associates.

Pale, his mouth quivering, the agent pointed down the corridor and shook his head no. Relieved that the American had said nothing, Jeno stormed past the German and sent him sprawling to the stone floor with a shove.

Jeno turned a corner, glanced back to where the agent was still lying on the floor, and leaned against the cold, wet granite wall. Closing his eyes for a moment, he inhaled deeply and slowly exhaled. Step one was complete.

He walked up to Arthur's cell and reached into his pocket for his keys. With a metallic rasp, the heavy, scarred steel door opened. Arthur was crumpled on the bare stone floor in the fetal position, his clothes tattered and his swollen face streaked with blood. For a moment, Jeno feared that the American was dead, but then Arthur groaned.

Jeno moved with a speed unusual for a man of his size. The crunch of boots against stone signaled that other Gestapo agents were rushing down the corridor to assist him with the prisoner. As soon as they arrived at the open cell, Jeno kicked the prone American in the back and ordered him to his feet. Behind him, several officers stared and inched back a few steps—Jeno intimidated even the most sadistic of his fellow Gestapo agents.

He reached down, grabbed Arthur's collar, and hauled him to his feet as if the prisoner weighed merely a few pounds. As the other Gestapo agents scattered, he dragged the groaning Arthur out of the cell and down the hall. Without looking back, Jeno informed anyone within earshot that he was transferring the prisoner to solitary in a smaller Gestapo building reserved for captives about to disappear.

No one followed him. None of the Gestapo men believed that the prisoner would even make it to solitary. Jeno's special interest in him meant that the massive French collaborator had likely decided to take the man somewhere, torture and kill him, and then dump the body. Jeno was counting on that belief. Several times before, he had removed prisoners, and they had "disappeared." His Gestapo colleagues never suspected that each of those prisoners had been a Morhange operative whom Taillandier could not afford to lose or to have reveal secrets under torture. Arthur was the first American Taillandier had ever ordered Jeno to remove.

Jeno yanked the barely conscious Arthur out the front door of the headquarters and tossed him into the backseat of a dark sedan. Groggy, but certain he was about to be killed, Arthur lifted his blackened, bloody eyes and suddenly realized that the Gestapo agent was Jeno. For a moment, he thought that he was hallucinating, that the man could not possibly be who he thought he was. Then the man behind the wheel inclined his head slightly back toward Arthur and nodded. Arthur recognized Robert, Taillandier's "chauffeur."

Then, from the front passenger seat, another man leaned over toward Arthur and smiled. Marcel Taillandier's face was the last thing Arthur saw before he passed out.

At that moment, Arthur was far more fortunate than Gisèle Chauvin and Pierre Dupin. Dupin was languishing in solitary confinement at Fresnes Prison, left naked, battered, and unfed for days at a time until the next round of torture began. He had not given up anyone's name.

The Gestapo had whisked Gisèle from Lesparre to the Villa Calypso for her first round of questioning, and as Arthur was being arrested and subsequently rescued from the Gestapo, she was being held at Fort du Ha, an ancient stone prison in Bordeaux. Her cell was one of those reserved for "select prisoners": "The bars were flat and held together by a traversed pair palming the vertical ones. There was also a wooden box, trapped in front of it, preventing the prisoners from looking down [i.e., outside] as well as drawing attention to a little light coming in from the sky."[1]

She and the other select prisoners, most of them captured Resistance members, had no toilet, no cot, no blanket, and were denied the once-a-week communal showers that other prisoners were allowed to take in the bastion's oldest tower, where the Germans forced prisoners to walk in a circle as ice-cold water cascaded down on them.

Around the dank, tiny cells where Gisèle and other special prisoners were suffering "were lots of guards, a small army around [them] and within the fort itself."[2] Much worse was in store for Gisèle Chauvin, who had not surrendered one name or any other information about the Resistance to her Nazi torturers.

Another Fort du Ha inmate, a Jewish man slated for transportation to the concentration camp at Buchenwald, wrote, "Sometimes, we could hear prisoners being taken away early in the morning. We often heard brave women patriots singing the 'Marseillaise' [the French national anthem]. These women helped to boost our morale and pride in the cause, which was all we had left!"[3]

Battered, deprived of sleep, and poorly fed, Gisèle heard those voices one morning. Through her cracked, swollen lips, she mouthed the words of her anguished nation's anthem.

CHAPTER 18

THE MAQUIS

Taillandier's driver, Robert, navigated the black Citroën through Toulouse's late-afternoon traffic, darting past buses, German Army trucks and troop carriers, and other cars. As Taillandier and his eighty-two Morhange operatives knew and used to their advantage, few people other than officials, police, or Gestapo could drive automobiles because of the severe shortages of gas. Even the authorities assumed that any large Citroëns or Mercedes sedans on the road belonged to them, not French civilians. Taillandier's deft use of the black market ensured that he always had enough gasoline hidden away for ambushes and essential "errands." He had long ago decided that Arthur's safety and eventual escape were essential, and no one thought to stop Taillandier's car as it headed toward the outskirts of the city, whose pink-tinged bricks almost seemed to glow in the oncoming twilight.

Arthur's quick thinking at the Frascati—dropping his photo identification card and papers to the floor and under the table—ensured that the Gestapo agent who had recognized him was the only one who could actually identify him as Georges Lambert. Jeno would solve that problem quickly and mercilessly. The Gestapo man would simply disappear or turn up as one more bullet-riddled Morhange target dumped lifeless into a ditch or even cut down in broad daylight on the streets of Toulouse. Before exiting the city, Robert pulled over and let Jeno out to take care of the matter. Once again, Taillandier's judgment that the American airman could think fast on his feet had proven correct.

Arthur, slumped in the backseat and sliding in and out of consciousness, sensed little except the car's motion. Robert drove out of the city and followed a series of back roads that he knew with a native's familiarity. He sped past vineyards and pastures framed by tree-lined ridges and hills.

Some fifteen miles from Toulouse, he darted onto a road that was little more than a cow path and stopped in a small clearing nearly surrounded by trees. He and Taillandier got out of the car, opened one of the passenger doors, and quickly but carefully slid Arthur out of the backseat and half carried him to a long, low-slung structure with gray, battered walls and a partially collapsed roof. They had brought Arthur to a maquis, a remote hideout used by Resistance groups to elude capture and lie low when things were getting too hot. Throughout southern France, Resistance groups would cleverly conceal maquis in the woods and hills.

The word *maquis* refers to a thicket, bush, or scrub growth and was originally a Corsican term that had made its way to mainland France. Resistance historian François Marcot, a professor of history at the Sorbonne, writes: "The term *maquis* signified both the bands of fighters and their rural location. The term established the image of a '*maquisard*' as a 'committed and voluntary fighter,' a *combatant* . . . Members of those bands were called *maquisards*. The term meant 'armed resistance fighter.' The *Maquis* have come to symbolize the French Resistance."[1]

Inside the maquis, Arthur was greeted by twenty or so men hiding from the Gestapo and the Vichy police. He was able to open his swollen eyes just enough to find a familiar and welcome face smiling at him. Far from Lesparre, Pierre Delude had fled to the Morhange refuge out of fear that the Gestapo would be at his door following the arrest of the Chauvins and the destruction of Brutus.

Taillandier and Robert left the hideout as quickly as they had arrived, planning to bring Arthur back to Toulouse once he was recovered and once they were sure that the Gestapo agent had been "removed." He would be safer in the city because German foot and air patrols constantly combed the countryside for any sign of the maquis. As Arthur would soon learn, the hideout's inhabitants were armed with rifles, pistols, and even a few submachine guns to mount a fight if the Nazis discovered them. Shortly before Taillandier departed, he had slipped a small pistol into one of Arthur's pockets.

Marcel left Arthur in good hands with the other men of the maquis. They were a colorful group of Frenchmen ranging from sophisticated urban physicians, lawyers, and businessmen to waterfront toughs and roughhewn farmers. Within a few days, with the doctors in the band tending to Arthur, he regained his strength, and the other men embraced the American as one of their own.

From Pierre Delude, Arthur learned the horrifying details of what had happened in Lesparre a few weeks after he had been removed. He was devastated at the news that the Gestapo had taken Gisèle prisoner and that no one knew where she was or if she was still alive. Arthur was unable to close his eyes that night, staring at the walls and ceiling of the maquis, shaking his head from time to time.

Over the next two weeks, until the end of March 1944, Morhange agents stealthily brought supplies and scraps of information to the maquis. As his strength slowly returned, Arthur, like the others, tensed every time he heard a car or truck outside the hiding place. They always feared the Nazis would burst in after being tipped off by a local collaborator.

The isolation and apprehension permeating the maquis made Arthur and the others crave a return to the city. The camaraderie helped quell some nerves, but being stuck in the hideout was an ordeal, the very minutes, let alone hours and days, interminable. Several of the men spoke excellent English, but there were long stretches when the only sounds inside the damp, dark lair were coughs and snores. Whenever anyone left to relieve himself outside, he made certain that he found a spot completely concealed by woods and brush. Several times a day, the drone of small Henschel scout planes low in the sky above the tree line provided a stark reminder that they were all wanted men. No one left the maquis during the day except for a few armed men posted as sentries concealed outside. At night, a fresh set of guards kept up the vigil. Arthur was relieved that if the Germans showed up, he had a weapon.

Whenever it rained, water pounded against the hideout's roof, and Arthur and the others were grateful that the rain did not leak through it. Still, dampness permeated the shelter. They could not even start a small fire to dry out their clothes, out of fear that the glow might reveal their location. The one indulgence they allowed themselves was a smoke, but only one man at a time and only in the one corner of the building, where neither rain nor light penetrated. The only way the burning ash or whiffs of smoke could be seen there was if someone was literally looking inside the maquis.

A few farmers sympathetic to the Resistance sneaked in cooked but cold pails of potatoes, radishes, and carrots for the men, as well as an occasional skinned and boiled rabbit or quail that the locals trapped in the woods. Several times, the locals brought eggs and bread. The men's stomachs were constantly growling, the meager portions barely enough to subsist on.

Fortunately, farmers scrounged enough bottles of wine hidden from the Germans to allow Arthur and the others to ward off the chill from gusts that found their way into the windowless hiding place. Locals even furnished the occasional bottle of cognac on the chilliest evenings as the men huddled beneath soggy woolen blankets against the bare stone walls.

On those walls, men had defiantly scratched patriotic messages: *Victoire!* and *Vive de Gaulle!*

Over and over, several men assured Arthur that he would soon be out of France and safe. He wanted to believe them, but as days went by without word from Toulouse, doubt seeped into him. Still, he believed that Taillandier would come for him. The Morhange leader had always kept his word.

Eventually, Pierre Delude decided he needed to be closer to his family in Lesparre, and decided to take the risk. Arthur was deeply saddened to see him go, but the urge to return to loved ones was one that he shared with Pierre. In the maquis, his own thoughts were always less about himself than about how his parents, Seymour, and especially Esther were holding up. It helped when he and his new comrades spoke in low, hushed tones about their families, but those moments were few compared to the long hours each man was alone with his fears. No matter how deep the camaraderie of the maquis, in those awful, endless moments, each man was utterly alone.

In the apartment house on Findlay Avenue in the Bronx, Rose Meyerowitz refused to abandon her conviction that her son Arthur was still alive. She simply felt that he was too intelligent and street-savvy not to have survived.

She continued to write letters to the War Department, imploring officials for any scrap of information about Arthur. The replies were

always the same. He was "missing in action." Each day that passed
without the most feared Western Union telegram of all—the
Killed-in-Action notification—allowed Rose to hope for another day.

The noncommittal replies from the War Department, signed by
or for Adjutant General Robert H. Dunlap, were discouragingly
similar to his response of April 21, 1944:

Dear Mrs. Meyerowitz:

*It has been my fervent hope that favorable information would be
forthcoming and that you might be relieved from the great anxiety
which you have borne during these months. It is therefore with deep
regret that I must state that no further report in his [Arthur's] case
has been forwarded to the War Department.*[2]

The family also enlisted the help of friends and neighbors to inquire
about Arthur's status. Max B. Goldman wrote to a War Department
contact in early 1944:

*I would consider it a great favor if you could obtain any further infor-
mation possible in connection with this case [Arthur's status] and
either call me by phone or wire me.*[3]

David Meyerowitz went to work each day, trying to hold his own
fears in check. For Seymour Meyerowitz, the wait was gut-wrenching.
He prayed every day for his big brother's safe return, as Rose insisted
he do. Still, Seymour saw the papers and the movie newsreels, the news
of heavy losses in bombing raids over Hitler's Fortress Europe. He
tried to emulate his mother's faith that Arthur would come home.
Alone at night with only his own thoughts, he was gnawed by doubt.

For Esther Loew, the strain was growing worse. David, Rose, and
Esther's family grew increasingly worried about her as the weeks

dragged on and still no word came of Arthur's whereabouts. Esther knew other young women who had already received the news that boyfriends, fiancés, and husbands were never coming back.

Rose constantly consoled Esther, urging her to hold on for Arthur's sake. Although Rose had nothing but her faith to sustain that belief, it kept her going. She was convinced that her son was just the one who would beat the odds and make it home to them again.

||||||||||||||||||||||||||

At the beginning of April 1944, Taillandier decided that it was time to bring Arthur back to Toulouse. Jeno had arranged for a transfer of the two Gestapo agents who had interrogated the airman, and the agent who had stalked him had simply vanished without a trace.

Arthur was elated when Taillandier came for him. He was ready physically and mentally to resume life as Georges Lambert and glad to hear that he was even returning to 96, boulevard Deltour. Although a few twinges of emotion tugged at him when his maquis comrades hugged him and bade him a heartfelt *bonne chance*, he understood that they actually envied him because he was leaving.

In another maquis, a few miles outside of Lesparre, one of Arthur's early benefactors had been hiding from the Gestapo. Dr. Pierre Chauvin had endured about two weeks of abuse at the Gestapo's hands after he and Gisèle had been seized. He did not reveal anything about Brutus or Arthur and was released; Gisèle, however, remained imprisoned. They had been unable to break her at the Villa Calypso or the Fort du IIa, but now she had been transferred to Fresnes Prison. There, a new and even harsher regimen of starvation, sleep deprivation, and beatings awaited her as the Nazis attempted to pry information from her about her comrades. If she survived that, a concentration camp awaited her next.

At Fresnes, some of the toughest Resistance captives had finally given in to the abuse and blurted out names in hopes that the Nazis would end the agony with a bullet to the head. As Gisèle and other female Resistance fighters had heard, the Gestapo at Fresnes had cut off the heads of several women who refused to betray their comrades, and had done this slowly.

Pierre returned home to find his mother-in-law, Mercédes; his maid, Simone; and his three children still at the house. Perhaps suspecting that the Gestapo had released him solely to shadow him in hopes he would lead them to other Resistance operatives, he managed to sneak away undetected to a maquis about an hour from Lesparre in order to protect his family.

He spent several weeks at the maquis, providing medical treatment to other escapees. After his arrival, two of Simone's brothers came to the hideout after the Gestapo cracked down hard in and around Lesparre. They had been kicking down doors in search of Brutus operatives and dragging them off to the Villa Calypso. As a message to the locals, the Germans seized several people who allegedly sympathized with the Resistance and warned the townspeople that anyone who did not provide information about the shattered unit was under suspicion.

With her daughter already arrested and perhaps dead and with Pierre in hiding, Mercédes was worried that the Gestapo would return to the Chauvin home and haul her away, too. She took the three children to a Lesparre neighbor. However, a few days later, she learned that the neighbor, likely concerned that she was also under suspicion, had taken the children a mile and a quarter away to a house in the town of Liard. It was near the maquis. Nervously, Mercédes rushed there as fast as she could to pick up the children, pushing a small cart for the infant, Patrick.

On the road to Liard, several black sedans roared past her, followed by troop carriers filled with steel-helmeted German soldiers in their field-gray uniforms. Half-tracks—armored cars—with swivel turrets and heavy-caliber machine guns brought up the caravan's rear. Mercédes realized that they were headed for the maquis, but she could do nothing about it. It was too late. She had no idea whether Pierre was still there or not. She kept pushing the cart the last half mile to the house and waited for the first echoes of gunfire and explosions.

Within ten minutes the sudden shrieks of birds pouring from trees to the rear alerted her. The din crashed down the road and all around her.

Someone had likely managed to alert the men in the maquis just before the Germans started to encircle the shelter. As covering fire from small "firing holes" punched into the lair's stone walls pelted the Germans, men spilled outside and scattered in all directions. Machine-gun blasts downed several men as bazooka rounds pummeled the maquis. Flames began to flare and then engulf the shelter. Defenders staggered out of the building, still firing, and were quickly cut down by the Germans. Gestapo officers strode up to the fallen fighters, kicked them, and put a single Luger round into each man's head just to be sure. One of Simone's brothers lay dead near the maquis. The other was still running.

Dozens of soldiers pursued Frenchmen deeper into the woods or across farmland. Only a handful eluded the relentless Germans. Pierre Chauvin was one of them.

Just as she reached the house, she saw Jean-Claude and Monique peering out a window and heard Patrick wailing inside. Mercédes turned as heavy footsteps thudded close by. A young man, panting, his eyes wide and bulging, stumbled past her and fell against the door of a barn just across the street. Three plainclothes Gestapo men in long, black leather jackets were closing fast on the Frenchman and nearly knocked down Mercédes in their pursuit. Each of the Germans held a gleaming Luger.

One of the Nazis paused, aimed carefully, and squeezed off one round. It slammed into the young man's back and knocked him down onto the road. He lay there, thrashing, trying to get up, his legs useless. Slowly, the trio walked up to him and pumped several bullets into his head.

Mercédes ran into the house. Clutching the squalling Patrick, she told the older children to cover their eyes and to get into the cart. She handed Patrick to Monique and pushed the cart past the dead freedom fighter and the blood pooling around him. She looked straight ahead, refusing for the sake of the children to let the Gestapo see any trace of the fury and contempt simmering inside her.

As Robert guided the Citroën from the maquis, Marcel handed Arthur something—his identification card and papers. The American was headed back to Toulouse, but with no idea of how long he would have to remain there. He understood that when Taillandier believed the moment was right, he would orchestrate Arthur's escape immediately. Once again, Arthur would have to remain patient but be ready to move in an instant. It could not come soon enough for him. The arrest at the Frascati and the torture at the hands of the Gestapo had both terrified and enraged him. He wanted the chance to pay back a Gestapo agent or two before or even during the escape attempt. His hatred of the Nazis and their treatment of his French friends nearly matched his desire to see home again.

||||||||||||||||||||||||||||||||||||||||||||||||

CHAPTER 19

MEET LIEUTENANT CLEAVER

In early April 1944, Arthur resumed his life as Georges Lambert in Toulouse. He left the house at 96, boulevard Deltour each day except Sunday to help Monsieur Thoulouse at the paint store. He constantly looked around on the streets for any sign of the Gestapo agent who had trailed him in March; after a week or so, the airman realized that Taillandier and his men had taken care of the problem. Thoulouse had told neighbors that Georges had returned after a visit to family in Soulac-sur-Mer. Judging by the friendly nods and waves from them, Arthur was comfortable with the belief that locals took his host at his word.

Although heartened by his sense that the Gestapo operative was not coming back, Arthur never let his guard down. Morhange operatives came and went from Thoulouse's home. Just as before, Arthur knew them only by their first names. During his weeks at the maquis, a major change had occurred for the people of Toulouse and the Nazi occupiers. The Allies had unleashed the controversial Transportation

Plan full bore, with B-24s, B-17s, and British Halifax, Lancaster, and Stirling bombers pummeling any French rail centers that might help the Germans send reinforcements to the Atlantic coast after D-Day. Although the raids never targeted the center of Toulouse, they pounded rail lines, factories, German supply depots, bridges, and other military targets just outside the city. At night, the walls of Arthur's bedroom quaked from the not-so-distant bomb blasts, tiny bits of plaster falling around him.

In the last days of March 1944, animated meetings at Thoulouse's house among Taillandier, Jeno, and other Morhange agents indicated that something big was up. It seemed especially true when Taillandier took Arthur to lunch at the Frascati on April 2, the first Sunday of the month. Arthur had not been back to the bistro since his return to Toulouse. If the Frenchman believed it was safe enough to take Georges Lambert to the café again, Arthur trusted his judgment.

With the weather unseasonably warm, the bistro was packed. Even though the Frascati teemed with Nazis, this was the way that Taillandier and Morhange operated. Still, Arthur could not help but scan the café for any sign of the Gestapo agent who had seized him a few weeks earlier. Taillandier smiled and shook his head at the notion that he would have left such an important detail to chance.

Taillandier was certain that on this mild Sunday afternoon, the police and Germans were more concerned with controlling revelers and enjoying the unofficial celebration of spring themselves. He had invited Jeno and several other Morhange leaders to meet him in the Frascati to plot a daring raid against the local Gestapo. Arthur, wearing his well-rehearsed blank expression, was able to piece together just enough French to realize that Taillandier was detailing a coming ambush against the Gestapo; if he pulled it off, the action could yield more intelligence about the Gestapo, the police, and their collaborators than ever before.

After lunch, Taillandier walked back with Arthur to 96, boulevard Deltour and stepped inside to speak with Thoulouse. Arthur turned to Taillandier and asked, "Can I go with you?"[1]

Marcel smiled faintly, respect glinting in his hard brown eyes, and shook his head. It was simply too risky.

Arthur did not see Marcel for nearly a week after the meeting. The Frenchman finally reappeared at Thoulouse's house the following Sunday. The Morhange strike, against a heavily guarded Gestapo outpost on the fringe of the city, had yielded two large briefcases crammed with top-secret documents. The contents outlined upcoming Gestapo and police operations as well as the names of informers.

Over several glasses of wine with Arthur and Thoulouse, Taillandier, speaking first in French and then in English, for Arthur's sake, informed them that on the raid, Morhange had rescued a "top-priority" prisoner from the Nazis. He was a Royal Air Force bomber squadron leader named Lieutenant Richard Frank Wharton (R.F.W.) Cleaver. Cleaver and his squadron, whose specialty was not unloading bombs but delivering munitions and supplies to drop zones for the French Resistance, were crucial components of the preparations for D-Day, in June 1944. He was part of the 644th Tactical Bomber Group and the Germans knew how badly the British wanted him back and had intended to turn his capture into a propaganda coup through newsreels and radio conduits such as "Axis Sally" (the collective name American GIs gave to the German and Italian women who broadcasted propaganda for the Axis powers during the war).

Taillandier told Arthur that it was vital that Cleaver be returned to his command and that Morhange was entrusting him to help with that mission. It was up to Arthur to show Cleaver the ropes and for the two men to protect each other, Taillandier explained.

Inwardly, Arthur was elated that now he could actively help his French friends. The fact that Taillandier and his operatives trusted him to aid the escape of such a high-priority asset as Lieutenant Cleaver showed how highly they respected the American airman for his courage and endurance, as well as his ability to keep his head under stress. His instinctive decision to drop his photo identification and papers while being arrested by the Gestapo had proven his mettle to Morhange. Further, his ability to keep quiet and not give up any information was a telling sign of the grit of the American.

⁞⁞⁞⁞⁞⁞⁞⁞⁞⁞⁞⁞⁞⁞⁞⁞⁞⁞⁞⁞⁞

On the evening of Wednesday April 5, 1944, at 10:30 p.m., the British crew of a Halifax B Mk V Bomber, of the 644th Squadron, boarded their aircraft. At the throttle of the Halifax LL228 "A" for code name "Able," was twenty-four-year-old Squadron Commander Lieutenant R.F.W. Cleaver. As they soared down the runway of the Royal Air Force base at Tarrant Rushton, Dorset, in central England, Cleaver guided the bomber aloft and took the lead position in a formation of forty-four Halifax and Stirling bombers bound for targets in southern France. Cleaver, just four days short of his twenty-fifth birthday, was one of the RAF's best bomber pilots, already known for his coolness under fire and deft reflexes in the cockpit. In October 1943, he had been awarded the Distinguished Service Order (DSO) "in recognition of gallantry and devotion to duty in the execution of air operations for No. 295 Squadron, Royal Air Force, during the invasion of Sicily." According to the citation, "after successfully dropping a glider [full of commandos] at the target in Sicily, he returned to North Africa with a badly shot up plane with three damaged engines."[2]

Cleaver's olive-drab-colored bomber, with the usual distinctive red, white, and blue British bull's-eye circles on both sides of the fuselage, could reach a top speed of 275 miles per hour and a top cruising altitude of 15,000 feet; but his plane and the others that night were not loaded with bombs. Instead, his Halifax was crammed with arms, ammunition, and explosives for the Resistance. The bombers' "targets" that night were designated drop zones in southwestern France where Resistance fighters would be waiting.

Cleaver and his fellow pilots that night had been specially chosen for one of the war's most dangerous tasks—to fly no higher than three thousand feet over the English Channel and Occupied France in order to muddle German radar on the way to the drop zones. At such a low altitude, the bombers were more vulnerable to flak than usual. Smaller and lighter than the B-24, whose tail structure was similar, the Halifax could deliver nearly as many five-hundred-pound bombs as the B-24.

Cleaver's mission fell under the command of Great Britain's Special Operations Executive (SOE). After the fall of France in 1940, the SOE was created to aid sabotage and subversion behind enemy lines in France; Cleaver's job was to drop vital supplies and munitions there so that the Resistance could blow up trains, bridges, and factories. If the Gestapo got their hands on pilots delivering supplies to the Resistance, they were treated no better than captured Resistance fighters.

As Cleaver led his squadron over the Channel, the crew settled in for their long flight to a drop zone in the department of Charente-Maritime, near the southwestern coast of France. They flew less than a thousand feet above the churning whitecaps. A Resistance unit called Bir Hacheim would be waiting at the drop zone—if all went according to plan. Cleaver noticed that "there was a good moon that night."[3] That meant that visibility for low-flying planes was good, but that German observers could spot the planes by eye, even if the radar did not pick up the formation.

|||||||||||||||||||||||||||

"Frank" Cleaver was proud of the 644th, whose motto was "We Sow the Seeds of the Dragon," a fitting term for the cargo in the Halifax's bomb bay. Flying with Cleaver that night was the five-man crew he had come to trust and respect on fourteen previous drops to the Resistance: Pilot Officer Norman Wyatt; navigator Flight Sergeant John Franklin; wireless operator Flight Sergeant Donald J. Hoddinott; rear gunner Sergeant Alan Matthews; and bomb aimer and flight engineer Sergeant Raymond Hindle. The copilot, Wyatt, like Cleaver, was university educated and hailed from Britain's upper middle class, which was still called the gentry.

The rest of the crew came from the lower reaches of Britain's class system, but in the Halifax, none of the social conventions held true. The men were united in purpose and tightly knit in the air and on the ground, and Cleaver insisted every crew member call him Frank.

If not for World War II, Richard Frank Wharton Cleaver's path would likely have ensconced him in a comfortable role in the family's shipping business, memberships at upscale gentlemen's clubs, and an equally comfortable marriage and home life in Kent. He was engaged to Dorothy Elliott, an attractive schoolteacher from an upscale family.

Cleaver was born on April 9, 1920, in Portland, Maine, while his parents were visiting relatives in that state and Boston. There was never a question of dual citizenship. He was English, pure and simple. A top student and gifted athlete with wavy blond hair and blue eyes, Cleaver was schooled at the Sevenoaks School, one of England's oldest and most prestigious private academies, where he was a star runner for the Kentish school's track team. He also had a passion for fast cars and airplanes. Against his parents' wishes, he took flying lessons while at university.

When World War II broke out, Cleaver's choice of service was clear. He enlisted in the Royal Air Force in the fall of 1940. His preference was fighter planes, but his leadership skills and calm personality led his superiors to believe that he was perfectly suited to lead entire crews into action rather than fly solo in a Spitfire or Hurricane fighter.

||||||||||||||||||||||

As Cleaver approached the coastline of France, he and the other bombers increased their altitude to three thousand feet and readied themselves for "the gauntlet"—the gut-wrenching flight above

Nazi 88s. Their luck held as they drew closer to the drop zone. Despite the glowing moon, there were no bursts of antiaircraft fire—yet.

Nearing the drop zone, bomb aimer Sergeant Hindle checked their "payload"—cylindrical C and H steel containers equipped with a parachute. The C's were sixty-nine inches long and loaded with rifles, pistols, and automatic weapons for the Bir Hacheim unit; each weighed up to 224 pounds. The H's were the same size, but could be broken down into five smaller sections for the fighters on the ground. Although the H container was easier to carry and conceal for the Resistance, the sections could not hold long items such as rifles. The H type was perfect for ammunition, explosives, boots, blankets, and radio equipment.

As the Charente River appeared on Cleaver's left side and the Atlantic on his right, he peered out for the tiny glint of six bicycle lamps, the prearranged signal for the drop zone. Standing in the cockpit right behind him, navigator Flight Sergeant John Franklin checked the distance to the drop zone on his map, using the river as a landmark, and gave Cleaver a report every sixty seconds. If Cleaver did not detect the contact signal or had any doubts about the drop zone, he had the option to abort the mission and lead the formation back home.

Franklin told Cleaver that the drop zone was directly ahead. From the ground, there was only darkness. Cleaver wondered if the Resistance had not reached the DZ [drop zone] because the Nazis had been tipped off somehow. He decided to scrap the delivery and turn back for England.

As the squadron banked back toward the coast, flak burst all around the bomber above a German airfield near Cognac. Cleaver immediately yanked the throttle hard to peel away from the 88s, but shrapnel tore into the starboard wing and set it ablaze. The bomber quaked violently and began to lose altitude.

Cleaver recognized immediately that the Halifax was finished. He ordered his crew to bail out while there was still—barely—enough

time and distance between the plane and the ground for their parachutes to deploy. Jumping from three thousand feet meant a hard or
even fatal landing, but it was his crew's only chance.

Remaining at the controls to allow his crew to escape, Cleaver
fought to keep the plane level, but she was losing height rapidly. With
all of his men out but the Halifax now at one thousand feet and plunging, he had no chance to jump. His only hope was to crash land. With
the bomber packed with the ammunition and the explosives intended
for the Resistance, Cleaver figured the Halifax would explode on
impact.

Unfamiliar with the ground, he attempted to put the lurching,
flaming Halifax down in a field cloaked in mist. In the darkness, only
the shadowy tops of trees were visible as he braced himself for landing.
The plane slammed against the ground and skidded to a stop. As
flames that would soon bring the Germans to the crash site engulfed
the plane, he crawled through the shattered glass windshield of the
bomber. He staggered into the brush as German armored personnel
carriers swarmed the site. Within minutes the bomber exploded in a
column of fire and smoke.

Several men in black Gestapo uniforms found Cleaver, beat him,
and handcuffed him. They threw him into a sedan and headed down
a road with several other vehicles. One of the Gestapo agents looked
at Cleaver's RAF identification card. He informed him they were
going to make a public example of him and show people what happened to those who aided "Resistance gangsters."[4]

The Nazis drove him just outside Toulouse and imprisoned him
in a stone blockhouse that adjoined a farmhouse and large stone barn
that the Gestapo used to interrogate prisoners and store files.

They stripped him of his clothing, and for the next two days he was
interrogated and beaten, either tied to a chair or chained by his ankle to
a wall.

On the third night, April 9, 1944, shouts and small-arms fire broke out from all directions outside the blockhouse. A grenade blast blew open the front door, the shock wave shook the walls around Cleaver and stunned him. Agonized screams echoed above submachine-gun bursts, and pounding footsteps neared the room where Cleaver lay slumped against a wall.

The wooden door was kicked open in a shower of splinters. A moment later several men rushed inside with automatic weapons. Cleaver thought they were about to kill him.

Instead, a Frenchman with a mustache and a beret pulled low across his brow freed the pilot from the chain with a single pistol shot. Two of the man's comrades helped Cleaver from the building to a dark sedan near several other similar cars.

At least ten Germans lay sprawled, bleeding, and motionless in and around the blockhouse. Several single shots from inside the adjacent farmhouse testified that no Nazis had been spared.

The Resistance group's leader, the man with the mustache, introduced himself to Cleaver in English as Marcel.

Arthur's mission to help the famed RAF pilot attempt an escape that could end fatally for both men was about to begin.

CHAPTER 20

UNLIKELY FRIENDS

The Morhange sedan carrying the injured RAF pilot sped across the Pont Neuf across the Garonne River and cut from the highway to a series of side streets close to the center of Toulouse. To the south, bright flashes lit the night sky. Concussive shock waves rolled through the city, shaking roads and buildings. The RAF was hammering German positions and railways outside Toulouse.

As usual, no one stopped the sinister-looking Citroën, the Nazis assuming it was one of theirs. Just a few blocks from the boulevard Deltour, the car stopped in front of a brick apartment house. Two Morhange agents hustled Lieutenant Cleaver inside the building and up to the top floor, where the door was slightly ajar. A slight, sixtyish woman with gray hair pulled back in a tight bun was waiting for them. The operatives led Cleaver into an annex, laid him atop an old, iron-framed bed, and raced back downstairs to the sedan. It vanished down the street seconds later.

A doctor was waiting inside and examined the Englishman, who was covered with bruises and cuts and whose blond hair was plastered with sweat and dried blood. The physician stitched several gashes and bound up several broken ribs. Then he injected the pilot with a small dose of morphine.

Although Cleaver was grateful to be in a real bed and safe for the time being, and despite his morphine-induced state, the window-rattling explosions of the RAF night raids pulled him in and out of a restless sleep. His muddled thoughts drifted back to the crash, and he strained to remember how many of his crew's parachutes he had counted as he fought to keep his burning Halifax in the air as long as possible.

He was certain that Pilot Officer Norman Wyatt, in the seat next to him, had gotten out. Cleaver thought he had counted five chutes, but was concerned that the jump from such a low altitude could have injured or killed his men. At least he had held the bomber aloft long enough to give them their only chance of survival.

As Cleaver hovered on the edge of consciousness, his own chances of survival hinged not only on the man named Marcel and his operatives, but also on the diminutive, slightly hunched woman in wire-rimmed glasses. Marie-Louise Dissard was a Resistance member responsible for running the most successful escape line for downed Allied airmen. At the moment that Cleaver had been brought to her, she was a wanted woman by the Gestapo and police. That fact had not slowed down her Resistance activities in Toulouse.

IIIIIIIIIIIIIIIIIIIIIIII

Sixty-four-year-old Marie-Louise Dissard was born in Toulouse in 1880. After the fall of France, in June 1940, Dissard, who burned with a fierce love of her nation and a hatred of the Germans and their Vichy collaborators, joined the Resistance. She would soon find herself working with British Special Operations Executive (SOE) officer Ian Garrow and Belgian naval officer Albert Guérisse in a clandestine escape network dubbed the Pat O'Leary Line. The name was coined by Guérisse, who had told German captors that he was "Pat O'Leary," a Canadian officer.

Using the code name "Françoise," Dissard operated out of her Toulouse apartment. There, she and Garrow set up a complex web of safe houses and couriers in Toulouse, Marseilles, and Perpignan, at the approaches of the Pyrénées Mountains between France and Spain. Both Garrow and Guérisse were eventually arrested, in 1941, and both escaped with the aid of "Françoise." Dissard took command of the O'Leary network. Her age and appearance worked to her advantage and to that of the more than 250 airmen she helped to escape. World War II historian Michael Grant writes: "Because of her relatively advanced age, the Gestapo did not suspect that she was a member of the Resistance. This gave her considerable freedom to travel throughout France, arranging escapes for airmen. Her customary procedure was to escort airmen to Toulouse, where, through the network, she arranged lodgings. From here, they were moved to Perpignan and transferred to the care of local guides for the trek across the Pyrenees."[1]

In the Toulouse annex, the injured pilot had no idea who the woman was and no idea that she was in even more trouble than he was. Cleaver assumed the apartment was hers, but she was, in fact, also hiding out there, several blocks from her own home. The Gestapo had seized one of the network's guides in Perpignan in January 1944 and found a notebook on him even though the guides were never supposed to write down any operative's name. Several pages contained Dissard's name. When a Morhange plant in the Toulouse Gestapo alerted Dissard that the Nazis had her name, Resistance leaders urged her to go underground.

For "Françoise" Dissard, keeping a low profile contradicted her very nature. Described as "an old woman with a very loud voice"[2] by one of the airmen she rescued, she had yelled at and cursed the Gestapo and police on a regular basis in the streets of Toulouse. Often, she walked up to German soldiers and especially Gestapo agents, wagged a finger in their faces, and unleashed a torrent of insults and swears at them.

Always, she went out with her cat, which led neighbors and Nazis alike to dub her as the cat lady. Because of her aged appearance, the Germans believed her to be eccentric or outright crazy and left her alone. Normally, they would have immediately arrested anyone else for such defiance. The Gestapo had never suspected that the verbally abusive cat lady was the main safe-house keeper and organizer for the Pat O'Leary Line in the south of France.

A British airman whom she helped to escape wrote: "Due to her efforts the line stayed open. She often gave abuse to the enemy, who thought her eccentric. She stood no nonsense, trusted no one. Her cat Miff went everywhere with her, and he lived to 18 years of age."[3]

Much of that changed when the Nazis seized the guide's notebook. Dissard went into hiding, but on her own terms, which meant she refused to abandon her work to help Allied airmen to safety. Taking refuge for several weeks in attics, cellars, and garages in and around Toulouse, she still ventured out from time to time with forged photo identification cards and papers. She correctly calculated that her appearance was that of any number of aging widows in the city, her features and manner of dress common and unremarkable. She made subtle changes to her appearance, arranging her hair in a bun instead of the coiled braid she wore in her original photo identification card. She donned wire-rimmed glasses that were absent in her original photo as well and let her hair go completely gray. The Gestapo was hunting for her, but she remained one step ahead of them.

Taillandier, who visited Cleaver several times during the pilot's first week in Toulouse, told Arthur to be ready to meet the Englishman soon. Arthur asked Taillandier about the man, wondering if Cleaver was one of those upper-class British officers whose air of superiority, even haughtiness, so grated on Americans who had grown up with little and worked hard for everything they had. At first, many raucous 8th and 15th U.S. Army Air Corps crewmen and pilots, reacting to the extreme manneredness and reserve of the British blue bloods, had mistakenly thought them effete. They quickly came to realize that many of those "lads of the finishing schools" had climbed into the cockpits of rugged Hurricane and sleek Spitfire fighter planes and bested the Luftwaffe in the Battle of Britain. Others, such as Cleaver, controlled the throttles of RAF bombers pounding Axis Europe with their Allies or running dangerous supply drops to the Resistance.

In Thoulouse's parlor, Taillandier described how Cleaver had stayed with his plane to make sure his entire crew had gotten out. Arthur's eyes met Taillandier's through the usual swirl of smoke from the cigarette in his hand. The fact that Cleaver had made sure his crew escaped first earned Arthur's respect instantly, sight unseen.

Taillandier explained to Cleaver that because the Gestapo knew his face and identity, the Englishman could not be allowed to go about the city. "They cut my hair a bit and dyed it black," Cleaver wrote. "[Taillandier] provided me with an ID card with the name Antoine Broussard, with the words 'slow witted' on it. If the Germans or police ever entered Mrs. Dissard's home, I was told to speak French with a stutter, that my command of the language was ample enough to pass."[4]

Since January 1944, when she'd been identified as a member of the Resistance, Dissard had curbed her confrontational demeanor toward the police and the Nazis, not wanting to call so much attention to herself. If any neighbors did recognize her despite her changed appearance, they kept silent—they knew that a "visit" from Morhange awaited anyone who informed on her. For Marie-Louise Dissard, lying low to help American and British airmen remained her mission. It has been estimated that even after her name appeared in the captured notebook, she planned the escapes of at least 110 airmen through the Pyrénées. In April and May 1944, Lieutenant Cleaver was one of the Frenchwoman's top priorities.

Every time that she brought Cleaver his meals or simply entered the annex to chat with him, she took her cat, Miff, with her, either carrying the animal or letting her walk along on a leash.

Unlike Arthur, who came and went from 96, boulevard Deltour every day, Cleaver's confinement meant that he could only move around the annex and Dissard's apartment beneath it. As Cleaver would write in an addendum to his RAF debrief, his stay there mirrored Arthur's in one way: "During my weeks at the house of Francoise [sic] Dissard, men and women of all ages came and went from the address. I assumed that they were couriers and other Resistance agents and fighters. Mrs. Dissard, while always friendly and solicitous of me, took great pains never to mention any of their names when I was in the same room or even within earshot. I understood the necessity of strict secrecy for the protection of myself and others."[5]

Cleaver recalled Taillandier explaining to him that "because matters had become more hazardous since the German occupation of Toulouse, every Resistance band had necessarily become more organized and security conscious. In arranging escapes, many pilots and airmen never knew the real names of our handlers and couriers. We simply were handed off to the next link in the Escape Line chain. Many never even knew the name of their safe-house keeper."

Cleaver was never allowed outside, spending "most of my days and nights in a comfortable but Spartan bedroom in the attic annex of the house. Always the sound of sirens was outside."[6]

The wailing sirens were not just air-raid alerts. With the rumors of the Allied invasion swelling every day and with increased sabotage and executions by the Resistance, the police and the Gestapo stepped up efforts to arrest suspected Resistance fighters and their supporters. At any time of the day or night, the Germans and the police stormed into apartment houses and single homes to mount room-by-room searches.

Cleaver wrote, "Numerous times I heard the pounding of Gestapo agents on Mrs. Dissard's front door and harsh German shouted at her. She spoke some German, as well as English, and did not back down from Gestapo men's challenges. They always left her house without searching upstairs, though at those times I was always certain they would rush upstairs and find me."[7]

On the streets of Toulouse, Gestapo and police stop-and-checks turned from routine to incessant. Arthur had never been ordered to produce his photo and papers so often, and each time the Nazis or police hurled question after question at him before they finally accepted that he was deaf and dumb. As with virtually everyone in Toulouse, Arthur was constantly looking over his shoulder. Even though he knew that the Gestapo agent who had trailed him had been removed, he sometimes stiffened when he caught a glimpse of large Gestapo agents who, for a moment, resembled the man who had arrested him.

When he shaved at Thoulouse's house, he saw the strain in his own face, where there were furrows that had not been there before. He could not help asking Taillandier when an escape could be arranged. Every time, Taillandier's only answer was that Arthur needed to be patient and that the moment was coming. As always, it could not come soon enough for Arthur. He got out of bed each day, tucked his photo identification card and papers into his coat pocket, caught the bus to the city center, reported to work at the paint store, and retuned to 96, boulevard Deltour. He worried that with so many stop-and-checks, the odds were increasing that his luck would run out.

In mid-April 1944, Taillandier appeared at Thoulouse's house and told Arthur to come with him to meet Lieutenant Cleaver. Arthur scrambled to put on his coat and follow Taillandier out the door, the American's spirits rising with the possibility that an escape might be in the works if Taillandier was introducing him to Cleaver now.

Arthur and Taillandier walked just a few blocks to a red-brick apartment house on a dead-end side street and climbed several flights of stairs to the top floor. Taillandier knocked twice on a scarred wooden door, and it opened a crack to reveal an elderly woman wearing glasses and cradling a gray cat. Nodding at Marcel, she let them in and closed the door quickly.

Wordlessly, she took them to another door, opened it, and led them into a cramped passageway and up a creaking stairway to yet another door. She rapped once on it and called out Cleaver's name softly. A bolt on the other side of the door slid open with a rasp, and Marcel, Dissard, and Arthur entered. In the middle of the small annex, not unlike the ones where Arthur had stayed, a wiry man with pale blue eyes and cropped, dyed dark hair faced them. He was wearing civilian clothes, and his face still bore bruises and cuts.

Arthur walked up to him and shook his hand. Cleaver insisted that Arthur call him "Frank." Marcel and Madame Dissard left the two men alone.

When Taillandier came back upstairs to get Arthur, he opened the door to find the two men engrossed in conversation. "Time to leave," Taillandier said.[8]

Disappointment flashed across Arthur's face. The kind of rapport he had quickly developed with Cleaver was exactly what the leader of Morhange wanted. Both men would have to rely on each other in their escape attempt, and it would be easier if they liked each other.

Throughout late April and into May 1944, Arthur visited Cleaver several times a week. According to Cleaver, "Mrs. Dissard, Marcel, and Sergeant Meyerowitz were the only people with whom I conversed for nearly a month.

"Most of my information about the world outside, such as it was, came from Meyerowitz. He was out and about frequently as 'Lambert,' and sometimes went with Marcel to the Frascati . . . I marveled at how effectively Meyerowitz played his role as a deaf mute. Somehow he fooled the Germans, the police, and even the local crowd time after time. Despite the danger he confronted every time he went out, I envied him a tad. Hidden away as I was, each moment of each day varied between tedium and sudden bursts of fear every time I heard a vehicle pull up near the house."

Arthur could relate to all of Cleaver's feelings of isolation punctuated by sheer anxiety. Cleaver found an escape of sort in the large number of books in Dissard's apartment, remarking that he "read more than at any time since my schoolboy years." Marcel hinted at just how fortunate they all were to have Madame Dissard still operating as the chief organizer for the entire Resistance escape line in southwestern France. Without her efforts, the southern escape routes might not have been open. Luckily for both Cleaver and Arthur, they had been brought to Toulouse to be helped by the O'Leary Line in the south of France. The English and American airmen were even luckier that Marcel had taken a personal interest in getting them out of France.

As Arthur and Cleaver's trust and friendship grew, they talked about their lives, about Esther and Dorothy, and other deeply personal matters. Arthur reminded Cleaver "in a number of ways" of Cleaver's own flight engineer, Sergeant Raymond Hindle. To Cleaver, "aside from a bomber's pilot . . . the most important man aboard is the Flight Engineer. He knows both the inner and outer workings of the craft as well if not better than the pilot, and the training for the job requires both high intelligence and the knack of thinking quickly under the most unimaginable duress."

Arthur became comfortable enough with Cleaver to discuss the biggest disappointment in the American's military life: "how he had been accepted as a pilot candidate but had been forced out by an injury."

Cleaver was not surprised at all that Arthur had wanted to be a pilot: "Aside from his genuine intelligence—as with so many Americans, the lack of university does not reflect a second-rate intellect—his ability to pass himself off as 'Lambert' shows his knack for thinking quickly on his feet and never letting down his guard." Courage and a quick mind were the cornerstone traits of the best pilots.

Cleaver remembered that he and Arthur talked without letup for hours and credited those conversations with helping him keep his sanity. Jokingly, the pilot wrote that there were days when the only conversation he had was with Miff, the cat.

To Cleaver, Arthur detailed how he had come to Toulouse and how so many brave French men and women had helped him every step of the way. "To his utmost credit," Cleaver wrote, "he never revealed one name of any man or woman who had aided him. We both knew the necessity for such secrecy."

Both the American and the Englishman recounted the events of the nights their planes had been shot down. When Arthur stopped for a moment, he seemed lost in his own private reverie. He then looked at Cleaver "and said he only wished that the pilot and co-pilot of his B-24 had behaved as selflessly as I had."

Cleaver was genuinely flattered, though surprised by Arthur's vivid description of Lieutenant Philip Chase's conduct as *Harmful Lil Armful*'s demise unfolded. Cleaver found Chase's actions unfathomable—it had never occurred to him *not* to stay in the cockpit as long as possible. He had been trained in the principle that "as with a Naval Captain, the pilot should be the last man off."

"I also told him that his pilots merited court-martial for their abysmal performance and cowardice," Cleaver wrote. "The crew merited far better." He "had no doubt that if Meyerowitz had been able to go through pilot training without injury, he would have behaved far differently than his pilot in January."

Both Arthur and Cleaver were united in two purposes: to see their girlfriends and families again and to get another chance to fight the Nazis. For Arthur, the rumors of the wholesale murder of Jews filled him with a rage he could not fully articulate. He had lost count of how many times he had seen Gestapo agents hauling off men, women, and children simply because they were *Juden* (Jews). Although most citizens of Toulouse despised the Nazis and Vichy police and would do nothing to help them, a deeply anti-Semitic streak through-out Vichy France led collaborating officials to help the Nazis locate and deport French Jews to the concentration camps.

Cleaver's anger toward the Nazis was also personal. London lay in ruins after the Blitz of 1940–1941, tens of thousands of his fellow British men, women, and children dead or maimed. Even now, in the spring of 1944, German "buzz bombs," V-1 rockets, and a newer, even more lethal missile, the V-2, indiscriminately rained down and slaughtered people all over England.

At the beginning of May 1944, Taillandier repeatedly assured Arthur and Cleaver that the invasion was nearly at hand. The step-up in bombing raids all around the region attested to that welcome news for all three men. However, at the same time, the Germans grew ever more relentless in their search for Resistance saboteurs and escaping Allied airmen. Cleaver could hear and Arthur could see the increase in Nazi armored cars and troop carriers patrolling the city streets. Every day, Arthur was finding himself stopped and ordered to show his papers.

Life in Toulouse grew tenser and more dangerous throughout May, and the Gestapo was planning a brutal crackdown in June against anyone suspected of cooperation with the Resistance. At the top of the Nazis' hit list was the mysterious "Ricardo," and they were already rounding up and torturing "suspicious" men and women in an attempt to ferret out the identities of the shadowy Resistance leader and his operatives.

With things in and around Toulouse guaranteed to worsen once the Allies stormed ashore somewhere in France, Taillandier was determined to get Arthur and Cleaver moving before the invasion.

In mid-May, Taillandier brought both sobering and heartening news to Cleaver about his crew. Flight sergeant and rear gunner Donald Hoddinott had perished when his parachute failed to open in time. Cleaver hoped that Hoddinott's family might find some measure of comfort in the knowledge that "he died in the brave performance of his duty."[9]

Cleaver learned that Flight Sergeant and Wireless Operator John Franklin and Flight Engineer and Sergeant Raymond Hindle had parachuted safely near Châteauneuf-sur-Charente, buried their parachutes, and been taken in by the local Resistance. Taillandier told Cleaver that both of his men had been guided over the Pyrénées to Spain, but the Frenchman did not reveal the names to Cleaver of anyone who had helped the pair.

In the final week of May, Taillandier vanished. Thoulouse told Arthur that he was not to go out for a few days, but to stay put. After several days went by without Cleaver receiving a visit from Taillandier, and Madame Dissard brushed away the pilot's questions, he began to fear that something had happened to the Frenchman. Arthur worried about the same thing, agonizing that the worst had overtaken his friend and that he and Cleaver might be left stranded.

As it turned out, a British submarine had taken Taillandier and Jeno to Algiers for a meeting with Colonel Paillole to discuss pre-D-Day sabotage operations and ambushes around Toulouse. With the invasion date slated for early June, Taillandier decided on the return trip to France that he could no longer wait to move Arthur and Cleaver.

On May 28, 1944, an unnamed female courier delivered a message from Taillandier to both the American and the Englishman: be ready to move out at any time.

For Arthur, relief that Marcel was alive mixed with equal measures of anticipation and nervousness. After nearly five months in Occupied France, it was time. He was finally getting the chance to escape.

||||||||||||||||||||||||||||||||||||||||

CHAPTER 21

"IT'S TIME"

Taillandier simply could not wait any longer to move Arthur and Cleaver. With the long-awaited Allied invasion of France—Operation Overlord—at hand, the Resistance was awaiting their final orders to arrive from London. Secrecy surrounding the invasion site and date was so tight that Paillole could not reveal either the location or the date to his top operatives throughout France until literally a few hours before the Allied armada left ports along the southern coast of Great Britain.

For Arthur and Cleaver, the danger in Toulouse had never been greater. Paillole had warned Taillandier that the Germans, alerted by the staggering increase in Allied bombing runs along the entire French coastline, knew the invasion was perhaps just hours away. They just didn't know where. The Gestapo, Abwehr counterintelligence agents, and the police were cracking down harder than ever on the Resistance and rounding up hundreds of people in hopes that someone, anyone, might reveal information about the invasion under torture. That was precisely the reason that even Taillandier and Resistance leaders in France itself had not been told where and when the strike would come.

In and around Toulouse, Morhange was launching increased attacks on German convoys, trains, munitions depots, and other military installations. Their intention was to pin down as many troops as possible and prevent them from rushing to whichever coastal spots the Allies invaded. The Gestapo and Vichy police were launching building-to-building searches for Resistance safe houses and hidden Allied airmen.

The escape routes across the Pyrénées to Spain were hazardous and an arduous trek under the best of circumstances, but now the Germans were scouring every road and every mountain pass for any hint of Resistance activity.

After a restless night, Arthur arose early in the morning of May 29, 1944, shaved, bathed, and got dressed. He went downstairs and ate a small breakfast of grapes and bread with Thoulouse, who told him that he was not to leave the house and that someone would come for him early in the evening. Arthur went upstairs and packed his few belongings and secondhand clothes in the battered suitcase.

He was ready to leave Toulouse. His constant brushes with the Gestapo and police were beginning to chafe at his psyche, as did the memory of his merciless beating by the Gestapo. With luck, he might be able to make it home by his birthday, in August.

Just after twilight, Thoulouse returned from his paint store, and a knock on the door a few minutes later brought Arthur out of a parlor chair and to his feet. Thoulouse opened the door and Taillandier and Jeno stepped inside quickly.

They walked up to him. Although Marcel was "someone who was afraid of nothing," there was no mistaking the grim intensity fixed on his features. Jeno stepped behind a parlor window, opened a shutter an inch or two, and scanned the street.

"It's time . . ." Taillandier said.

Arthur stared at them for several moments, his emotions churning as he weighed those longed-for words. Nodding, he replied: "I'm ready."

He shook Thoulouse's hand, thanked him for all he had done, and followed Taillandier and Jeno outside to a now-familiar black Citroën. Both Frenchmen looked in every direction as Arthur climbed into the backseat. Robert was not at the wheel this time. Instead, the glowering face of Andrés Fontes peered straight ahead. He was wearing the long black leather overcoat and fedora favored by plainclothes Gestapo and police.

A dark van that Arthur recognized as the same official type used by the Nazis and the police to transport prisoners was parked behind the Citroën. Taillandier and Jeno got into it and trailed the car as Fontes pulled away from the curb. Within seconds, Arthur realized they were heading toward the street where Cleaver was hiding.

Cleaver was waiting, too. He had received the same message as Arthur: be ready to move out in the early evening. He opened the annex door in response to a soft but insistent knock from Madame Dissard and followed her downstairs to the hall of the apartment building. Like Arthur, he was clad in civilian clothes and a beret. Madame Dissard pointed at the Citroën outside.

Taillandier got out of the van and into the Citroën with Fontes, Arthur, and Cleaver. Fontes slipped the sedan into gear and pulled away from the curb, followed by the van, which Jeno was driving. No one said a word.

Before departing Toulouse, the car and the van made two more quick stops. At a safe house they picked up a haggard-looking Frenchman who had been jailed for aiding the Resistance, escaped, and been taken in by Morhange. At another safe house on the eastern edge of the city, Andres and Jeno stopped again, this time to pick up two Belgian men wanted by the Nazis. The pair were pale and trembling as they were loaded into the van with the Frenchman.

Arthur breathed a bit easier as the two vehicles finally left Toulouse behind and swung onto a dirt road winding into the countryside. Then, after twenty minutes, he was surprised when they left the rural road to merge onto a highway. Taillandier turned to the American and the Englishman and told them that they were driving 209 kilometers (130 miles) directly southwest to Perpignan, a city near the Spanish border. If all went well, the trip should take around two or three hours.

Everywhere they looked, German tanks and other armored vehicles were rumbling west along both sides of the highway. The route was safe because Allied bombers were not targeting the plains, foothills, and peaks of the central and eastern Pyrénées because they were not close enough to the anticipated invasion landing sites on the Atlantic coast. That meant that the Germans were trying to move troops closer to the coast by night and also that they were searching for any hint of Resistance activity between Perpignan and the border. The bombers would wait until the armored columns passed west of Toulouse.

If the cars were stopped, Taillandier and Fontes had forged police papers that would inform the Germans that the car was transporting prisoners to Perpignan for questioning by the Gestapo. In the van behind them, Jeno, with his German identification documents, would back them up by saying that he was personally transporting additional prisoners with Taillandier and Fontes.

En route to Perpignan, Arthur could make out little of the passing landscape in the darkness, but had a sense of the car climbing upward. The two vehicles slowed down and pulled to the side of the highway three times to stop and pick up four more men, who hopped into the van. Taillandier said that they were "four guides for our trek across the mountains."[1]

At several German checkpoints, soldiers waved the vehicles to a stop. Turning their flashlights on the occupants, the Germans judged that the haggard passengers were, in fact, prisoners being transported.

The forged police papers produced by Fontes and Jeno convinced the sentries to let the car and van continue on their way. Finally, lights twinkled ahead of the car.

Arthur was correct that their route had started with a climb and had now leveled off. Much of the drive from Toulouse to Perpignan wound through the foothills and ridges of the approaches to the hulking Pyrénées. Perpignan was a city of some three hundred thousand people on the Roussillon plain, eight miles from the Mediterranean Sea and eighteen miles from the Spanish border.

Even in the darkness, Arthur could make out the looming mass of foothills and mountains between the city and the border.

They drove deep into the city and stopped at its southernmost fringe at one of the modest stucco homes that appeared to be the type virtually everyone in the city lived in. As soon as the two vehicles entered a garage and parked, Taillandier led Arthur and Cleaver into a bulkhead at the rear of the house and into a dank, musty basement cluttered with stacked wood, old furniture, and a heap of old blankets in one corner. Just before descending through the bulkhead, Arthur had taken another quick glimpse at the towering mass of the Pyrénées, wondering again how they were supposed to get over them. He told himself that Taillandier knew what he was doing and that if other escapees had made the trek, he could manage it as well, no matter how grueling.

When the Frenchman and the two Belgians piled into the cellar, followed by the four guides, Arthur and Cleaver were both dismayed at the two Belgians' behavior; they seemed to be arguing with each other and with one of the guides. Taillandier glared at them, and they shut up, but continued to shoot angry glances at the guide.

Taillandier ordered everyone to get as comfortable as they could and be ready to move out before dawn. They would have to risk daytime travel to the foothills as the Germans were stopping every vehicle that tried to head out at night for the mountain approaches. In the past, they would have risked the nighttime passage, but the Germans' heightened alertness in late May and early June had resulted in several failed escapes by Resistance members and Allied airmen.

If they were challenged in the daylight—as they probably would be—Jeno and Fontes would bluff that Arthur, Cleaver, and the rest of the passengers were informers leading them to suspected safe houses near the border. If the bluff failed, the three Morhange men would have to try to shoot their way out of it. Arthur would not hesitate to use his pistol against the Germans.

In the "evasion classes" in which he had learned what measures to take while attempting to escape the Nazis, Arthur and the others had been instructed that if they were captured in civilian clothes, they were to identify themselves as Allied airmen and invoke the Geneva Convention for treatment of POWs. They were strongly warned, however, that if the Gestapo seized them in civilian clothes and they were holding or concealing a gun, they would probably be executed on the spot.

As Arthur lay beneath an oily, rancid wool blanket that made every exposed part of his hands and neck itch, he reflected on those classes and the warning about a gun. No matter what, he decided, he would hang on to the pistol. If things went bad tomorrow, the Germans would probably kill them all anyway, and if that were to happen, he intended to take as many Nazis with him as he could.

Alongside him, Cleaver did not say a word that night, lost in his own thoughts, shifting his position against the stone wall and atop the dirt floor from time to time. The Frenchman and the four guides were propped against the wall, a few of them snoring. The two Belgians whispered and muttered to each other all night, one of them a sallow-looking man with an almost feral face, the other a thin man whose unkempt, gaunt appearance testified that he had been through some grim ordeal.

Arthur was tempted to tell both of them to shut up or even smack the one with the pallid face, but finally ignored them.

A loud engine and grinding gears alarmed everyone in the cellar around 4:30 a.m. The Belgians began shouting, and this time Arthur hissed at them to shut their mouths. In French, one of the guides growled the same at the pair.

Arthur waited for the crunch of hobnailed Nazi boots outside and the sound of the bulkhead doors being pried open. The doors did in fact open, but all that came down the steps of the cellar was Tail-landier's voice, telling them to come outside quickly and to leave any baggage in the cellar.

Arthur sprinted for the stairs with only his coat, his identification papers, and his pistol. Cleaver was right behind him, his presence a reassuring one. As the men spilled from the cellar, Taillandier pointed to a large, mud-stained, open-backed truck with wooden posts and rails on each side. They ran to the back and climbed into it. One of the guides took the wheel, next to Fontes and Jeno. Taillandier sprang into the back and sat next to Arthur against the rails. On his other side was Cleaver.

The truck lumbered into motion, a dark, oily puff of smoke rising from the engine, and clattered off down a rough dirt road whose every bump sent the men in the back banging against each other. They were scarcely a few minutes on their way toward the foothills when one of the guides, a short, square-shouldered man whose weather-burnished face made it impossible to tell if he was thirty or sixty, asked Taillandier something in French. In an almost annoyed tone, Taillandier replied.

Whatever he said caused the two Belgians to erupt in a torrent of words, pointing at the thick, fur-lined boots the guide was wearing and at a satchel he was carrying. The guide had asked Taillandier where the boots, walking sticks, and heavy hiking socks, hats, and sweaters for the escapees were. Taillandier had told him that they should be stockpiled at the safe house in the foothills where they would spend the evening.

One baleful look from Taillandier silenced the Belgians, but they still whispered back and forth, shooting furtive glances at Taillandier and shaking their heads.

Arthur glared at the two men.

As the truck pitched along one dirt and rock-strewn road after another, the route was not directly toward the foothills ahead of them, but appeared to track alongside the mountain range, never turning directly to the peaks. Several times German fighter planes passed high overhead but did not swoop down. The planes were only tracking vehicles or parties on foot if they were moving straight at the foothills, not along them. After several hours, the truck still had not made that turn.

CHAPTER 22

MISERY IN THE MOUNTAINS

Around 1 p.m. on May 31, the farm truck rattled to a stop some eight hours after setting out to the west of Perpignan. A highway viaduct rose from the rim of a forested valley and toward the craggy foothills of the Pyrénées. Taillandier jumped from the truck's open bed, and the rest of the men followed.

The guides took them to a tiny clearing beneath one of the viaduct's mammoth steel and concrete arches. They were told that they must all wait there till nightfall because German patrols and aircraft scoured the area between the valley and passes through the foothills to the mountains from dawn to dusk.

As they sipped water from canteens and munched on hard cheese and bread, all they could do was wait for darkness. Throughout the long day, they tensed up every time a fighter plane droned overhead or the road atop the viaduct shook from approaching troop carriers. The guides instructed the escapees to try to rest as much as they could; any hope they had of eluding the Germans hinged upon reaching the foothills under cover of darkness and making it as far as the mountain approach the guides had selected.

While the weather had been warm in the early afternoon, the air began to change within a few hours. The temperature was dropping close to the mountains. To pass the time before nightfall, the men began to talk in low voices and to swap stories. The guides listened, sometimes chuckling at a joke or anecdote, but the two Belgians said nothing, frowning.

Arthur, able to follow French conversations enough to get the gist of what was being said, had Cleaver translate anything he had a hard time understanding. When Taillandier and the others turned to Arthur, he relied upon Cleaver's fluent, finishing-school French to regale the Frenchmen with descriptions of the colorful characters and incidents from his Bronx neighborhood. Street-hardened Andrés and Jeno, who both might have deemed Cleaver a snob before the war, were now mesmerized as he told not only Arthur's stories, but also described nail-biting flights to aid the Resistance. The Frenchmen's eyes glinted with respect for the RAF pilot and American airman who had put their lives in jeopardy for the French people.

Even the reserved Cleaver was captivated by the stories of Taillandier's daring missions and narrow escapes. On one of Morhange's most audacious ambushes, Taillandier and a handpicked hit team had donned stolen police uniforms, stopped a three-car Gestapo motorcade several miles outside of Toulouse, and in a flurry of submachine-gun and shotgun fire cut down a notorious SS colonel named Wilhelm Messack, his French mistress, Paulette Bordiet, and several Gestapo agents and collaborators. It was a "message assassination" that made "Ricardo" the most wanted man in Toulouse—but one whose identity remained a mystery to the Nazis.

One thing in which Taillandier, Fontes, and Jeno all evinced pride was that no Morhange operative captured and tortured by the Gestapo had ever given up their comrades. Several had killed themselves before the Gestapo could break them.

Left unsaid was that the tough Frenchmen trusted Arthur and Cleaver to uphold the same Morhange credo.

As night came on and the growls of the Germans fighters' engines ceased, the guides rose at the same time. Jeno and Fontes walked up to Arthur and Cleaver and embraced them. Without a word, they stepped out of the sheltered clearing when a Citroën pulled up along the adjoining dirt road and flashed its headlights. Fontes, who turned briefly to meet Arthur's eyes, nod, and flash a tight, approving smile— the first hint of anything except taciturn toughness he had ever shown the airman—got inside with Jeno. They were gone in seconds.

The guides led Arthur, Taillandier, Cleaver, and the other three men onto a woodland path only wide enough for the men to walk single file. Each guide had reached into his knapsack and put on a hat, a sheepskin coat, thick socks, and mountain boots; from those bags, each had pulled out a small carbine and slung it over a shoulder.

In complete silence except their own breathing and the crunch of their shoes against dirt and leaves, the procession wound higher and higher until the viaduct was far beneath them, a distant sliver in the moonlight. Already Arthur's lungs were starting to burn; Cleaver was also breathing hard. If these were just the foothills, how bad would the mountains be? Every pilot and airman who had attempted the climb had asked the very same question. All came up with the same answer— a nightmare that could only be worse if the Germans spotted them.

Pyrénées guides taking men through the passes preferred moonless nights, trusting their own knowledge of every twist, every turn, every fissure along the route. German alpine troops camped throughout the mountains and, when the moon shone, scanned the passes and peaks with binoculars for any sign of men or movement.

Arthur, Cleaver, and the other escapees were growing more concerned with how ill prepared they were for the climb. They had been whisked in such haste from Toulouse that there had been no time to properly outfit them with warm attire, hiking boots, or even gloves. Although they were still far below the actual mountains, their feet and hands were stinging from the gathering cold and starting to go numb. They kept moving, laboring for each breath the higher they climbed and hoping that the mountain gear and clothing Taillandier had promised would be at the first shelter.

Taillandier shared their misery, knowing that it was not the guides' job to provide clothing and footwear for escape parties. That was the task of the Resistance, but with the crackdown in Toulouse, there had been no time.

Arthur lost all track of time. He just kept one foot moving in front of the other as the group inched up narrow paths stretching ever higher into the foothills. At some point—he was not even sure when— every step was into deepening snow. The air grew colder and thinner.

Arthur's hands had gone from a painful throb to complete numbness, and his fingers were swollen and a deep shade of scarlet. Below the snowline, icy groundwater had seeped through his work boots; now ankle-deep snow filled them. One thing did not change, except to intensify: despite the cold, the pain that ripped through his back felt like flames.

His hatred of the Nazis and a desire for the chance to kill more of them prodded Arthur up the frigid trails. So, too, did loyalty and love for the French who were helping him. Along with all that was his determination to return to Esther and his family.

The guides did not allow them to halt even once. Canteens filled with water were passed up and down the line from time to time with a warning that each man take only a sip. Gulping it could cause already oxygen-deprived lungs to expand and contract so violently that a climber could suffer a seizure or worse.

As they trekked through shin-deep snow up paths discernible only to the guides, streaks of gray began to pierce the inky night sky. The guides stopped as the gray tinges turned lighter. Grateful to stand still even for a moment, Arthur and the other hikers spotted a long, gabled farmhouse with an ancient barn just ahead. One of the guides pointed at the structure and headed toward it. The others trudged behind him. They had reached their first safe house just minutes before sunrise.

Once they were inside the abandoned farmhouse, the guides told the men that they could not light the fireplace for fear of attracting squads of German alpine troops searching for escapees and Resistance members in the passes. Smoke from a vacant old home was a dead giveaway. They could not even dry out their sodden clothes with a fire. Even worse, there were no mountain boots, warm clothes, caps, or any gear except walking sticks.

All the furniture in the house was long gone, but several thick wool blankets were strewn across the floor. Several of the guides disappeared for a few minutes and returned with armfuls of dry hay from the barn. They laid the piles on the floor. Arthur, Cleaver, Taillandier, the Belgians, and the other Frenchman stripped off their coats, shirts, trousers, and socks. Then they wrapped themselves in the blankets, made makeshift mattresses with the hay, used the remainder to place their clothes atop in the hope that it would absorb some of the wetness, and slumped on the floor on top of their "beds."

In French, with Taillandier translating for Arthur, a guide told them that even though the group had traveled as a unit so far, the next day they would split up into pairs, with two men per guide. They would travel by night along trails hopefully not used by the Nazis, and reassemble at the next resting place the following morning. Taillandier nodded at Arthur to let him know that he would travel with him and Cleaver, the only group with three instead of two per guide.

CHAPTER 23

‖‖‖‖‖‖‖‖‖‖‖‖‖‖‖‖‖‖‖‖‖‖‖‖‖‖‖‖‖‖‖

"ONE OF THE WORST DAYS IN MY LIFE"

When Arthur awoke in the afternoon, every muscle in his body ached. The party rested until just before dusk, and while the guides had no heavy clothing to offer the escapees, they did have several days' portions of hard biscuits, equally hard cheese, and dried fruit for each man. Though the portions were scanty, they would have to suffice. They were also handed two leather flasks, each one smeared with sheep fat to prevent cracking or freezing in the mountain chill. One flask contained water and could be refilled along the way by simply scooping snow into the opening.

The second flask held brandy, and they were urged to use it sparingly, only when the cold seemed unbearable. They were warned that drinking any of it before sleeping was a complete waste, as the liquor was meant to be used on the trail.

Each man was provided with a walking stick for support wherever the trails narrowed and one misstep could send a climber hurtling thousands of feet into a valley or a ravine.

The route the party was to follow cut from the central Pyrénées to the eastern edge of the range, from the Aran Valley, above which the old farmhouse was perched, to the Col du Somport pass. One of only three major passes across the mountains to Spain, Somport would not have been the guides' first choice under normal conditions. The easiest route would have been directly across the eastern edge of the chain from Perpignan to Figueres, the closest Spanish town to the border crossing, but the Germans had choked off virtually all chances of escaping that way, forcing the Resistance to attempt escapes on a hazardous course winding eastward from the central Pyrénées.

If escape parties could have stayed on the pass for the entire journey, their odds would have increased; however, the Germans patrolled the trail day and night with alpine troops who carried skis and long-range sniper rifles. Henschel 126 scout planes, whose narrow wingspan and small fuselage made them ideal for maneuvering through breaks between the peaks, flew less than fifty feet above the trails. Even worse for Arthur and the others, the aircraft were equipped with powerful lights that allowed them to scout the passes in the darkness. The guides would have to rely on their knowledge of little-used paths off the main trail for any hope of getting Arthur, Cleaver, and the rest of the party to safety in eastern Spain.

As dusk neared, the guides imparted final instructions to their charges. They were not to stop unless ordered to do so by their individual guide. If they had to relieve themselves, they were to find a rock to go behind. No matter where they were in the pass or on a side path, the line had to keep moving. If a man did find a boulder behind which he could urinate or defecate, it was his job to catch up with the rest. The guides warned them not to leave their extremities exposed for too long in the bone-chilling night air.

Their route was to take them up and down some of the Pyrénées' highest peaks, some as high as eleven thousand feet. The moment they heard a Henschel scout plane—whose drone sounded like a loud washing-machine, they were told to fling themselves into the deep snow on the trail, behind a boulder, or flatten themselves against a rocky wall.

The guides knew the likeliest spots where alpine troops encamped along the pass, and tried to lead the party along goat paths and hidden routes known only to locals. Some of these paths, the guides warned, were less than two feet wide. The snow would be deep everywhere until they approached the eastern edge of the Pyrénées, and tonight's passage would pose constant hardship because the northern-facing French slopes of the chain were blanketed by snow deep enough for skiers until late June.

The last warning from the guides was the most sobering. If they did not reach the next safe house by sunrise, the Germans would undoubtedly spot them in the daylight.

Shortly after dusk, the first party, that of the two Belgians, set out with two guides. With Jeno and Fontes gone, there was one more guide than was needed. Taillandier, having mulled over the Belgians' difficult behavior, decided that two guides might be necessary to keep them moving.

Arthur, Cleaver, and Taillandier went out next, a half hour later, with their guide, a small, compact man named Emil. His movements were quick and sure, inspiring confidence that he knew every inch of the route. Snow was falling heavily, an ominous obstacle in their quest to reach their next stop before daybreak. Their first steps proved slow and difficult. No matter how much Arthur and Cleaver wished that they had boots, gloves, a hat, and a thick coat like Emil, it did not matter. They headed up a trail one behind the other, Emil at the head, Cleaver next, Arthur third, and Taillandier at the rear. The moon lay hidden behind glowering dark skies.

As the path steepened, an opening a few hundred feet ahead loomed between two jagged peaks. They needed nearly an hour to plod through knee-deep snow to reach the gap, and when they did, a stunningly beautiful and terrifying panorama greeted them. The pass itself, though covered in snow, was wide. At one edge, however, was a "cirque," a sheer drop of several thousand feet to a tree-lined valley that was framed by a semicircle of near-perpendicular cliffs.

Despite the frigid temperature, torrents of water called *gaves* gushed downward from fissures in the cliffs, the noise like that of hundreds of fire hoses turned on at once.

The pass continued upward, the track forcing every man to lean forward with all his weight on his walking stick. The energy expended in climbing just a few feet was harder than any of the physical tests Arthur had endured during pilot training. The freezing air made every breath a torment.

Except for the guide, everyone battled vertigo, the heights so disorienting that the men constantly felt that they were lurching to either side. The mental strain was as bad as the physical. The realization that even one slip or stumble could send you plunging down into ravines or the valley caused hesitation with every step. As Arthur inched along, his fingers and toes on fire, the likelihood of frostbite grew.

Arthur and his companions listened during every step of their route for the unmistakable drone of the Henschel 126 scout plane. With no sense of time, he was not sure if the clatter of the plane's single engine came an hour or several hours into the trek. As the noise grew louder and the plane's beacon flashed across the pass, he dove behind a boulder as instructed. The scout plane buzzed no more than fifty feet above them with its light sweeping the trail. The men lay flat in the snow or behind the boulders and waited for the craft to make another pass, with no way of knowing if they had been spotted. If Henschels had not been too lightweight to carry a cumbersome machine gun, Arthur and the others might have already been cut down.

At least ten minutes passed. The plane was apparently not coming back. The guide pushed himself off the trail, brushed the snow off his clothes, and took a step. Suddenly he flung himself back down, and the others, who had just started to climb back to their feet, flopped back into the snow as well. The Henschel swooped back above the trail, the beacon illuminating the pass, and vanished again. The party lay in the snow for a short time, and as soon as the guide stood up again, they followed his lead. Whether or not they had been discovered, they had to move out again immediately. If the German pilot was already radioing their position, their only chance was to reach the safe house before German troops searched the pass in daylight.

They stayed on the pass, having lost at least a half hour because of the scout plane, leaving no time for the guide to escort them to the safe house by circuitous back trails before sunrise.

Fear sent a rush of adrenaline through Arthur and the other men, and while he could not completely ignore the pain in his hands and feet, he kept pushing forward, keeping Cleaver's back in sight and fighting the impulse to look down at the sheer drops from the pass.

The sky began to lighten. Emil veered from the pass and through a fissure nearly invisible to the naked eye but just wide enough for a man to push through; behind the fissure and shielded by a granite outcrop stood a small stone lean-to known only to local mountain climbers.

They had made it after what Arthur would call "one of the worst days in my life."[1]

They staggered inside the windowless shelter to find the Belgians and their two guides shouting at each other. As the Belgians yelled and pointed fingers at the guide, one of the guides explained to Taillandier that the pair did not want to go on and that if they did want to continue, the guides were demanding more money than the Resistance had agreed upon.

The Belgians declared that they wanted to turn back to hide and wait for warmer weather. Taillandier argued that they were halfway to Spain and that the distance was roughly the same in the cold either

way. Still, they were determined to turn back at nightfall the following day.

For a time, Taillandier tried to persuade them to reconsider, warning them that the Gestapo had already begun an unprecedented crackdown on the Resistance and escapees. They were as good as dead if
they turned back now, he warned.

The debate stopped for a few minutes as the Frenchman and his
guide stumbled into the hut just as the horizon lightened. Then the
Belgians went at Taillandier again and utterly refused to continue
into Spain.

The Belgians tried to convince the rest of the group to turn back
with them, insisting that the journey was suicidal with so many Germans in the mountains and too many dangers posed by the snow and
the cold. Although Arthur could commiserate about the cold—his fingers and toes were grotesquely swollen—there was nothing anyone
could say to make him turn back. He knew without asking that Cleaver
felt the same. From the scornful expression on Taillandier's face, it was
clear that he agreed wholeheartedly with Arthur.

Cleaver wrote: "The Belgians did not want to continue and wanted
to turn back. They refused to change their minds. I thought them
utter fools. We were closer to freedom, so why go back when we were
getting close to Figueres?"[2]

Though *neutrality* in World War II Spain was an ambiguous term,
Figueres was the closest major town to the French border, which was
roughly twenty-four miles away. It was also a place whose population
had fiercely battled Franco's army during the Spanish Civil War and
loathed his ties to Hitler. The townspeople sympathized with the
Allies and aided the Resistance and Allied escapees.

Arthur, Cleaver, and the Frenchman bluntly declined the offer to
head back with the Belgians. Enraged that no one supported them, the
two men cursed Taillandier and stepped toward him in an aggressive
way. Arthur and Cleaver moved immediately to his side.

As one of the men lunged at Taillandier, Arthur stepped in front of him and drove a hard right hand into his face. The man staggered to his knees, but quickly got back up and swung at Arthur. Arthur blocked the punch with his left arm, stepped closer to the Belgian, and delivered a short and swift right to his stomach. The Belgian gasped and sank to his knees. This time he did not get up, with Arthur standing over him with both fists clenched.

Cleaver had grabbed the other Belgian and pinned his arms.

Whether it was Taillandier's contemptuous, chilling glare or the obvious intent of the American and Englishman to protect him, the Belgians stopped struggling. Arthur let the man get up off the floor. Cleaver released the other. The Belgians backed away to a corner and sat on the earthen floor against a wall. Two of the guides agreed to take them back down the way they had come.

For Arthur and Cleaver, the choice was simple. They preferred to die attempting to escape than to return to Nazi-infested Toulouse or the countryside.

Later, Emil, through Taillandier, told Arthur and Cleaver that if they were not spotted and if they maintained their nightly pace, they could reach Figueres in a day and a half, two at the most. Of course, that depended on the weather and the "roadblocks" they encountered.

As Arthur lay against a wall and tried to close his eyes, he realized he had not sipped his brandy even once yet. Hoping that the liquor might warm up his hands and feet at least a little, he drank just a tiny shot, reveling in the fiery warmth that slid down his throat and into his growling stomach. For a few welcome minutes, the liquor did seem to help. He sank into a deep, dreamless sleep.

CHAPTER 24

//////////////////////////////////////

PARTING WAYS

Near ten o'clock on the morning of June 2, 1944, Taillandier woke up Arthur and Cleaver with a gentle shake of their shoulders. The only sounds inside the lean-to were the snores and groans of the other men, who were scattered across the floor in deep, weary sleep. Wispy clouds of frost swirled above each man with every breath.

Crouching in front of the American and the Englishman, Taillandier told them in a hushed tone that he would not be accompanying them on the final leg of the journey. He had kept this to himself. Matters in Toulouse required his immediate presence, but he assured them that in Spain, arrangements to receive the "Marcel-Jeno party" had been made.[1]

Still, simply reaching Spain did not ensure freedom, Taillandier warned them again. Even though the country was technically neutral, the Fascist regime of General Francisco Franco identified with Hitler's Germany. Spanish authorities not only turned the other way when Gestapo agents kidnapped Allied escapees and took them back to Occupied France, but also aided them directly by arresting airmen and pilots and turning them over to the Nazis.

The "matters" that Taillandier had mentioned had to do with the coming Allied invasion, and he and Morhange were undoubtedly receiving orders from London right up to the eve of what would be the largest amphibious landing in recorded history. Arthur wished that he could be on a B-24 softening up Nazi targets before the strike, and Cleaver likely wanted to be dropping munitions for the Resistance rather than sitting in a freezing hut high in the Pyrénées.

Although Taillandier did not need to do so, he reminded Arthur and Cleaver that they had to watch out for and protect each other not only across the mountains, but also in Spain.

Cleaver, unable to keep his eyes open any longer from exhaustion, clasped Taillandier's hand. Neither man said anything more. They didn't have to.

Taillandier moved next to Arthur and leaned back against the wall. Both men craved a cigarette but could not light up out of fear that even the tiniest spark of flame or telltale puff of smoke might reveal their hiding spot.

For an hour or so, Arthur and Taillandier reminisced about their months together, now coming to an end. From Thoulouse, Arthur knew that the Nazis were mounting a savage and desperate manhunt for "Ricardo." Just one slip of the tongue by anyone associated with Taillandier or a torture-induced confession by someone in Toulouse would mean the end of the Morhange leader. For Taillandier, the safer course would have been escape to Spain with his friends. He never even entertained that thought. He intended to continue his personal reign of terror against the Gestapo and the traitors in Toulouse.

Taillandier uncorked one of his flasks and handed it to Arthur. Arthur took a sip of brandy and returned it to him. Smiling almost imperceptibly, the leader of Morhange nodded and drank. He clutched

Arthur's shoulder for a moment, smiled, leaned back against the wall, and closed his eyes.

Arthur did the same.

||||||||||||||||||||||

Arthur was awakened by Cleaver rustling around and gathering his scanty supplies. Despite the endless pain in his back, Arthur was ready to get going.

As he sat up and started to stretch, he suddenly realized that he, Cleaver, and Emil were the only ones left. The other guide had just set out with the French escapee, and Taillandier, the two guides, and the two Belgians had also departed.

Arthur was hit with an array of emotions as he quickly grabbed the knapsack with his remaining food and his flasks. He made sure that his pistol was still in his coat pocket; he wouldn't have put it past the Belgians to have rifled through his and Cleaver's belongings.

The only way to truly thank Taillandier was to make it home safe and to make sure Cleaver did the same.

The American and the Englishman started to follow Emil to the thin wooden door. All three men suddenly stood still as the jarring tone of a scout plane's engine vibrated overhead. The sound ebbed as fast as it had approached, but it served as a warning that they were nowhere near out of danger. Ahead, somewhere across the snow and crags, if their luck held, lay Figueres, the first stop for any hope of escape through Spain.

CHAPTER 25

|||||||||||||||||||||||||||||||||||||||||

A PERILOUS TREK

The guide led Arthur and Cleaver up another steep, snowy trail in the early evening of June 2, 1944, and halted at a gap exposing a path that twisted downward at a dizzying angle. As the three began their descent, the knee-deep snow slowly decreased in height. Within a few hours, it rose barely over their ankles.

Approaching the semicircular peaks of a cirque, the men spied lights along the opposite rim of the yawning chasm beneath the crags. They flattened themselves on the trail and waited, inclining their heads just high enough from the snow to trace the lights. They were flashing in a downward direction and eventually disappeared. The Germans had no qualms about revealing their presence as they searched for Resistance fighters or escapees.

Arthur pushed himself back onto his feet, ignoring the pain in his back, fingers, and toes, and with Emil in the lead and Cleaver in front of him, continued the descent. Another hour or two into the trek, the snow no longer came over their shoe tops and bare patches of earth and rock peeked through the trail.

Emil was piloting Arthur and Cleaver southeast, the granite and limestone peaks of the central Pyrénées giving way to granite walls colored by gneiss, multicolored mineral formations that gave the appearance of stripes on the rocks. The three men were now traversing a wild, barren maze of mountains that were lower elevation than they had seen before. Trudging below the snowline, which started at roughly 8,800 feet above sea level, they welcomed the absence of snow but strained not to slip on the loose little rocks that seemed to be everywhere. Every step downward and eastward brought subtle drops in the icy temperatures.

The men kept walking, sipping water and munching bread and cheese on the move. When they entered a wide-open valley surmounted by another series of peaks that were not as high as the earlier ones the three men had crossed but were still daunting, the trail leveled out. The terrain turned barren except for patches of scrub grass and wizened gray trees. The guide was hiking toward several foothills fronting a peak at the left edge of the valley.

Occasional flashes of lights from the crags above them signaled that the alpine units were patrolling in force that night. Despite this, the guide did not appear too concerned, likely because the Germans were too high up to spot him and his two charges.

No one relished the prospect of traversing such a long, open valley even with the night providing cover, but Emil, pointing at the valley, confirmed that they had no choice.

The sudden drone of a Henschel 126 froze all three men in place. They hurled themselves onto the dirt and sharp little rocks of the path, holding their collective breath, straining not to move at all.

With ample room to operate between the peaks and gaps above the broad valley, the scout plane came in low, the pilot throttling down to a near glide less than a few hundred feet above Arthur and his companions. The Henschel appeared to literally hover above them, its beacon illuminating the ground in all directions around them. The plane banked away a short distance and then turned to pass over them again. Finally it climbed and faded away over the peak toward which the three men were traipsing.

After a few minutes went by without the plane's return, they resumed the trek. They would know soon enough if they had been spotted. Emil picked up the pace, Arthur and Cleaver's sore, stiff legs straining to keep up.

White and violet cistus flowers (rock roses) filled the foothills, wild green thyme peeked out from the rocks, and rows of vines stretched up to the edge of the peak. The climb grew steeper.

With the stark granite face of the mountain looming directly above them, Emil suddenly seemed to vanish. On his heels, Arthur and Cleaver followed him into a passage barely wide enough for one man to wriggle through; a ripple of claustrophobia gripped Arthur momentarily. Again, he took several deep breaths. He squeezed through the opening into another, much wider gap.

Across a sheer-walled ravine, a second peak faced the one on which Arthur stood. Similar in height and mass, the two peaks looked identical. Like diminutive, demonic eyes, yellow lights flared along the upper reaches of the opposite crag. More alpine troops had appeared, perhaps alerted by the scout plane that someone was trying to cross the valley.

The hike across the lower elevation of the valley had allowed Arthur and Cleaver to catch their breath despite the appearance of the scout plane. Now, as they climbed higher and higher again, their lungs began to burn in the thinning air. Stretches of snow greeted them the higher they hiked, but nowhere near what they had already experienced. Snowfall in the eastern Pyrénées, which were closer to the warmer climate of the Mediterranean Sea, was less than the rest of the range. Still, there was enough to make every step treacherous.

Several hundred feet from the summit, Emil turned onto a hiking trail that curled around the northern slope to the southern wall, which faced Spain. The view was breathtaking. At that height, a chain of foothills far below undulated toward a massive plain dotted with vineyards, fields, and trees. The Spanish border lay just beyond where the foothills met the plain.

To Arthur's and Cleaver's horror, the horizon was already tinged with gray. Unless Emil was leading them to a cave or another hut, the American and the Englishman had to wonder if they were going to make the final leg of their journey in daylight. Across the ravine, lights still flared on the adjoining slope—and were moving downward, in the same direction as the three men.

Leaning back, using his walking stick as both a support and a brake, Emil began to half step, half slide in the thin blanket of snow. Cleaver and Arthur followed.

The sun began to rise, and still the three men snaked their way down the trail. Perhaps a quarter of the way down the jagged slope, the roar of an engine all too familiar to Arthur and Cleaver pealed from the direction of the adjoining mountain. An Me 109 with tan and white camouflage paint, one of the many German fighter planes that patrolled both the northern and southern passes and trails of the Pyrénées as soon as dawn broke, ripped past the first mountain just a few hundred yards in front of the trio. The pilot raced past them, banked away from the mountains, and bore right back at them for another look.

Emil did not press himself against the rock wall or fling himself facedown onto the path; if they had scattered for cover, the German would have opened up immediately on them. They could only pray that the pilot could not get a close enough look to decide if they were Germans, mountain dwellers, or escapees. Arthur and Cleaver emulated their guide by staying upright, too.

As the Nazi pilot surged past the second peak, he waggled his wings and vanished.

He had signaled the alpine soldiers that someone was on the neighboring peak and climbing down toward the border. Probably unable to determine just who was on the mountain and not wanting to pour machine-gun fire accidentally into his own troops, the Me 109 pilot had simply tagged the three men. The white uniforms of Nazi alpine soldiers and their shiny ski goggles flashed in the strengthening sunlight.

Emil began to move faster in small but quick steps through the snow and loose rocks. Behind him Arthur and Cleaver stumbled, keeping on their feet and fighting to make sure not to lose sight of the guide. Several sharp rocks tore through the beaten leather soles of Arthur's shoes, but his feet were so swollen and numb that he barely felt the gashes. Every brutal step now to the bottom of the mountain and to the Spanish border was a race against highly trained soldiers with sturdy, fur-lined mountain boots and sniper rifles.

At one point roughly halfway down, the gap between the two mountains dwindled to just five hundred yards, close enough that Arthur, Cleaver, and Emil could see the small silhouettes of their pursuers. Several of the Germans paused, slid their long-range Mauser rifles from their waterproof shoulder sheaths, knelt, squinted through telescopic lenses, and aimed the barrels across the divide. The trio dove onto the trail just as the sharp cracks of the Mausers echoed in the rarefied air.

The bullets whistled across the gap, slammed against the granite walls beneath the three men, and ricocheted with grating whines below. For the moment the three men lay just out of the effective range of the Germans, who needed to close the distance by perhaps a hundred yards in order to pick off their targets. The guide crawled into a small opening that led to a trail shielded from the attackers by a curve of the wall. Cleaver and Arthur crept on their bellies right behind him as another Mauser volley slammed into the rock below them.

As the sun rose ever higher, the three men snaked down one of the tightest, sheerest paths they had encountered on the journey. Emil's familiarity with every inch of the terrain was keeping them out of the Germans' sight and range for the present, but at some point, the rarely used hiking trail would inevitably turn back toward the middle of the peak and put them back in eyeshot of the soldiers. Equally disturbing was the possibility that the alpine troops were simply heading down the adjacent slope in order to reach the bottom first and cut off the escape route.

With roughly two thousand feet of mountain left, Emil had no choice but to lead them back on a hiking trail within sight of the Germans again. It was the only route down.

Instead of a half-dozen German soldiers moving single file down a trail on the opposite slope, there were at least three or four times that number. If Arthur or Cleaver expected a barbed-wire fence with sentry posts along the border, they were relieved to see that only a few signs marked the crossing from France to Spain. A swift-flowing river raced along the border, and an uncovered bridge carried travelers from one country to the other.

Of course, the two escapees had no reason to believe that the absence of a fence would stop the Germans from pursuing them past the boundary. The only certainty for the American and the Englishman lay in their need to reach the border bridge ahead of the Nazis and hope for the best. They and their guide had to get there first or not at all.

They could no longer worry about falling. They slipped, stumbled, and slid down the final trail in a spray of snow, cracking twigs, and rocks that tore their clothes and their flesh. Whenever the trail proved too steep for them to stay upright or even dip into a crouch, they slid along on their rear ends or crawled across the rocks. The three men's sole thought was to keep pushing forward. Across the divide, the Germans were also moving as fast as they could, staggering, too, but their footing aided by their boots.

His breaths coming in gasps and pants, his heart pumping so fast that he was afraid it would literally burst, Arthur scrambled closer and closer to the bottom behind Cleaver and Emil. Somehow, Emil led his two men at least a hundred yards closer to the bottom than the Germans, but as he, Arthur, and Cleaver lurched closer to the Spanish border, the Germans were closing fast.

While most of the soldiers tottered down the slope, several again knelt on one knee, braced their long-range Mausers against their shoulders, and took their bearings through their sniper lenses. The rifles barked just as the three men nearly toppled down the last few yards of the mountain. Bullets slammed into an ancient tree in front of them and a stinging spray of splinters and sheared-off bark cut their faces and hands. All three staggered, recovered their balance, and ran with their last reserves of strength and adrenaline the few hundred yards toward the bridge. The shots whizzed just a few inches above their heads. The Germans finally had the range.

As the half-dozen snipers readied their second volley, the rest of the alpine troops pursued the three men. Cleaver wrote that the Germans "were moving fast down a trail on the far side of a ravine to cut us off at the border bridge across a deep chasm. We did not need our guide's muttered exhortations to prod us to expend our remaining energy to reach that bridge before the Germans."

Cleaver continued: "Our guide was relentless, pushing us far past what either Meyerowitz or I could have imagined as our physical limits.

"As we finally neared the border, matters worsened quickly. We got there ahead of the Germans but several aimed their long-range rifles at us. I was certain our end was here."[1]

Arthur, Cleaver, and the guide pounded across the rough wooden planks of the bridge and crossed into Spain.

More than a dozen German soldiers had stopped running toward them and were arrayed in a loose semicircle, pondering whether to cross the bridge and seize the three men or shoot them on the spot.

One of the Nazis bellowed curses at them, placed his Mauser to his shoulder, and pointed it at them. Arthur and the others figured they were finished. After all they had gone through, their lives would end in Spain.

"We crossed less than a hundred and fifty meters ahead of them," Cleaver wrote. "Why they did not cut us down, I will never understand."[2]

In all likelihood, the snipers who had opened up a minute or two earlier had held their fire as their comrades chased the escapees to the bridge. Still, as Cleaver wrote, why the Germans did not finish off the three men would always remain a mystery. Perhaps because the alpine troops were not SS or Gestapo, some semblance of human decency made them hesitate.

The likeliest reason was that the crossing was patrolled by heavily armed Spanish partisans who could appear with lightning speed and seemingly out of nowhere. They despised the Nazis as much as they did Franco, and on numerous occasions, tore apart German soldiers who crossed onto Spanish soil in pursuit of escapees from France.

The Germans did move right up to the other side of the bridge. Then, an officer who had to be wary that he and his men might already be in the gunsights of partisans concealed in several stands of trees and brush beyond the bridge shouted an order. The soldiers formed a double line and marched back toward the mountains. Like Cleaver, Arthur would never understand why the Germans, so relentless in his long months in France, simply turned around and left.

A new set of dangers faced them, however, and Arthur and Cleaver understood the necessity of safe houses even in "neutral" Spain. With Spain crawling with Nazi and Allied agents alike, the Germans would be sure to try and make a grab for the two escapees.

<hr />

In Toulouse, Marcel Taillandier did not yet know whether Arthur and Cleaver had survived the first leg of their escape. The leader of Morhange had suffered a devastating blow on June 2, the very day that the American and the Englishman made their break for the border. One of Taillandier's most important lieutenants, Achille Viadieu, whom Arthur had met at 96, boulevard Deltour, had been unmasked by the Gestapo.

The thirty-three-year-old Viadieu, on Taillandier's orders, had tricked the Germans and Vichy police into believing that he was a staunch collaborator. He so won the enemy's trust that he was appointed the regional director of the RNP, an ultra-Fascist and collaborationist unit that wore black uniforms similar to the Gestapo. Several times on Paillole's orders, Viadieu had assassinated notorious traitors in Toulouse.

Paillole wrote: "The enemy had just figured out that Viadieu . . . had been a penetration agent of French counterespionage for the past two years."[3]

Two Gestapo agents walked up to Viadieu and shot him down in the center of Toulouse.

Taillandier had moved Arthur and Cleaver out of Toulouse just in time. Through torture and murder, the Gestapo was closing in on Morhange and other Resistance units. Three-quarters of all Resistance fighters who would die during the war fell from June to August 1944. Viadieu was one of the first of Morhange to be executed in that time frame. He would not be the last.

CHAPTER 26

STRANDED

Arthur and Cleaver fell in step with Emil. Continuing eastward, he brought them deeper into the Spanish province of Catalonia, across a wide-open plain eventually leading to stands of fig trees and one vineyard after another. They skirted a two-lane highway that cut between the vineyards and the foothills that edged the plain. Occasionally, cars and clattering farm trucks piled with hay passed along the highway, but not once did a military vehicle of any sort appear. To the northeast, the now-muted drone and muffled growl of Nazi scout and fighter planes grew even fainter.

For the first time in three days, the sun's warmth beat down from a dark blue sky and on Arthur, whose frostbitten fingers and toes alternately ached or went numb. Sweating, he removed his overcoat, slipped his pistol into a trouser pocket, and slung the coat over his shoulder. He was exhausted, hurting from head to toe. Still, the realization that every step farther from the border heightened his chance for escape and for freedom drove him onward.

Emil kept them walking between rows of grapevines and trees. Flowers bloomed everywhere, turning the landscape into a carpet of myriad, almost dizzying colors, a stark contrast to the snow and barren rocks of the mountains.

After an hour or so, Emil turned toward the highway and pointed to several gnarled fig trees flanking the roadway. Attuned by now to every hand signal and gesture from the Frenchman, Arthur and Cleaver understood that he wanted them to wait. They sat behind the trees, screened from the highway by the trunks and by the twisted strands of Catalan grapevines. Emil crouched just off the road, watching and waiting for something or someone.

Glad for the chance to rest, Arthur and Cleaver waited, too. Soon a nondescript old car with a dusty windshield slowed down and pulled off the road a few feet away from Emil. He rose from his crouch and approached the vehicle. As the front passenger window rolled down, he leaned in and began to converse with the driver.

Emil stepped away from the window and waved in the direction of the American and the Englishman. Struggling to get to their feet again, their legs wobbly and twitching from spasms, Arthur and Cleaver leaned against each other to steady themselves. After a few moments, they limped over to the car.

When Emil opened the rear passenger-side door, the two eased themselves into the worn, ripped backseat. Emil slid in alongside them. The car slipped back onto the road and headed off at a leisurely pace.

Emil, pointing forward, looked at Arthur and Cleaver and said one word: "Figueres."

The driver, in a beret and with a shirt whose sleeves were rolled up to reveal thick, heavily veined forearms, did not say anything, but his nose was slightly twitching.

They all knew the reason for the man's reaction. The American longed for a bath or shower, but was almost too tired to care or even notice the stench wafting from him and his companions, none of whom had seen soap or water for nearly four days and nights.

Less than an hour later, they reached the outskirts of a town and a gargantuan fortress that loomed from a dark ridge above the streets. Figueres had once been a picturesque blend of medieval and nineteenth-century buildings and homes. The town that greeted Arthur, however, was one battered by the Spanish Civil War.

The thick-walled castle, Sant Ferran, had served as the outpost where the region's Republican forces had made their last stand against Franco's Fascist army. With Stuka and Heinkel dive bombers supplied by the Nazis, Franco's air force had gutted Figueres, which had once been a bustling town of forty thousand people. Only about half that number now remained among the ruins.

The car crawled down rubble-strewn streets and stopped in front of a stucco house whose tan walls were scorched but remained intact beneath a patched red-tile roof. The guide opened the car door and beckoned for Arthur and Cleaver to follow. From behind the scarred shutters of other houses in various states of disrepair, Arthur sensed people watching. It was a hangover from the ceaseless stress of collaborators everywhere he had turned in France. Weariness flooded Arthur's thought and limbs, but he could not let down his guard, not even for a second.

Once they stepped inside the house, the guide quickly shut the door as the car drove off slowly. The first floor of the building was virtually empty, a few broken chairs on their sides and backs. Dense dust cloaked every inch of the house. A collapsed staircase had once led to the second floor. In one corner, an old cast-iron stove was shrouded by cobwebs.

The guide walked over to the far wall, faced the front door, unslung his carbine, and sat down with the weapon cradled in his lap. Arthur and Cleaver sat down and leaned back against a sidewall.

Half dozing but still alert, Arthur was suddenly startled by several short, sharp raps on the door.

A small man who looked like a clerk in his white shirt, dark tie, and black pants entered with a much larger man in a beret and a leather jacket.

The man in the tie introduced himself to Arthur and Cleaver as "Louis—Louis *petit*. I am a courier for Marcel."

He walked over to the guide and stretched out his hand. Then he asked, "Do you have something for me?"

Emil reached into his pocket and pulled out an envelope. Louis opened it and, in English for Arthur and Cleaver, said, "It says that the 'Marcel and Jeno party has arrived in Figueres.'"

Another set of knocks alarmed Arthur and Cleaver. They relaxed as Louis opened the door to let in two more men, both also wearing berets and leather jackets. The pair also carried large canvas satchels packed with food and a few bottles of wine. There was no mistaking the bulge of revolvers in both men's jacket pockets.

Inclining his thumb at the two newcomers, Louis said, "I will take this note to the British consulate in Barcelona. These two men will remain with you until I make arrangements for you to leave here.

"You are not to leave this house. Stay away from the shutters and do not open the door for anyone—my men know who to let in."[1]

Louis departed as quickly as he had arrived. Emil went with him, offering a wave and a smile to the two men he had led over the mountains, two more of the many he had taken this way before.

Arthur and Cleaver remained in the house for the next two nights, resting, recuperating from the harrowing trek across the mountains. They needed to sleep, to prepare themselves emotionally as well as physically for the next leg of the escape. Once again, all they could do was to wait for a knock on the door.

Arthur and Cleaver drank a little of the dark red, robust wine and munched soft cheese, bread, and olives from the satchels; they were eating a meal in an unoccupied nation for the first time in months. "Neutral Spain," however, was far from being free.

CHAPTER 27

GOOD-BYE, GEORGES LAMBERT

In June 1944, Arthur's and Cleaver's lives became a grueling waiting game. Their new guide, a dour middle-aged man named Miguel, returned to Figueres two days after their arrival to drive them the eighty-six miles to Barcelona, where Taillandier had made arrangements for an agent to meet them with new identification papers.

No longer would Arthur have to rely upon his "Georges Lambert" photo ID even though he still had it. No one had asked him to give it back. Escapees were usually required to return their IDs to their guides or the resistance groups so that the documents could be reused with different photos. With D-Day so close at hand, it is possible that neither Taillandier nor Emil believed it was necessary for Arthur to give back his ID.

In Spain, escaping airmen and pilots needed papers and a photo card with their actual names and citizenship on the documents. If the Spanish police or Civil Guard seized anyone with forged identification or none at all, they immediately arrested him. German agents tipped off by bribed Spanish officials were allowed to "identify" Allied airmen as "escaped criminals" and return them to Occupied France.

A Spaniard named Joan Garcia Rabascall who worked as an agent for the British consulate in Barcelona often had to rush to various prisons with papers identifying RAF escapees whom the Germans were about to seize. To the terrified airmen, he explained, "In this country the presence of these Germans is more legal than British consulate activities."[1] Barcelona native Roberto Garcia handled the "extrication" of captured escapees for the American consulate in the city. Any man who required their help was in a dire situation, and many times the Gestapo had removed prisoners before Rabascall or Garcia could arrive.

Every mile between Figueres and Barcelona posed a threat to Arthur and Cleaver if they were caught without proper identification. Cleaver had no way to know that two of his crewmen had experienced this frightening predicament a month earlier.

Thanks to Cleaver's decision to stay at the controls of the crippled Halifax in April, John Franklin and Ray Hindle had parachuted safely near Cognac and had been taken in and helped by the Resistance (not Morhange). Guides had taken them into Spain by crossing the Pyrénées above the Pont de Rei, farther west than Arthur and Cleaver's route. In the Spanish town of Vielha, Franklin and Hindle—with no identification—were arrested by the Spanish Civil Guard and moved to the Seminari Vell prison, in Lleida, where German agents often plucked airmen from cells and shipped them back to France.

Hindle, who so reminded Cleaver of Arthur, and Franklin got lucky. Joan Garcia Rabascall raced from Barcelona to the prison with papers for both men and removed them before the Nazis could do so.

Arthur and Cleaver also got lucky on the drive from Figueres to Barcelona. They arrived in the sprawling, beautiful city without being stopped and ordered to show identification. Then, in a safe house, their guide suddenly told them that he had to go to the British consulate, which, like the U.S. consulate, provided papers for both escaping British and American airmen and their documents. Arthur and Cleaver had to be concerned. This was not the plan Taillandier had explained to them. They were supposed to be met by another guide in Barcelona who would have their new identifications and other paperwork on his person.

As always, Taillandier came through for the American and the Englishman. The photos and papers did arrive, and over the course of nine days in Barcelona, Arthur and Cleaver had the option of staying in the house or moving warily around the city with their new IDs. Many Allied airmen were being harbored in Barcelona, but Arthur and Cleaver's guide had cautioned the duo to be careful whom they befriended there. The Germans could ply unwitting airmen with liquor at any of the city's countless cafés and bars and lure the men to a brothel. Many of them soon found themselves trussed up in the German consulate and smuggled out of Spain and on their way to a prison camp. During their time there, Arthur and Cleaver avoided trusting the wrong "friend."

As with all Allied airmen in Barcelona, Arthur and Cleaver were told that if they chose to go out, they must never break the city's curfew. Historian Alberto Poveda Longo, in his book *Paso Clandestino* ("secret pass"), states: "[Airmen] had to respect the curfew rules. The foreigners shouldn't have been in the street from 9 p.m. but during the summer they could be in the street until 11 p.m."

Once again, in Barcelona, Cleaver's crewmen Franklin and Hindle made a mistake that Arthur and Cleaver avoided: "One day the friends decided to visit the local cinema. When the film had finished, a couple of civil guards [Spanish] were waiting for them and moved the young men to the prison."[2] Franklin wrote that they had "broken the curfew rules . . . to visit the local cinema. We were escorted to jail through the main street, I thought with some satisfaction by the civil guard."[3]

Their luck held, thanks once more to Joan Garcia Rabascall, who liberated them from "the small stone cell and the tiny grill window" before the Nazis could make a move. "You can imagine our relief," Franklin added.[4]

On June 13, Arthur and Cleaver finally left Barcelona. By that time, they had to know that the Allied forces had stormed ashore along Normandy on June 6, and were craving the chance to get back into the thick of it.

Arthur wrote tersely that they "then went to Madrid with Cleaver and 3 Belgians."[5]

Cleaver remembered, "We were worried that German agents would seize us. Meyerowitz, a trio of Belgians, and I reached Madrid . . . We had several near-disastrous run-ins with Spanish police sympathetic to the Germans, as well as spying Gestapo agents many times. We were challenged several times."[6]

As Taillandier's carefully crafted escape plan for Arthur and Cleaver unfolded, the Frenchman and Morhange were fighting for their very survival in and around Toulouse.

CHAPTER 28

||||||||||||||||||||||||||||||||||||||||||||

DEATH TO FRANCE

On June 2, 1944, about the time that Arthur and Cleaver were racing the pursuing Nazis toward the Spanish border, Taillandier, identified as a "person of interest" based on a tip from a collaborator, was approached in Toulouse's Place du Capitole, the city's main public square, by six Gestapo agents. He pulled out a revolver and opened fire on them.

As crowds scattered, he dashed down several streets where he knew every turn and alley, ran into a building, and climbed the stairs to the roof. Leaping from roof to roof, he slipped away from the Germans and fled the city.

He hid for most of June in a maquis near Quérigut, in the department of Ariège, in a rugged stretch of the Midi-Pyrénées. From the hideout, he directed Morhange ambushes and executions that "quickly scrubbed 150" Nazis and collaborators.[1]

Taillandier left on July 11, to meet in Toulouse with several of his Morhange lieutenants including Fontes, and "entrusted the command [of the maquis] to one of his deputies, André Audebaud."[2] Accompanying Taillandier was an operative named "Georges" and twenty-four-year-old Léo Hamard, one of Taillandier's most trusted and valiant agents. He had been with Morhange since 1942, and his experience as a police inspector had proven invaluable in their infiltration of the Vichy gendarmerie.

As the three men drove out of the Toulouse neighborhood of Saint-Martin-du-Touch in a black Citroën, the streets teemed with Gestapo and German soldiers. The car slowed near the dam at the edge of the neighborhood and then stopped in front of a guardhouse where four *Feldjägers*, uniformed Nazi military policemen with Schmeisser submachine guns, approached the car.

One of the policemen demanded that Taillandier and the others hand over their identification papers. Suspiciously eyeing the Frenchmen, he grabbed Taillandier's card and walked over to the guardhouse to crank the field telephone inside. According to operative Pierre Saint-Laurens, Taillandier understood that he "was trapped like a rat."[3] There was not even time to draw their pistols. He ordered Georges and Léo Hamard to run. Instead, the two jumped from the left side of the car and rushed the officers so that Taillandier could try to get away and Morhange would not lose its irreplaceable commander.

As his two men punched and kicked the police and others swarmed them, Taillandier slipped out the right side of the Citroën and sprinted back down the street. By the time that the Germans finally overpowered his two companions, Taillandier had vanished.

He ducked into a blacksmith's forge, and the blacksmith told him to turn down a driveway that led to a church and an alley through which he could escape the police and Gestapo fanning out across the streets. Taillandier reached the front of the church and spotted the alley "to the left . . . the narrow passage between the wall and that of the building."[4]

He ran halfway down the alley and then paused. He thought that he had strayed into a dead end, and before reaching the bottom of the alley, he turned back.

He skirted the church to his right and down another passageway—only to find, Saint-Laurens writes, "the terrible surprise that he was in a cul de sac."[5] With the harsh shouts of approaching Germans and the snarls and barks of attack dogs coming closer, Taillandier scaled a large cross next to the church and climbed onto the steeply pitched roof, flattening himself onto it as Gestapo and police rushed past the church. Once again, it looked as though "Ricardo" had eluded the Nazis.

A window suddenly opened on the house across the street from the church. A woman's shouts caused some of the Germans to stop and run back toward the sound.

"There he is!" she yelled, pointing at the roof of the church.[6]

As Taillandier squeezed off several shots from his revolver, the Germans opened up with rifles, submachine guns, and Lugers. Tiles shattered as rounds ripped into the roof and slammed into Taillandier from head to toe. He tumbled from the roof, dead before he hit the street, riddled with bullets. The Gestapo dragged away his body. Days later, the long, dried-out trail of blood left by the body remained in the street, a warning to other men and women of the Resistance. The warning went unheeded.

On August 30, 1944, in the garden of a building of Maignac Street, in Toulouse, Taillandier's corpse was tossed by the Gestapo into a shallow ditch. A crudely lettered sign was tied to him. It read, *Death to France.*

Marcel Taillandier was far more fortunate than Georges and Léo Hamard. The Germans kicked Georges to death outside the car and hauled Hamard off to Gestapo headquarters in Toulouse. For a week, he was tortured in every savage way his captors knew. Hamard would not break, never revealing information about Morhange.

When the Gestapo realized that he would never talk, they did not end his agony with a bullet to the head. They chose instead to bury him alive.

||||||||||||||||||||||||||||||||||||||||

CHAPTER 29

"WELCOME BACK TO THE WAR"

Packed into a van with the three Belgian escapees, Arthur and Cleaver endured their longest time on the road since the eight-hour drive with Andrés Fontes from Perpignan to the central Pyrénées. The van, driven by a guide who worked with the British and American consulates, made an uneventful 332-mile, seven-hour trip from Madrid southwest to the river port of Seville despite the presence of Spanish Civil Guard and army trucks and armored cars along the route.

Arthur and Cleaver had been told that the authorities rarely stopped vehicles on the highways between the two cities. Along with Gestapo and Abwehr agents, pro-Nazi Spanish officials and military preferred to lie in wait in Seville, which was the "clearing house" where pro-Allied Spaniards planned the last leg of the journey for airmen and pilots. The final destination was the legendary British fortress "the Rock of Gibraltar," which commanded the passage between the Atlantic Ocean and the Mediterranean Sea. If an escapee made it to Gibraltar, he was as good as home. The Nazis and their Spanish supporters knew it, too, searching every route to Gibraltar in their effort to seize any unfortunate Allied pilots and airmen.

There was a reason that both Madrid and now Seville served as way stations for fleeing Allied airmen. Both cities were so large that it was relatively easy for escapees to either hide or walk the streets before curfew with their identification papers. Still, exploring the two cities carried risks, as Gestapo agents often trailed English-speaking men and grabbed them in alleys, took their identification papers, summoned Spanish police on the Nazi payroll, and announced that the prisoners had no papers and were going to be taken to German territory.

In his two days in Madrid, Arthur "didn't see any Americans."[1] Wary of going out in public as Americans and British airmen had done in Barcelona, he decided that it was better to lie low in Madrid until they left for Seville.

As their van neared Seville, a vast plain stretched toward the Guadalquivir River, with the city sprawling in every direction along both banks, which flowed eighty miles to the Atlantic. The van turned along the western side of the Guadalquivir amid a breathtaking blend of civil buildings and houses whose architecture ran from Roman and Moorish to neoclassical and modern.

The deeper they headed into the city, the narrower the side streets, or "closes," became. The driver pulled into the Triana neighborhood, the birthplace of flamenco and famous for its unique style of ceramics, a place where medieval-era apartment houses still crowded against each other. Since the fall of France, in 1940, Triana had served as a haven for Allied airmen because the neighborhood was a fervent bastion of anti-Franco, as well as anti-Nazi, sympathy. During the Spanish Civil War, working-class, Republican Triana had fiercely fought Franco's forces before the resistance was crushed by merciless reprisals. Now the seething hatred along the river's west bank for

Franco and Hitler meant that Arthur and Cleaver would find any number of men and women to help them escape Spain.

From Seville to Gibraltar, the usual escape route for Allied airmen was a dangerous 119-mile drive from the city to the Rock along roads heavily patrolled by the Spanish Army and the Civil Guard. Luck played a huge role if soldiers or militia stopped a car or van with escaping Allied airmen and pilots; the consulates in Barcelona had provided Arthur and Cleaver with Spanish pesos to bribe border patrols to let them cross into Gibraltar. Sometimes, though, German agents who paid police, soldiers, and Civil Guards far more than the amount the escapees could offer accompanied the authorities—especially when the Nazis were searching for a specific high-value person. Cleaver fell squarely into that category. The Gestapo knew he was in Spain and their agents were undoubtedly waiting along the road to Gibraltar with Spaniards on the take.

Getting Cleaver to safety meant that his and Arthur's guides would have to use a second, far more hazardous escape route, one that meant a 115-mile drive from Seville to the southwestern port of Algeciras and then a seven-mile trip by boat to Gibraltar through waters where U-boats still prowled and Spanish planes could order a vessel to turn back to Algeciras. Nazi agents were stationed all along the docks of the port to hunt for any hint of Allied airmen and pilots boarding a fishing boat, or "smack." Vessels carrying any such escapees were frequently sunk if a U-boat was alerted in time by coded messages from onshore.

Arthur could have opted to go with the Belgians by the easier route, entirely by car. His chances of reaching Gibraltar were far better that way. For him, however, there was no question which route he would choose. He would stay with Cleaver, running the gauntlet from Algeciras to Gibraltar by boat.

Before dawn on Friday, June 16, a car pulled up at the safe house in Seville. Arthur and Cleaver, in worn but clean clothes and decent shoes provided by their hosts, climbed into the car, having carefully checked that they had their identification papers and their cash.

As the car waded into the crowded streets of the city and turned south along the coastal road for the drive to Algeciras, the American and the Englishman had already traveled over a thousand miles on their winding journey from Toulouse to Seville. They knew that the final seven, from Algeciras to Gibraltar, could well prove the most nerve-racking and lethal.

High above the shoreline of southwestern Spain, every mile on the roadway brought vistas of the sun glinting off the Atlantic. As always along the highways leading south, cars, vans, and trucks were pulled over by police and militia for inspection of travelers' papers, an unnerving sight for the American and the Englishman, who both tensed every time an official-looking car or a military vehicle suddenly appeared alongside or behind them.

Approaching Algeciras near 7 a.m., some three hours after departing Seville, the car hit traffic that had come to a near standstill. Several police cars and army half-tracks were parked on both sides of the highway, and police officers and Civil Guards, in dark blue uniforms and German-issue jackboots, and toting German submachine guns, were questioning the occupants of every car, van, and truck. Every now and then they waved vehicles to pull over to the side and ordered the drivers and passengers to step outside. Most ominously, several men in fedoras and dark suits challenged travelers. Arthur had seen enough of their type in Toulouse to recognize them instantly as Gestapo agents.

The presence of Nazis would spoil any attempt to bribe Spaniards working with the Nazis up ahead. While Arthur and Cleaver did have the correct identification to pass through "neutral Spain," this wouldn't matter if the Spanish police and soldiers looked the other way as the Gestapo seized the identification documents. Cleaver's face and actual name were on his papers, and the Toulouse Gestapo wanted him back. Arthur had no doubt that the Germans would extradite him along with the RAF pilot. A Jewish airman carrying a concealed weapon would not fare well back in Nazi territory.

The turn of Arthur, Cleaver, and their driver came after an interminable wait of over an hour. Even if they got through the checkpoint, they had to be at the dock before nightfall because the U-boats would surface only at night to recharge their batteries and replenish the air inside or to stop and board a suspicious vessel. By day, it was too dangerous for the submarines to surface, with Allied fighter planes from the airfield at Gibraltar combing the waters below. Under the relative cover of darkness, sometimes a U-boat simply sank ships that matched the descriptions from Nazi agents dockside at Algeciras.

At the order of a Civil Guard, Arthur, Cleaver, and the driver handed over their papers. The Spaniard looked them over and returned them. He waved the car forward.

No matter how much relief filled Arthur and Cleaver, the feeling ebbed quickly. Nazi agents were waiting along the port's docks, studying every man and woman there.

The car traveled down several streets that were filled with cafés and shops and turned onto the Avenida del Carmen, the large commercial roadway running along the waterfront. Spanish Navy destroyers were anchored at large piers, and countless freighters and fishing vessels of all shapes and sizes clogged the harbor. Directly east across the Bay of Gibraltar, the massive algae-flecked, granite face of the Rock jutted from dark blue, almost violet waters, a small bank of fog covering the summit, where the British fortress stood. Freedom lay within sight of Arthur and Cleaver, but running the gauntlet to Gibraltar promised to be seven of the longest miles of both men's lives.

The driver stopped in front of a dilapidated fishing boat with peeling red and green paint and barnacles encrusting the hull just above the waterline. A rusty crane and winch hovered above the stern, and patched-up nets were fastened to the gunwales. Surprisingly, the vessel's engines were already running and humming strongly, creating a large backwash from the propellers at the stern.

Arthur and Cleaver sprang from the car and hustled up a swaying gangplank and onto the vessel. As instructed, they did not look around for watchful Nazi agents, avoiding any movement that could arouse suspicion. The car had left by the time they turned around.

Within a few minutes, the captain, standing in the wheelhouse, throttled the craft into reverse near 9 a.m. and eased it from the pier and into the channel. As with all Allied escapees on a fishing boat, Arthur and Cleaver were handed woolen sailor's watchcaps and oily smocks that reeked of grease and fish.

Slowly gathering more speed, the vessel churned down the channel for the waters of the Bay of Gibraltar. No one said a word to the two passengers. Unsure what to do, Arthur and Cleaver stood together by the port gunwale and fought to keep their balance as the vessel plowed into choppy, whitecapped waters.

Several planes flew in low circles above the bay, some with the all-too-familiar hum that Arthur recognized as that of the Henschel 126. Much of the Spanish military's equipment, vehicles, and planes had come from Germany. For the first few years of the war, the Nazis had pressured Spain to enter the fray on Hitler's side and capture Gibraltar; however, Franco's determination to keep the German Army off Spanish soil thwarted Hitler's Operation Felix, the Nazis' plan to capture Gibraltar. Franco became increasingly concerned that he faced the threat of invasion from both the Germans and the Allies, playing a skillful but dangerous game of duplicity with both sides until he gauged which way the war was going. In June 1944, the landings at Normandy cemented the dictator's decision: Hitler would lose, and Spain would do as little as possible to help the Nazi war effort henceforth. Still, Spanish officials collaborating with the Nazis were aiding Gestapo efforts to take back escaping Allied airmen. The

Gestapo prowled ports and other escape routes for Allied airmen for several months to come.

As planes darted down over the plodding fishing vessel and circled it several times, Arthur hoped that from above, he and Cleaver looked like ordinary Algeciras fishermen. On every run to Gibraltar with Allied airmen aboard a fishing boat, one of the crew stood at the bow and another at the stern, peering at the water in every direction. They were searching for the tiny, telltale wake of a U-boat's periscope among the whitecaps.

The boat felt like it was trying to blow through cement, and for a long while the mass of the Rock did not appear to be getting any closer. Halfway there, the currents grew heavier, the vessel's progress seemingly slowing to inches. A scout plane was dogging the craft, passing slowly over her and back again and again. The pilot had to be looking for something, or someone.

To throw off pesky scouts, crewmen would lower a few nets into the water in an attempt to trick the pilots into believing that a fishing run, not an escape, was under way. The scout above was apparently not buying it, keeping the boat squarely in view. The captain, the crew, and the two passengers had no way to know if the pilot was playing games or tracking the vessel for a German U-boat. There was another distressing possibility. For the first two miles into the bay, sleek, speedy German E-boats—coastal patrol craft—with Spanish Navy crews, could stop and board any vessel they wanted to in Spanish waters. Several E-boats were on the water around Arthur and Cleaver, but were battling the rough waters, too.

With stomach-knotting slowness, the fishing boat lumbered past the halfway point to Gibraltar. There were just a few miles left, but the boat was getting there at a near crawl.

The Spanish scout planes peeled away, not willing to risk being mistaken for Germans by RAF Spitfires or Hurricane fighter planes.

British patrol boats now appeared ahead of the fishing vessel. From the flagpoles at their sterns, the Union Jack snapped in the gusts. As comforting as the sight was, Arthur and Cleaver were still not safe. A U-boat could have them in the crosshairs of a periscope a mile or more away. Also, the Royal Navy had heavily mined the waters around Gibraltar from past fears of German or even Spanish assaults.

Like all of the Spanish skippers sneaking Allied escapees to the Rock, the seaman ferrying Arthur and Cleaver knew the safe passages among the minefields. Allied agents provided the captains with secret charts of the routes, and after the skippers memorized them, the charts were destroyed to prevent them from falling into the hands of collaborators or the Nazis.

Suddenly the Rock of Gibraltar loomed right in front of and above Arthur, 1,398 feet of stark cliffs that commanded the path between the Atlantic and the Mediterranean, one half of the ancient Greeks' and Romans' mythic Pillars of Hercules. The fishing boat slowed even more as it neared several long, steel piers where more patrol boats and several Royal Navy frigates and destroyers were moored.

A town that appeared completely deserted stretched from the harbor to the foot of the mountain. The town was in fact deserted. When the war had broken out, the British government had evacuated Gibraltar's civilian population, mainly to London and also Morocco, Madeira, and Jamaica. Now, with complete Allied control of the skies above Gibraltar, the Royal Navy no longer had to worry about Luftwaffe strikes against the port. The biggest threat rested with the U-boats. While there was little question that a German submarine had spotted the fishing boat at some point of the trip and may well have been tipped off that a high-priority British escapee was on the vessel, the skipper would not have risked a torpedo attack that would have revealed his location with so much daylight still left.

The boat throttled down and eased against one of the piers with a gentle thud. As crewmen lowered the gangplank, a jeep rattled onto the dock and alongside the vessel. Two officers stepped out of the jeep, boarded, walked straight up to Arthur and Cleaver, and asked for their identification from the Barcelona consulate. One wore the olive-drab uniform of the U.S. Army, the other the tan-hued issue of the Royal Army.

After checking the photos and papers, one of the officers gave the escapees the customary greeting: "Gentlemen, welcome back to the war."[2]

CHAPTER 30

||||||||||||||||||||||||||||||||||||

"IT IS THEREFORE *SECRET*"

As Arthur and Cleaver settled into the backseat of the jeep, the fishing boat pulled away from the pier and churned back out into the channel.

The jeep surged forward, and Arthur and Cleaver hung on as it shot toward an opening at the base of the Rock. Seconds later, they were moving up the mountain through a labyrinth of illuminated tunnels. Other jeeps moved through the tunnels, the American and British uniforms everywhere emphasizing the fact that Arthur's and Cleaver's long months on the run were truly ending. A giant clock affixed to a bone-white limestone wall read 1 p.m.

Inside the Rock of Gibraltar, miles of limestone had been blasted to create a vast underground city, with "huge man-made caverns, barracks, offices, and a fully equipped hospital." About thirty thousand British and American soldiers dwelled within the complex.

The government of Gibraltar's records for "The Great Siege Tunnels" state: "This 'town' inside the Rock contained its own power station [and] water supply . . . Some soldiers posted here would not

see the light of day for months on end . . . engineer companies . . .
with diamond-tipped drills . . . added some 30 miles of such tunnels,
a feat thought impossible at the time."[1]

At the foot of the mountain's northern walls, the engineers had
carved out an aerodrome, where Arthur and Cleaver were to be put on
transport planes bound for London. First, though, an arduous debriefing and interrogation, and a round of paperwork to complete, awaited
both men.

After an examination at the hospital, they were issued uniforms,
shoes, and watches and were fed a hot meal in a massive mess hall—
with cups of the first real coffee either man had tasted in months—
and a clerk showed up to escort Arthur to the Military Liaison Office
of the American consulate. Someone would arrive shortly to take
Cleaver to the RAF debriefing office. The American and the Englishman understood that the time had come for them to part ways
and return to their squadrons. Well aware that they would likely not
see each other again, they stood and shook hands. No words were
necessary.

Later, with emotion simmering beneath understated words, Cleaver
wrote, "I would add that without Taillandier and Meyerowitz in par-
ticular, I would never have reached safety. Of their valor and friendship,
I can hardly begin to render fitting words."[2]

As Arthur followed the clerk to the limestone-walled office of
Colonel Horace W. Forster, the American liaison in Gibraltar, his
thoughts turned to Esther, his parents, and his brother, Seymour. He
checked his new GI watch—it was just after 2:30 p.m. The airman
wanted to know when he could get word to them that he was alive.

Forster, after his initial conversation with Arthur, sent a cablegram
to London. Dated June 16, 1944, the cable informed the "Commanding General, European Theater of Operations, U.S. Army" that "the
enlisted man named below, Staff Sergeant Arthur S. Meyerowitz . . .
448th Bm.Gr. [Bomb Group] having reported to this station . . . will

proceed by first available transportation to LONDON, ENGLAND. Where he will report to the Commanding General."[3]

The colonel allowed Arthur to write a few brief lines for a cable to his family—so long as he revealed nothing about his whereabouts or where he had been since December 31, 1943.

Arthur was handed a detailed questionnaire in which he was required to recount the events aboard and loss of *Harmful Lil Armful*, all of his own actions on the mission, his parachute jump, and everything he could recall about the conduct of every member of the crew.

He battled whether to reveal the loss of nerve and cowardly conduct of the pilot, Second Lieutenant Philip J. Chase. Having discussed Chase's actions with Cleaver, a man who did everything that a pilot was supposed to do and had harshly criticized Chase's conduct as related by the B-24's flight engineer, Arthur wondered whether he should come clean about the skipper of *Harmful Lil Armful*.

Not certain if Chase was even alive but certain that Air Corps brass might not place much credence in the charges of an airman against an officer, Arthur held back. He filled out the questionnaire without criticizing Chase. It was a decision that would haunt him for the rest of his life. It would have been worse years later if he had ever seen Chase's classified account of *Harmful Lil Armful*'s final flight, a retelling that stood in stark, self-serving contrast to everything Arthur knew about that mission.

Required to write an account of his ordeal in France, Arthur related every moment from his painful landing in the trees to the journey to Gibraltar. He listed and described everyone who had helped him, the places he had stayed (96, boulevard Deltour was the only actual address he knew), the escape route he had taken, and the ways in which he had evaded the Nazis and the police.

Arthur was on a transport plane out of Gibraltar the next day, June 17, and landed at Bristol, England, that night. His back blazed with pain that would bedevil him for the rest of his life, and he was still suffering from frostbite. It was too early for him to start processing all that had happened from the inspection of *Harmful Lil Armful* on the airstrip at Seething on December 31, 1943, to the moment he had set foot on Gibraltar.

Letting his guard down still seemed impossible at that moment, if ever. The constant fear of discovery and death was not something a person could shake overnight. He was far from doing that, but for the moment, the realization that he would see Esther and his family again pushed back all the other emotions with which he was grappling. Marcel Taillandier, Gisèle, and all the men and women who had so gladly risked their lives for a stranger from the States would remain a part of him for the rest of his life. Safe now, he felt guilty that his French friends still lived in moment-to-moment danger—in Gisèle's case, if she still lived at all.

Arthur scarcely stepped from the plane at Bristol before he was led to the office of First Lieutenant Charles A. Byron, of the Adjutant General's Office. Byron slid a pen and single-page, typed document with the word *RESTRICTED* emblazoned across the top of the sheet.

As Arthur studied the document, he realized that he would never be able to reveal the true story of how Philip Chase's decision to fly with a bum engine and to jump from the crippled B-24 before his crew had sealed the bomber's fate. He did understand the need to keep secret the names of the French men and women who had aided him. Some of them were likely doing the same for other downed pilots and airmen at that very moment.

When he signed the document, he accepted the fact that the details of his "escape or evasion from capture *could be useful to the enemy* and a danger to your friends. It is therefore *SECRET.*"

His signature proved he grasped and accepted the classified status of his debrief:

You must therefore not disclose . . .

    (1) The names of those who helped you.

    (2) The method by which you escaped or evaded.

    (3) The route you followed.

    (4) Any other facts concerning your experience.[4]

The Western Union cablegram Arthur had sent from Gibraltar the previous day would not reach New York for over a week.

CHAPTER 31

||||||||||||||||||||||||||||||||||||||||||

ROCKAWAY BEACH

On Monday, June 26, 1944, Seymour Meyerowitz walked home to 1205 Findlay Avenue from Robert Morris High School. A sultry sun washed across the Bronx as he neared the yellow-brick apartment house.

Each day that passed without any word from Arthur, Seymour prayed for his brother's safe return. However, he battled doubts that his prayers would be answered. Seymour marveled at their mother Rose's faith that Arthur was alive. She never lost her faith that God would bring him back, and she would not allow anyone else to question it in her presence.

Arthur's girlfriend, Esther Loew, was having perhaps the roughest time as neither a letter from Arthur nor any word from the War Department arrived. The silence ripped at her and wore her down. As she grew more distraught, her family and the Meyerowitz family feared that she was teetering on the verge of an emotional breakdown. It was understandable, Seymour observed. "She was deeply in love with my brother," he would later say.[1]

To try to cheer Esther up, the Loews had rented a bungalow at Rockaway Beach and invited the Meyerowitz family to join them for a few days. Seymour was supposed to meet everyone at the cottage later in the day with his uncle Max, who would drive. Seymour was glad to have an afternoon off from his after-school job assembling expensive fluorescent fixtures at a lamp factory. As he reached the building on Findlay Avenue, ran up the front stairs to the entryway, and stepped inside, all he knew about his older brother's fate was that Arthur was still listed as MIA, missing in action.

Seymour had a task to perform for his mother. Before he left for school that morning, Rose instructed him to check for any telegrams from the War Department that might arrive during the day. Seymour did not expect to find one. Why should today be any different from all the others since the family had last received a communication from the Army? Still, a part of him feared that a message could come at any time, and he wondered how he would react if grim news arrived, how he could tell his mother. What if today *was* the day?

He could not and did not want to imagine life without his older brother. Even though Arthur was missing, no one could yet say he was gone.

One thing Seymour could easily imagine was what would happen if he did not check for the telegram. "No place to hide if I didn't," he recalled.[2]

He climbed the three flights of stairs in the hot, sticky building and walked down the hall to 1205. He pushed his key into the lock, and as the latch clicked and the door swung open, he saw a telegram lying at his feet. A scream exploding from him, Seymour "got kind of hysterical."[3]

From down the hall, Mrs. Baden, a neighbor, rushed from her apartment to see if he was all right. Shaking, terrified of the telegram's contents, sixteen-year-old Seymour stared down at the envelope. "I was afraid," he would remember.[4]

Several neighbors looked out their doors to find Seymour now standing rigid and looking down at the yellow piece of paper. The neighbors immediately understood.

Mrs. Baden bent down, picked up the envelope, and opened it to find a Western Union cablegram. She asked Seymour if he wanted her to read it, and he nodded.

She said, "It's from your brother . . ."

"I was stunned," Seymour would say.[5]

Mrs. Baden read the message, addressed to "Mrs. Dave Meyerowitz," out loud:

```
DEAR FOLKS AND SEYMOUR EVERYTHING OKAY HERE
HOPE TO BE SEEING YOU ALL VERY SOON MY LOVE
TO EVERYONE LOVE ARTIE MEYEROWITZ[6]
```

His head swimming with a torrent of emotions, Seymour tried to focus on what to do next. It was not easy—his elation blurred his ability to reason for a few moments, and his eyes kept filling up. Then he calmed down. His first action was to get word to his mother and father and Esther at the beach, but it would take at least a couple of hours by bus or Uncle Max's car to join up with them. This news could not wait.

"We needed a telephone line," Seymour said.[7] The only person in the building who had one was a neighbor on the first floor, and he raced down the stairs and pounded on her door. When she opened it, he breathlessly explained to her that his brother was alive and he needed to reach his parents immediately but they were on the beach at Rockaway.

Everyone with a serviceman overseas knew how important a moment like this was, and the neighbor dialed the operator, told her that we have "a missing airman telegram," and put Seymour on the line.[8] When he related that his parents were somewhere on the beach, the operator, who must have known her way around Rockaway, suggested calling a candy store close to the beach and see if anyone there might be able to go look for the family and Esther. She called the shop, and when a clerk who was there alone answered, she told the youth that she had an emergency—she needed his help to find the parents and sweetheart of an airman who had just turned up alive after being MIA for six months. Then she put Seymour on the phone.

Without hesitation, the clerk agreed to help. He found a large piece of cardboard, scrawled a message in large letters, locked up the store without even considering lost business, and raced onto the beach with his sign.

There, more than an hour later, a middle-aged couple and a pretty, black-haired young woman rushed through the thick white sand toward him. Tears streamed down their sun-darkened faces. Rose, David, and Esther had spotted the words scribbled on the cardboard sign: *MR. & MRS. MEYEROWITZ—YOUR SON IS ALIVE!*

While the candy clerk was trying to find Rose, David, and Esther, Seymour thanked Mrs. Baden and the downstairs neighbor profusely. Now he needed to get out to Rockaway. He dashed back upstairs to lock the apartment and then ran back down and out the front door of the building. He sprinted several blocks to his uncle Max's building and, his breaths coming in ragged gulps, half staggered to Max's door. When his uncle opened it, the sweating teenager blurted out, "Artie is safe! You need to get me to Rockaway!"[9]

Max grabbed his car keys.

When Seymour and Max pulled up to the Loews' beach bungalow a few hours later, they waded into what Seymour called "a sea of relatives." Everyone was crying, laughing, hugging, and kissing, the news that "Artie" was alive making the night "emotional beyond belief."[10]

On June 29, 1944, another Western Union message arrived at

the door of the Meyerowitz family. The Office of the Adjutant General officially confirmed that Arthur was safe:

```
AM PLEASED TO INFORM YOU YOUR SON STAFF SER-
GEANT ARTHUR S MEYEROWITZ RETURNED TO DUTY
SEVENTEENTH JUNE UNDOUBTEDLY HE WILL COMMU-
NICATE WITH YOU AT AN EARLY DATE CONCERNING
HIS WELFARE AND WHEREABOUTS[11]
```

Rose Meyerowitz had somehow known. She knew her son Arthur and believed that he would be just the one to beat the odds.

Staff Sergeant Arthur S. Meyerowitz had beaten odds that neither Rose, his family, nor Esther could ever fully comprehend and would never know the details of. Seymour would be the only one to learn the full extent of Arthur's ordeal, some seventy years later. Arthur should have been dead several times over, and he understood that. As with most veterans of the Greatest Generation, he grasped that he was one of the fortunate ones. He was coming home—but the war was coming back within him.

In late July 1944, Arthur was sent to a hospital to recover from his injuries. "His back was bad," Seymour said decades later. "He could not do a lot physically."[12]

Typical of the men who returned from World War II, Arthur "never complained or whined about anything."[13]

When he limped out of a New Jersey military hospital in late July 1944 and hailed a cab, he instructed the driver to take him to 1205 Findlay Avenue. It would be the first time he had seen his family since a brief furlough in the early fall of 1943. He had the driver circle the apartment building three times before finally stepping from the cab. He was afraid that his mother was not all right because of her worry about him. The moment he knocked on the door and was swarmed by his parents, his brother, and Esther, his fears evaporated.

Seymour caught a glimpse of just how much his older brother had suffered overseas and just how much he wanted to talk about it, but could not yet do so. He had signed a pledge to secrecy until such time as the Army declassified his debrief and written accounts. Overhearing a late-night conversation between Arthur and his father, Seymour heard Arthur say that he "wished he could get a pistol and kill both pilots."

"Dad," Arthur related, "they were the first two guys out of the plane . . ."[14]

There were also the nightmares. Arthur slept fitfully, the faces of McNamara and Dunham, Gisèle and Pierre, Taillandier, Cleaver, and all the others always with him. Although his cablegram home had assured his family "Everything Okay Here," the memories he brought back with him were never to be fully "okay."

Arthur Meyerowitz had indeed come home, but part of him remained in France—and always would.

EPILOGUE

Awarded the Purple Heart for the severe back injury he suffered on his parachute jump into France, Arthur S. Meyerowitz spent nearly a year in various military hospitals. He longed to rejoin the 715th Bomber Squadron, but the Army Air Corps did not allow men to return to combat if they had been shot down and managed to escape from the enemy. Even without that policy, military doctors would have deemed Arthur's injuries too severe for a return to combat. He was offered administrative jobs if he opted to remain in the Army Air Corps as a career, his superiors recognizing his courage, his initiative, his toughness, and his intelligence. Few airmen or pilots could have fooled the Gestapo, the police, and collaborators in Vichy France into believing that "Georges Lambert" was the deaf mute he claimed to be. Arthur was awarded the Purple Heart and promoted to Technical Sergeant.

Even if he had wanted to remain in the military, he knew he could not put his mother and Esther through such an ordeal again. He was honorably discharged in the fall of 1945, and that same year he married Esther Loew. They raised a family, a daughter, Carole, and a son, Mark.

Letters from Arthur's French friends began to arrive in 1945 after the liberation of the nation and the final defeat of the Nazis. In all likelihood, Arthur learned of the death of Taillandier from Madame Rigal and Mademoiselle Thoulouse. On December 16, 1945, Madame Rigal wrote: "Well, darling, the man who has done so much for you, who was called Marcel Taillandier and was really the commandant *Morhange* has been killed by the German Gestapo. It has been a terrible loss for us. He was killed near Toulouse."

Mademoiselle Thoulouse wrote on March 28, 1945: "Taillandier died, and LEO and GINOUX (Jeno), cleaned [killed] by the Gestapo . . . This is unfortunate and the death of Taillandier did great harm to our entire team, which is now almost completely disorganized."

The news of Taillandier's death undoubtedly had a profound impact on Arthur.

He corresponded with his French friends throughout 1945 and 1946, and the letters that he received, as well as one Madame Rigal sent to Rose Meyerowitz, brimmed with love, respect, and admiration for the airman.

On January 21, 1945, Madame Rigal wrote to Rose from Beaumont-de-Lomagne: "[Arthur] is such a nice young man. I considered him as my son. Poor dear, we were obliged to hide him and I did my best so he could have the most comfort we could offer him. It has been a great trial for him but he was so courageous and a real soldier. I admired him so much you must be so proud."

Charlotte Michel, from Lesparre, wrote on May 5, 1945: "My Dear Arthur, I have just received your letter written on the 27th of March.

"Arthur, do you remember your departure from Bordeaux to

Moissac . . . with all the police around you? It was cold but you were very hot . . . and the crossing of demarcation line . . . ? The control of the identity cards by the police captain? So you remember, Monsieur Georges Lambert? . . . we speak very often of those things . . . we hope to see you again in France one day. All your friends would be happy to see you paying a visit to them."

Charlotte was delighted to hear of Arthur's engagement to Esther, writing on June 3, 1945: "We have heard of your [engagement] with a real pleasure. We wish you to be very happy and all your friends from France are sending you their best wishes. With our wishes I am sending too a little gift for your [fiancée] and yourself. I should have liked to send you a case of old wines, but we are not allowed to do it now. I wonder when all those things are going to go normally again?"

In a July 17, 1945, postcard from teenage Christiane Michel, the deep bond between Arthur and all the friends who helped him escape from France was apparent: "Dear Arthur, Now I must tell you that from all the parachutors [sic] we had at Lesparre you are the only one to send us news. So, please go on in being charming and do write to us, we are waiting for a long letter, soon followed by your arrival in France."

Sadly, Arthur never returned to France. As the demands of his own life and family took center stage and the postwar years passed, the correspondence between New York and France dwindled and eventually stopped. Perhaps the death of Taillandier weighed so heavily on Arthur that the thought of visiting was simply too painful. In January 1945, he had requested that the Army return "the small gun which is a very highly prized possession of mine." It was the pistol that Taillandier had given him in the maquis: "If you [Captain Dorothy Smith, an administrative officer, WAC—Woman's Army Corps] can send it to me it would be very much appreciated and if not would you tell me how I could go about claiming it in the near future?

"As you no doubt remember, it holds very fond memories and I would like to have it when [the war] is all over so that I can look back upon those days when it came in handy."

Captain Smith replied on March 13, 1945: "We can't send a gun through the mail. We don't know how or when it will get to you, but don't worry about it because we fully appreciate your attachment to it."

The Meyerowitz family does not know if Arthur's pistol from Taillandier was ever returned.

Along with the crushing reports of Taillandier's death, Arthur was certainly affected by the disturbing news in the spring of 1945 about Gisèle Chauvin. Arthur's Bordeaux friend and helper Robert J. Ardichen and Charlotte Michel told Arthur that Gisèle had not yet come home to her family. Ardichen wrote, "Mrs. Chauvin of Lesparre has also been deported [sent to a concentration camp] in June 1944."

Charlotte Michel informed Arthur that "Mrs. Chauvin (Dr. Chauvin's wife) was arrested by the Gestapo one year ago and deported in Germany. Nobody heard from [her] since . . ."

Rose Meyerowitz passed away in September 1962, and David almost a year later, in August 1963. They knew how fortunate they were that their son Arthur had defied the longest of odds to come back to them.

Seymour Meyerowitz married, raised a family, and is now retired after a long career as a chiropractor. Of Arthur, he says, "He was my brother, my idol . . ."[1]

In January 1968, Esther died, and Arthur, the dashing airman who had won her heart shortly before he was shipped to England in 1943, followed her in March 1971. Their two children, Mark and Carole, have three and two children respectively. Arthur worked hard to support his family the best he could, fighting to make a good life for them. Always, he remembered how lucky he was to even have that opportunity.

||||||||||||||||||||||

Shortly after the liberation of Toulouse from the Nazis in the fall of 1944, the body of Marcel Taillandier was exhumed from the shallow mass grave where the Gestapo had so ignominiously buried him. His grateful nation would reinter his remains beneath a graceful monument in Toulouse, the city he had loved and fought for so fiercely and so valiantly.

Survived by his wife and two daughters, Taillandier would be posthumously made a Knight of the Legion of Honor and a Companion of the Liberation and was awarded the Croix de Guerre with Palm—France's highest military honor—the Military Medal, the Medal of the Resistance, and the U.S. Medal of Liberty. He is revered today as one of France's greatest World War II heroes and stands as a symbol of the Resistance.

Arthur Meyerowitz revered him not only as a benefactor, but as a friend.

||||||||||||||||||||||

Richard Frank Wharton Cleaver returned to his unit after his escape with Arthur Meyerowitz and went on to cement his reputation as one of the RAF's finest and most courageous pilots of World War II. Having already earned the Distinguished Service Order (DSO) for his "gallantry and devotion to duty" during the invasion of Sicily, in 1943, Cleaver was awarded the Distinguished Flying Cross on October 3, 1944, for staying at the controls of his burning Halifax bomber in April 1944 near Cognac, France. His "skill, courage, and devotion to duty of the highest order" saved all but one of his crew that night. All except one made it back home to Great Britain.[2]

Like Arthur, Cleaver married his sweetheart, Dorothy, in 1946. He remained in the RAF after the war and became one of his nation's first jet test pilots. In 1953, Cleaver was killed in the crash of an experimental and highly unstable jet fighter. The accident was front-page news throughout the United Kingdom. The oldest of his three children was four years old at the time of his death.

⸻

Gisèle Chauvin miraculously returned to Lesparre from the "Road of Death," surviving torture and deprivation at three concentration camps in Germany: Neubrem, Ravensbrück, and Sachsenhausen, where she was liberated by Allied troops in 1945. She came back a virtual scarecrow to Pierre and their children and never fully regained her strength. Her survival testified to her courage and her indomitable will to see her family again and to see France a free nation.

Her son Patrick, an infant at the time when Arthur ended up in the Chauvin home, remembers his mother as a heroine of the Resistance. So, too, does France.

⸻

Except for Sergeant Thomas McNamara and Sergeant William Dunham, the other crewmen of *Harmful Lil Armful* survived the conflict. The pilot, Second Lieutenant Philip J. Chase, was debriefed after his liberation from a German stalag (prison camp). His account of the day that his B-24 went down presents a matter-of-fact portrait of a steady pilot doing everything he could to keep his crippled bomber aloft and everything he could to make sure his entire crew had a chance to parachute from the plane.

Harmful Lil Armful's top-turret gunner and flight engineer knew differently. To his dying day, Arthur S. Meyerowitz never wavered in his certainty that Chase and his copilot had jumped first from the bomber and abandoned their crew. Nightmares of that horrible mission above Occupied France tormented him for the rest of his life. Arthur wished he had told everything he knew in his debrief, and he carried the regret for not doing so to his grave. Some forty years after his death, his grandson Seth Meyerowitz, whom Arthur never had the chance to meet, uncovered the full, long-hidden saga and became Arthur's voice to tell the story.

ACKNOWLEDGMENTS

I would like to dedicate this book, first and foremost, to the people of France who saved Arthur's life in 1944. Arthur may never have made it home without them and for that my whole family (and countless others) owes a huge debt of gratitude to you.

To the Chauvin family who, both in 1944 and over the past few years, have taken the Meyerowitzes in and shown us unparalleled hospitality, love, and respect, we thank you sincerely for all that you have done. Additionally to the memory of Marcel Taillandier and the Morhange/Brutus men and women who risked their lives protecting Arthur—you brought Arthur home and we thank you.

To the countless individuals in France who have helped with research, and hosted me and my family over the past couple years; Guillaume Agullo of the Musée Départemental de la Résistance (Toulouse), Bernard Boyer, the Hautefeuilles, and more, we thank you for your contribution to our project.

To my Spanish family and my *chachis*, without you this entire quest would never have begun. Thank you for hosting me time after time and always making me feel like part of the family.

To my agents, Daniel Bodansky and Anthony Mattero, my writer Peter Stevens, editors Charlie Conrad and Brent Howard, and all the support staff at Dixon Talent, Foundry Literary & Media, Gotham, Penguin, and Berkley who worked their butts off to bring this project to fruition, thank you for your efforts.

To my parents, Mark and Karen, whose support over the years has allowed me to follow my heart wherever it wanted me to go, thank you. Now you have something easy to explain to your friends when they ask, "What does Seth do, exactly?"

Finally, I would like to dedicate this book to my uncle Seymour. Your amazing ability to recall stories of Arthur and therefore keep his story alive all these years is what prompted me to begin my search. I hope this is a fitting tribute to the man you loved so deeply and I am so pleased that I can present this to you in his honor and in his memory.

SOURCES

||||||||||||||||||||||||||||||||||||||||||||||||||

ARCHIVAL

U.S. National Archives

Records of the Army Air Forces (AAF), Record Group 18, 1903–64 (with the bulk of the material from 1917–47).

Record Group (RG) 18.7: Records of Headquarters U.S. ARMY AIR FORCES (AAF) 1917–49.

1940 U.S. Census: Meyerowitz Family.

Service File 32000985, 1941–45, Sergeant Arthur S. Meyerowitz, 137 pages.

Sergeant Arthur S. Meyerowitz, Debrief and Escape and Evasion Report, No. 758, June 17, 1944, marked "Secret," 18 pages.

Letter from Captain Dorothy Smith to Sergeant Arthur S. Meyerowitz, March 13, 1945.

Letter from Sergeant Arthur S. Meyerowitz to Captain Dorothy Smith, January 9, 1945.

Letter from Captain Dorothy Smith to Sergeant Arthur S. Meyerowitz, December 14, 1944.

Special Order 31: Arrival of Sergeant Arthur S. Meyerowitz at Gibraltar. Received by Military Liaison Office, American Consulate, Colonel Horace W. Forster, June 16, 1944.

Appendix (B) to Escape and Evasion Report No. 758, Sergeant Arthur Meyerowitz, January 18, 1944, 3 pages.

Secret American Questionnaire for Service Personnel Evading from Enemy Occupied Countries. Sergeant Arthur S. Meyerowitz, June 18, 1944, 2 pages.

Sergeant Joseph DeFranze, Escape and Evasion Report No. 581, 22 pages.

Second Lieutenant Harold O. Freeman, Escape and Evasion Report No. 553, 32 pages.

Second Lieutenant Hugh C. Shields, Escape and Evasion Report No. 554, April 12, 1944, 47 pages.

Meyerowitz Family Correspondence, 1941–47

Letter from Arthur Meyerowitz to David and Rose Meyerowitz, October 31, 1943.

Western Union Telegram, War Department to David and Rose Meyerowitz, "Missing in Action," January 14, 1944.

War Department Notice, "Still Missing in Action," to David and Rose Meyerowitz, April 21, 1944.

Western Union Cablegram from Sergeant Arthur S. Meyerowitz to David and Rose Meyerowitz, June 17, 1944.

Letter from Mademoiselle Thoulouse (in Toulouse, France) to Rose Meyerowitz, March 28, 1944.

Letter from Madame Rigal (Beaumont-de-Lomagne, France) to Arthur Meyerowitz, December 14, 1945.

Letter from Rigal Family (Beaumont-de-Lomagne) to Rose Meyerowitz, January 21, 1945.

Letter from Robert A. Ardichen (Bordeaux, France) to Arthur Meyerowitz, April 18, 1945.

Letter from Charlotte Michel (Lesparre, France) to Arthur Meyerowitz, May 5, 1945.

Letter from Charlotte Michel (Lesparre) to Arthur Meyerowitz, June 3, 1945.

Four postcards from Christiane Michel (Bayonne, France) to Arthur Meyerowitz, July 17, 1945.

Letter from Christiane Michel (Lesparre, France) to Arthur Meyerowitz, August 27, 1945.

Letters from Arthur Meyerowitz to Michel Family (Lesparre, France), July 19 and August 8, 1945.

Letter from Charlotte Michel (Bordeaux, France) to Arthur Meyerowitz, May 8, 1947.

Military Records Center: National Personnel Records Center, Military Personnel Records, St. Louis, MO 63132

United States Air Force Military Heritage Database, 8th Air Force in WW II: Names, Missions, Crew, Targets, Aircraft, Biographies, and Photos.

UK National Archives and Royal Air Force Service Records, RAF DPA SAR Sections

Officers of the RAF, RFC, RNAS, Second World War (1939–45).
Rolls of Honour.

Entries in the Air Force List for Officers.

Citations for Gallantry Awards.

Operational Record Books (ORBs).

Squadron Combat Reports Aircrews' Flying Log Books.

Details of Those Who Crashed Overseas: RAF Squadron Combat Reports, No. 644 Squadron, LL228 "A" for Able Piloted by Flight Lieutenant Frank Cleaver DSO.

Military Record of Lieutenant R.F.W. Cleaver, Service Number 1457098/124411, Royal Air Force (RAF).

Flight Lieutenant R.F.W. Cleaver, "(Secret) Evaded Capture in France," WO/ 208/3320, including Gibraltar Debrief, June 17, 1944, and Appendices B, C, D, and E (a long-classified and revised entry).

Seething Airfield (UK) Museum and Collection

448th Bomb Group Collection.

Lieutenant William H. Thomas, Debrief and Casualty Report, File No. 3093, Account of Loss of B-24 *Harmful Lil Armful*, 715th Squadron.

Statement (Confidential) of Lieutenant A. L. Northrup Jr., Headquarters 44th Bombardment Group, Testimony of Loss of *Harmful Lil Armful*.

Report of Operations Officer, 448th Bombardment Group, Mission of 24 December 1943, Labroye, France.

Report of Operations Officer, 448th Bombardment Group, Mission of 31 December 1943, Cognac-Chateaubernard and Landes de Bussac, France.

Archives Nationales de France, Paris

Archives of Algiers (File No. 3265-37) list are (AASSDN), "Information Services 1871–1944."

Musée Departemental de la Résistance et de la Deportation, Toulouse, France.

Musée de l'Ordre de la Libération, Paris.

INTERVIEWS

Seymour Meyerowitz, brother of Sergeant Arthur S. Meyerowitz.

Lou McNamara, brother of *Harmful Lil Armful* crewman Sergeant Thomas McNamara.

Patrick Chauvin, Son of Gisèle and Dr. Pierre Chauvin.

Pierre Delude, Resistance fighter and friend of Sergeant Arthur S. Meyerowitz.

Guillaume Agullo, director of the Musée Departemental de la Résistance et de la Deportation, Toulouse, France.

Patricia Everson, Historian of the 448th Bomb Group, Seething, England.

PUBLICATIONS

Ambrose, Stephen E. *The Wild Blue: The Men and Boys Who Flew the B-24s over Germany, 1944–45.* New York: Simon & Schuster, 2001.

Anson, Robert Sam. *McGovern.* New York: Holt, Rinehart & Winston, 1972.

Aubrac, Raymond, and Lucie Aubrac. *The French Resistance: 1940–1944.* Paris: Hazan Editeur, 1997.

Astor, Gerald. *The Mighty Eighth: The Air War in Europe as Told by the Men Who Fought It.* New York: Dell, 1998.

Baynes, Richard C. *Replacement Crew.* Irvine, CA: R. C. Baynes, 1993.

Binot, Jean-Marc, and Bernard Boyer. *Nom de code, BRUTUS: histoire d'un réseau de la France libre.* Paris: Fayard, 2007.

Birdsell, Steve. *The B-24 Liberator.* New York: Arco Publishing, 1970.

———*Log of the Liberators.* Garden City, NY: Doubleday, 1973.

Blue, Allan G. *The Fortunes of War.* California: Aero Publishers, Inc., 1967.

———. *The B-24 Liberator.* New York: Charles Scribner's Sons, 1976.

———. *Consolidated B-24 Liberator.* Crowood Aviation Series, 1998.

———. *Fields of Little America.* Cambridge, UK: PSI, 1977.

Bowman, Martin W. *The B-24 Liberator 1939–1945.* New York: Rand McNally, 1980.

———. *The Bedford Triangle.* Stroud, UK: Sutton Publishing, 1996, PSI, 1988.

Brett, Jeffrey E. *The 448th Bomb Group (H): Liberators over Germany in World War II.* Pennsylvania: Schiffer Military History Book, 2002.

Campbell, John M., and Donna Campbell. *Consolidated B-24 Liberator.* Pennsylvania: Schiffer Publishing Ltd., 1993.

Carigan, William, *Ad Lib: Flying the B-24 Liberator in WWII.* Manhattan, KS: Sunflower University Press, 1988.

Childers, Thomas. *Wings of Morning: The Story of the Last American Bomber Shot Down over Germany in World War II.* Reading, MA: Addison-Wesley, 1995.

Clark, Forrest S. *Innocence and Death in Enemy Skies: A True Story of WWII Adventure and Romance.* Jawbone Publishing Corp., 2004.

Cobb, Matthew. *The Resistance: The French Fight Against the Nazis.* UK: Simon & Schuster, 2013.

Copp, DeWitt S. *Forged in Fire: Strategy and Decisions in the Airway over Europe, 1940–1945.* New York: Doubleday, 1982.

Craven, Wesley Frank, and James Lea Cate, eds. *The Army Air Forces in World War II*, Vol. 2, Europe: *Torch to Pointblank*, August 1942 to December 1943. Chicago: University of Chicago Press, 1949.

———. *The Army Air Forces in World War II*, Vol. 3, *Europe: Argument to V-E Day*, January 1944 to May 1945. Chicago: University of Chicago Press, 1951.

———. *The Army Air Forces in World War II*, Vol. 6, *Men and Planes*, Chicago: University of Chicago Press, 1955.

Currier, Donald R. *50 Mission Crush.* Shippensburg, PA: Burd Street Press, 1992.

Davis, Larry. *B-24 Liberator in Action.* Carrollton, TX: Signal Publications, 1987.

Dorr, Robert F. *B-24 Liberator Units of the 8th Air Force.* Oxford, UK: Osprey, 2001.

Eisner, Peter. *The Freedom Line: The Brave Men and Women Who Rescued Allied Airmen from the Nazis During World War II.* New York: Harper Perennial Reprint, 2005.

Fittko, Lisa. *Through the Pyrenees (Jewish Lives Series).* Evanston, IL: Northwestern University Press, 2000.

Francis, Devon. *Flak Bait.* Washington, D.C.: Zenger Publishing, 1948.

Freeman, Roger. *B-24 Liberator at War.* Osceola, WI: Motorbooks, 1983.

———. *The B-24 Liberator.* Leatherhead, UK: Profile Publications, 1965.

Goodall, Scott. *The Freedom Trail: Following One of the Hardest Wartime Escape Routes across the Central Pyrenees into Northern Spain.* UK: Inchmere Design, 2005.

Goubet, Michel, and Paul Debauges. *L'Histoire de le résistance en Haute Garonne.* Milan: Éditions Milan, 1986.

Hastings, Max. *Bomber Command: The Myths and Realities of the Strategic Bombing Offensive, 1939–45.* New York: Dial Press, 1979.

"History of 501 Squadron: War Record of GW Shire's Own Flight Lieutenant: R.F.W. Cleaver." *Western Daily Press*, Bristol, UK, May 6, 1947, p. 3.

Hughes, Walter F. *A Bomber Pilot in WWI: From Farm Boy to Pilot, 35 Missions in the B-24.* Freemont, CA: privately printed, 1994.

Jablonski, Edward. *Airwar.* New York: Doubleday, 1971.

La Prison Saint-Michel. Musée Departemental de la Résistance et de la Deportation. Toulouse, France, 2012.

Mahoney, James J., and Brian H. Mahoney. *Reluctant Witness: Memoirs from the Last Year of the European Air War 1944–1945.* Trafford, 2001.

McDowell, Ernest R. *Consolidated B-24D-M Liberator.* New York: Arco Publishing, 1969.

McGovern, George. *Grassroots: The Autobiography of George McGovern.* New York: Random House, 1977.

Merritt, J. I. *Goodbye, Liberty Belle: A Son's Search for His Father's War.* Dayton, OH: Wright State University Press, 1993.

Miller, Donald L. *Masters of the Air: America's Bomber Boys Who Fought the Air War Against Nazi Germany.* New York: Simon & Schuster, 2007.

Moyes, Phillip J. R. *Consolidated B-24 Liberator Early Models.* Oxford, UK: Visual Art Press, 1979.

Ottis, Sherri Greene. *Silent Heroes: Downed Airmen and the French Underground.* University Press of Kentucky, 2001.

Paillole, Colonel Paul. *Services spéciaux (1935–1945).* Paris: R. Laffont, 1975.

Picardo, Eddie. *Tales of a Tail Gunner.* Seattle: Hara Publishing, 1997.

Rémy, Colonel (pseudonym of Gilbert Renault-Roulier). *Morhange: les chasseurs de traîtres.* Paris: Éditions Flammarion, 1975.

Rowe, John C. *A Replacement Crew in the ETO (European Theatre of Operations), World War II, 448th Bomb Group, 20th Combat Wing, 2nd Air Division, 8th Air Force.* Self-published, 1999.

Saint-Laurens, Pierre. *Conte de faits, X15, Réseau Morhange.* Toulouse: Éditions Signes du Monde, 1995.

Schoenbrun, David. *Soldiers of the Night.* New York: E. P. Dutton, 1980.

Smith, Ed. *Ball Turret Gunner, B-24 Liberator in Action.* Carrollton, TX: Self-published, 1987.

Stourton, Edward. *Cruel Crossing: Escaping Hitler Across the Pyrenees.* UK: Doubleday, 2013.

Stout, Lieutenant Colonel (Ret.) Jay A. *Men Who Killed the Luftwaffe: The U.S. Army Air Forces Against Germany in World War II.* Mechanicsburg, PA: Stackpole, 2010.

———. *Unsung Eagles: True Stories of America's Citizen Airmen in the Skies of World War.* Havertown, PA: Casemate Publishing, 2013.

Ten Haken, Mel. *Bail-Out! POW, 1944–1945.* Manhattan, KS: Sunflower University Press, 1990.

Tracas, Famine, Patroille. Musée Departemental de la Résistance et de la Deportation. Toulouse, France, 2012.

Ulanoff, Stanley M., ed. *Bombs Away!* New York: Doubleday, 1971.

Vinen, Richard. *The Unfree French: Life Under the Occupation.* New Haven, CT: Yale University Press, 2007.

Watry, Charles A. *Washout! The American Cadet Story*. Carlsbad, CA: California Arco Press, 1983.

Whitehouse, Arch. *The Years of the Warbirds*. New York: Doubleday, 1960.

Westheimer, David. *Rider on the Wind*. UK: Sphere, 1979; New York: Walker, 1984.

Wolf, Leon. *Low Level Mission*. New York: Berkley Publishing Corp., 1957.

Yedlin, Benedict. "In My Sperry Ball I Sit." *Briefing Journal of the International B-24 Liberator*, Spring 1999.

NOTES

━━━━━━━━━━━━━━━━━━━━━━━━━━━━━━

PROLOGUE

The chief source for the prologue is the author's and writer's interviews with Seymour Meyerowitz.

CHAPTER 1

The chief sources for Chapter 1: U.S. National Archives, Service File No. 32000985, 1941–1945, Sergeant Arthur S. Meyerowitz; Sergeant Joseph Defranze, Escape and Evasion Report No. 581; Seething Collections: Lieutenant William H. Thomas: Debrief and Casualty Report, File No. 3093; Account of Loss of B-24 *Harmful Lil Armful*, 715th Squadron. Statement (Confidential) of Lieutenant A. L. Northrup Jr., Headquarters 44th Bombardment Group. Testimony of Loss of *Harmful Lil Armful*. Report of Operations Officer, 448th Bombardment Group: Mission of 31 December 1943. Cognac-Chateaubernard and Landes de Bussac, France.

1. The quotations on page 4 are drawn from the U.S. National Archives, Service File No. 32000985, 1941–1945, Sergeant Arthur S. Meyerowitz; Seething Airfield (UK) Museum, 448th Bomb Group Collection; interviews of Seymour Meyerowitz.

2. U.S. National Archives, Service File No. 32000985, 1941–1945, Sergeant Arthur S. Meyerowitz; interview with Seymour Meyerowitz.

3. Interview with Seymour Meyerowitz.

4. U.S. National Archives, Service File No. 32000985, 1941–1945, Sergeant Arthur S. Meyerowitz.

5. Ibid.

6. Seymour Meyerowitz, as told to him by Sergeant Arthur S. Meyerowitz.

7. Ibid.

8. U.S. National Archives, Service File No. 32000985, 1941–1945, Sergeant Arthur S. Meyerowitz.

9. Ibid.

10. Ibid.

11. Letter from Arthur Meyerowitz to David and Rose Meyerowitz, October 31, 1943.

12. Seething Airfield (UK) Museum, 448th Bomb Group Collection.

13. "Lieutenant William Blum's Story," Seething Airfield (UK) Museum, 448th Bomb Group Collection.

14. Ibid.

15. Ibid.

16. Ibid.

17. Martin W. Bowman, *B-24 Combat Missions: First-Hand Accounts of Liberator Operations over Nazi Europe*, New York: Metro Books, 2009, p. 20.

18. Seymour Meyerowitz, as told to him by Sergeant Arthur S. Meyerowitz.

19. "Lieutenant William Blum's Story," Seething Airfield (UK) Museum, 448th Bomb Group Collection.

20. Martin W. Bowman, *B-24 Combat Missions: First-Hand Accounts of Liberator Operations Over Nazi Europe*. New York: Metro Books, 2009, p. 85 (account of Lt. William Carigan).

21. With the exception of Lt. Carigan's account (note 20), all quotations on pages 23–25 are drawn from U.S. National Archives, Service File No. 32000985, 1941–45, Sergeant Arthur S. Meyerowitz, interview with Seymour Meyerowitz.

CHAPTER 2

The chief sources for Chapter 2: U.S. National Archives, Service File No. 32000985, 1941–1945, Sergeant Arthur S. Meyerowitz; Sergeant Joseph Defranze, Escape and Evasion Report No. 581; Seething Collections: Lieutenant William H. Thomas: Debrief and Casualty Report, File No. 3093; Account of Loss of B-24 *Harmful Lil Armful*, 715th Squadron. Statement (Confidential) of Lieutenant A. L. Northrup Jr., Headquarters 44th Bombardment Group. Testimony of Loss of *Harmful Lil Armful*. Report of Operations Officer, 448th Bombardment Group: Mission of 31 December 1943. Cognac-Chateaubernard and Landes de Bussac, France.

1. The command or prompt always given by the pilot to or for the copilot as the plane took off.

2. The warning always used by the pilot or copilot to let the crew know they had crossed into hostile airspace.

3. All quotations from pp. 31–38 are drawn from U.S. National Archives, Service File No. 32000985, 1941–1945, Sergeant Arthur S. Meyerowitz; Sergeant Joseph Defranze, Escape and Evasion Report No. 581; Seething Collections: Lieutenant William H. Thomas: Debrief and Casualty Report, File No. 3093; Account of Loss of B-24 *Harmful Lil Armful*, 715th Squadron. Statement (Confidential) of Lieutenant A. L. Northrup Jr., Headquarters 44th Bombardment Group. Testimony of Loss of *Harmful Lil Armful*. Report of Operations Officer, 448th Bombardment Group: Mission of 31 December 1943. Cognac-Chateaubernard and Landes de Bussac, France.

CHAPTER 3

The chief sources for Chapter 3: Sergeant Arthur S. Meyerowitz, Debrief and Escape and Evasion Report No. 758, June 17, 1944, marked "Secret," 18 pages; Appendix (B) to Escape and Evasion Report No. 758, Sergeant Arthur Meyerowitz, June 18, 1944, 3 pages; Service File No. 32000985, 1941–1945, Sergeant Arthur S. Meyerowitz, 137 pages; interviews with Seymour Meyerowitz.

1. Sergeant Arthur S. Meyerowitz, Debrief and Escape and Evasion Report No. 758, June 17, 1944.

CHAPTER 4

The chief sources for Chapter 4: Record Group 498: Records of Headquarters, European Theater of Operations, U.S. Army (World War II), 1942–1947. POW Files: Lieutenant Philip J. Chase, Serial No. 745621, June 14, 1945; Lieutenant William H. Thomas, Serial No. 751190, June 8, 1945; Flight Officer Edward E. George, Serial No. 001527, July 4, 1945; Lieutenant Harry K. Farrell, Jr., Serial No. 688013, June 14, 1945; and Sergeant Howard R. Peck, Serial No. 39272980, June 12, 1945. Sergeant Joseph Defranze, Escape and Evasion Report No. 581, 22 pages. Lieutenant William H. Thomas: Debrief and Casualty Report, File No. 3093; Account of Loss of B-24 *Harmful Lil Armful*, 715th Squadron.

1. All quotations on page 45 are from the above-cited sources and from interview with Seymour Meyerowitz.

CHAPTER 5

The chief sources for Chapter 5: Sergeant Arthur S. Meyerowitz, Debrief and Escape and Evasion Report No. 758, June 17, 1944, marked "Secret," 18 pages; Appendix (B) to Escape and Evasion Report No. 758, Sergeant Arthur Meyerowitz, June 18, 1944, 3 pages; Service File No. 32000985, 1941–1945, Sergeant Arthur S. Meyerowitz, 137 pages; interviews with Seymour Meyerowitz.

1. All quotations on pages 48–51 are drawn from the above-cited sources.

CHAPTER 6

The chief sources for Chapter 6: Sergeant Arthur S. Meyerowitz, Debrief and Escape and Evasion Report No. 758, June 17, 1944, marked "Secret," 18 pages; Appendix (B) to Escape and Evasion Report No. 758, Sergeant Arthur Meyerowitz, June 18, 1944, 3 pages; Service File No. 32000985, 1941–1945, Sergeant Arthur S. Meyerowitz, 137 pages; interviews with Seymour Meyerowitz.

1. All quotations on pages 53 to the first quotation on page 57 are drawn from the above-cited sources.
2. Western Union Telegram, War Department to David and Rose Meyerowitz, "Missing in Action," January 14, 1944.
3. Interview with Seymour Meyerowitz.

CHAPTER 7

The chief sources for Chapter 7: "Marcel Taillandier," L'Association des Amis du Musée, Paris, p. 1; Colonel Paul Paillole, *Services spéciaux (1935–1945)*, Paris: R. Laffont, 1975; Colonel Rémy (pseudonym of Gilbert Renault-Roulier), *Morhange: les chasseurs de traîtres*, Paris: Éditions Flammarion, 1975; and Pierre Saint-Laurens, *Conte de faits, X15, Réseau Morhange*, Toulouse: Éditions Signes du Monde, 1995.

1. "Marcel Taillandier," L'Association des Amis du Musée, Paris, p. 1.
2. Karl-Heine Frieser, *Blitzkrieg-Legende*, Munich: R. Oldenbourg, 1995, p. 71.
3. Colonel Paul Paillole, *Services spéciaux (1935–1945)*, Paris: R. Laffont, 1975, p. 157.
4. Ibid.
5. Ibid, p. xviii.
6. Ibid, p. xviii.
7. Pierre Saint-Laurens, *Conte de faits, X15, Réseau Morhange*, Toulouse: Éditions Signes du Monde, 1995, p. 64.
8. Ibid.

CHAPTER 8

The chief sources for Chapter 8: "Marcel Taillandier," L'Association des Amis du Musée, Paris, p. 1; Colonel Paul Paillole, *Services spéciaux (1935–1945)*, Paris: R. Laffont, 1975; Colonel Rémy (pseudonym of Gilbert Renault-Roulier), *Morhange: les chasseurs de traîtres*, Paris: Éditions Flammarion, 1975; and Pierre Saint-Laurens, *Conte de faits, X15, Réseau Morhange*, Toulouse: Éditions Signes du Monde, 1995.

1. Pierre Saint-Laurens, *Conte de faits, X15, Reseau Morhange*, Toulouse: Editions Signe du Monde, 1995, p. 64.
2. Colonel Paul Paillole, *Services spéciaux (1935–1945)*, Paris: R. Laffont, 1975, pp. 288–289.
3. Saint-Laurens, p. 64.
4. Ibid.
5. Ibid.
6. Ibid.
7. Paillole, pp. 417–418.
8. Ibid.
9. Ibid.
10. Ibid, pp. 420–422.
11. Ibid, p. 422.
12. Ibid, pp. 420–422.
13. Ibid, p. 422.

CHAPTER 9

The chief sources for Chapter 9: Jean-Marc Binot and Bernard Boyer, *Nom de code, BRUTUS: histoire d'un réseau de la France libre*, Paris: Fayard, 2007; Sergeant Arthur S. Meyerowitz, Debrief and Escape and Evasion Report No. 758, June 17, 1944, marked "Secret," 18 pages; Appendix (B) to Escape and Evasion Report No. 758, Sergeant Arthur Meyerowitz, January 18, 1944, 3 pages; Service File No. 32000985, 1941–1945, Sergeant Arthur S. Meyerowitz, 137 pages; interviews with Seymour Meyerowitz; interviews with Patrick Chauvin, son of Gisèle and Dr. Pierre Chauvin; and interview with Pierre Delude, Resistance fighter and friend of Sergeant Arthur S. Meyerowitz.

1. Jean-Marc Binot and Bernard Boyer, *Nom de code, BRUTUS: histoire d'un réseau de la France libre*, Paris: Fayard, 2007; http://brutus.boyer.free.fr/; Dr. Pierre Auriac (officier de la Légion d'Honneur, Croix de Guerre, 1939–1945), *Le réseau BRUTUS à Bordeaux: 1943–1944*.

2. All quotations on pages 95–100 are drawn from Sergeant Arthur S. Mey-
    erowitz, Debrief and Escape and Evasion Report No. 758, June 17, 1944,
    marked "Secret," 18 pages; Appendix (B) to Escape and Evasion Report No.
    758, Sergeant Arthur Meyerowitz, January 18, 1944, 3 pages; Service File
    No. 32000985, 1941–1945, Sergeant Arthur S. Meyerowitz, 137 pages;
    interviews with Seymour Meyerowitz; interviews with Patrick Chauvin,
    son of Gisèle and Dr. Pierre Chauvin; interview with Pierre Delude, Resis-
    tance fighter and friend of Sergeant Arthur S. Meyerowitz.

CHAPTER 10

The chief sources for Chapter 10: Sergeant Arthur S. Meyerowitz, Debrief and
Escape and Evasion Report No. 758, June 17, 1944, marked "Secret," 18 pages;
Appendix (B) to Escape and Evasion Report No. 758, Sergeant Arthur Meyerowitz, January 18, 1944, 3 pages; Service File No. 32000985, 1941–1945, Sergeant
Arthur S. Meyerowitz, 137 pages; interviews with Seymour Meyerowitz; interviews with Patrick Chauvin, son of Gisèle and Dr. Pierre Chauvin; interview
with Pierre Delude, Resistance fighter and friend of Sergeant Arthur S. Meyerowitz.

1. The quotations on pages 102–106 are drawn from the above-cited chief
    sources.

CHAPTER 11

The chief sources for Chapter 11: Sergeant Arthur S. Meyerowitz, Debrief and
Escape and Evasion Report No. 758, June 17, 1944, marked "Secret," 18 pages;
Appendix (B) to Escape and Evasion Report No. 758, Sergeant Arthur Meyerowitz, January 18, 1944, 3 pages; Service File No. 32000985, 1941–1945, Sergeant
Arthur S. Meyerowitz, 137 pages; interviews with Seymour Meyerowitz; interviews with Patrick Chauvin, son of Gisèle and Dr. Pierre Chauvin; interview
with Pierre Delude, Resistance fighter and friend of Sergeant Arthur S. Meyerowitz.

    Letter from Robert A. Ardichen (Bordeaux, France) to Arthur Meyerowitz,
April 18, 1945; letter from Charlotte Michel (Lesparre, France) to Arthur Meyerowitz, May 5, 1945; letter from Charlotte Michel (Lesparre) to Arthur Meyerowitz, June 3, 1945; four postcards from Christiane Michel (Bayonne, France)
to Arthur Meyerowitz, July 17, 1945; letter from Christiane Michel (Lesparre) to
Arthur Meyerowitz, August 27, 1945; letters from Arthur Meyerowitz to

Michel family (Lesparre) July 19 and August 8, 1945; letter from Charlotte Michel to Arthur Meyerowitz, May 8, 1947 (Bordeaux).

1. The quotations on pages 108–120 are drawn from the above-cited chief sources.

CHAPTER 12

The chief sources for Chapter 12: Sergeant Arthur S. Meyerowitz, Debrief and Escape and Evasion Report No. 758, June 17, 1944, marked "Secret," 18 pages; Appendix (B) to Escape and Evasion Report No. 758, Sergeant Arthur Meyerowitz, June 18, 1944, 3 pages; Service File No. 32000985, 1941–1945, Sergeant Arthur S. Meyerowitz, 137 pages; interviews with Seymour Meyerowitz; letter from Charlotte Michel (Lesparre, France) to Arthur Meyerowitz, May 5, 1945; and letter from Madame Rigal (Beaumont-de-Lomagne, France) to Arthur Meyerowitz, December 14, 1945.

1. All quotations on page 123 are drawn from the above-cited chief sources.
2. Letter from Charlotte Michel (Lesparre, France) to Arthur Meyerowitz, May 5, 1945.
3. Letter from Madame Rigal (Beaumont-de-Lomagne, France) to Arthur Meycrowitz, December 14, 1945.

CHAPTER 13

The chief sources for Chapter 13: Sergeant Arthur S. Meyerowitz, Debrief and Escape and Evasion Report No. 758, June 17, 1944, marked "Secret," 18 pages; Appendix (B) to Escape and Evasion Report No. 758, Sergeant Arthur Meyerowitz, January 18, 1944, 3 pages; Service File No. 32000985, 1941–1945, Sergeant Arthur S. Meyerowitz, 137 pages; interviews with Seymour Meyerowitz; and letter from Madame Rigal (Beaumont-de-Lomagne, France) to Arthur Meyerowitz, January 21, 1945.

Jean-Marc Binot and Bernard Boyer, *Nom de code, BRUTUS: histoire d'un réseau de la France libre*, Paris: Fayard, 2007; "Marcel Taillandier," L'Association des Amis du Musée; Colonel Paul Paillole, *Services spéciaux (1935–1945)*, Paris: R. Laffont, 1975; Colonel Rémy (pseudonym of Gilbert Renault-Roulier), *Morhange: les chasseurs de traîtres*, Paris: Éditions Flammarion, 1975; and Pierre Saint-Laurens, *Conte de faits, X15, Réseau Morhange*, Toulouse: Éditions Signes du Monde, 1995.

1. Letter from Madame Rigal (Beaumont-de-Lomagne) to Rose Meyerowitz, January 21, 1945.

2. Joseph Robert White, *Humanities and Social Sciences Review* of *Confronting Captivity: Britain and the United States and Their POWs in Nazi Germany* (Chapel Hill: University of North Carolina Press, 2005), quoting Arieh J. Kochavi, p. 211.

3. Ibid.

4. Letter from Madame Rigal (Beaumont-de-Lomagne, France) to Rose Meyerowitz, January 21, 1945.

5. Ibid.

6. Sergeant Arthur S. Meyerowitz, Debrief and Escape and Evasion Report.

7. Colonel Paul Paillole, *Services spéciaux (1935–1945)*, p. 417.

8. Letter from Madame Rigal (Beaumont-de-Lomagne) to Rose Meyerowitz, January 21, 1945.

9. Paillole, p. 417.

10. Ibid.

11. Ibid.

CHAPTER 14

The chief sources for Chapter 14: Sergeant Arthur S. Meyerowitz, Debrief and Escape and Evasion Report No. 758, June 17, 1944, marked "Secret," 18 pages; Appendix (B) to Escape and Evasion Report No. 758, Sergeant Arthur Meyerowitz, January 18, 1944, 3 pages; Service File No. 32000985, 1941–1945, Sergeant Arthur S. Meyerowitz, 137 pages; interviews with Seymour Meyerowitz; interviews with Guillaume Agullo, director of the Musée Departemental de la Résistance et de la Deportation, Toulouse, France; and letter from Mademoiselle Thoulouse (in Toulouse, France) to Rose Meyerowitz, March 28, 1944.

Jean-Marc Binot and Bernard Boyer, *Nom de code, BRUTUS: histoire d'un réseau de la France libre*, Paris: Fayard, 2007; "Marcel Taillandier," L'Association des Amis du Musée; Colonel Paul Paillole, *Services spéciaux (1935–1945)*, Paris: R. Laffont, 1975; Colonel Rémy (pseudonym of Gilbert Renault-Roulier), *Morhange: les chasseurs de traîtres*, Paris: Éditions Flammarion, 1975; and Pierre Saint-Laurens, *Conte de faits, X15, Réseau Morhange*, Toulouse: Éditions Signes du Monde, 1995.

1. The quotations on page 141 are drawn from the above-cited chief sources.

2. Jean-Marc Binot and Bernard Boyer, *Nom de code: BRUTUS: Histoire d'un réseau de la France libre* (documents) (French Edition, 2007) (Kindle Locations 4306–4307), Fayard. Kindle Edition.

3. Ibid.

CHAPTER 15

The chief sources for Chapter 15: interviews with Patrick Chauvin, son of Gisèle and Dr. Pierre Chauvin; Sylvaine Dubost, "Le jour de l'arrestation de Gisèle Lacombe-Chauvin," *Sud Ouest* (daily newspaper), digital edition, July 5, 2011; Jean-Marc Binot and Bernard Boyer, *Nom de code, BRUTUS: histoire d'un réseau de la France libre*, Paris: Fayard, 2007.

1. All quotations on pages 147–148 are drawn from Sylvaine Dubost, "Le jour de l'arrestation de Gisèle Lacombe-Chauvin," *Sud Ouest* (daily newspaper), digital edition, July 5, 2011; interviews with Patrick Chauvin, son of Gisèle and Dr. Pierre Chauvin.

CHAPTER 16

The chief sources for Chapter 16: Sergeant Arthur S. Meyerowitz, Debrief and Escape and Evasion Report No. 758, June 17, 1944, marked "Secret," 18 pages; Appendix (B) to Escape and Evasion Report No. 758, Sergeant Arthur Meyerowitz, June 18, 1944, 3 pages; Service File No. 32000985, 1941–1945, Sergeant Arthur S. Meyerowitz, 137 pages; interviews with Seymour Meyerowitz; interviews with Guillaume Agullo, director of the Musée Departemental de la Résistance et de la Deportation, Toulouse, France; and letter from Mademoiselle Thoulouse (in Toulouse, France) to Rose Meyerowitz, March 28, 1944.

"Marcel Taillandier," L'Association des Amis du Musée; Colonel Paul Paillole, *Services spéciaux (1935–1945)*, Paris: R. Laffont, 1975; Colonel Rémy (pseudonym of Gilbert Renault-Roulier), *Morhange: les chasseurs de traîtres*, Paris: Éditions Flammarion, 1975; and Pierre Saint-Laurens, *Conte de faits, X15, Réseau Morhange*, Toulouse: Éditions Signes du Monde, 1995.

1. Sergeant Arthur S. Meyerowitz, Debrief and Escape and Evasion Report No. 758, June 17, 1944, marked "Secret," 18 pages; Appendix (B) to Escape and Evasion Report No. 758, Sergeant Arthur Meyerowitz, June 18, 1944, 3 pages.
2. Ibid.
3. All quotes from pages 157–162 are drawn from the above-cited chief sources.

CHAPTER 17

The chief sources for Chapter 17: Sergeant Arthur S. Meyerowitz, Debrief and Escape and Evasion Report No. 758, June 17, 1944, marked "Secret," 18 pages; Appendix (B) to Escape and Evasion Report No. 758, Sergeant Arthur Meyerowitz, January 18, 1944, 3 pages; Service File No. 32000985, 1941–1945, Sergeant Arthur

S. Meyerowitz, 137 pages; interviews with Seymour Meyerowitz; interviews with Patrick Chauvin, son of Gisèle and Dr. Pierre Chauvin; letter from Robert A. Ardichen (Bordeaux, France) to Arthur Meyerowitz, April 18, 1945; and letter from Charlotte Michel (Lesparre, France) to Arthur Meyerowitz, May 5, 1945.

Jean-Marc Binot and Bernard Boyer, *Nom de code, BRUTUS: histoire d'un réseau de la France libre*, Paris: Fayard, 2007; Sylvaine Dubost, "Le jour de l'arrestation de Gisèle Lacombe-Chauvin," *Sud Ouest* (daily newspaper), digital edition, July 5, 2011; "Marcel Taillandier," L'Association des Amis du Musée; Colonel Paul Paillole, *Services spéciaux (1935–1945)*, Paris: R. Laffont, 1975; Colonel Rémy (pseudonym of Gilbert Renault-Roulier), *Morhange: les chasseurs de traîtres*, Paris: Éditions Flammarion, 1975; and Pierre Saint-Laurens, *Conte de faits*, *X15*, *Réseau Morhange*, Toulouse: Éditions Signes du Monde, 1995.

1. *Une journée au fort du Hâ* (Bordeaux), World War, 1939–1945 Jewish Underground Resistance Collection, McMaster University.
2. Ibid.
3. Ibid.

CHAPTER 18

The chief sources for Chapter 18: Sergeant Arthur S. Meyerowitz, Debrief and Escape and Evasion Report No. 758, June 17, 1944, marked "Secret," 18 pages; Appendix (B) to Escape and Evasion Report No. 758, Sergeant Arthur Meyerowitz, January 18, 1944, 3 pages; Service File No. 32000985, 1941–1945, Sergeant Arthur S. Meyerowitz, 137 pages; interviews of Guillaume Agullo, director of the Musée Departemental de la Résistance et de la Deportation, Toulouse, France; interviews with Patrick Chauvin, son of Gisèle and Dr. Pierre Chauvin; and interviews with Pierre Delude, Resistance fighter and friend of Sergeant Arthur Meyerowitz.

Jean-Marc Binot and Bernard Boyer, *Nom de code, BRUTUS: histoire d'un réseau de la France libre*, Paris: Fayard, 2007; Sylvaine Dubost, "Le jour de l'arrestation de Gisèle Lacombe-Chauvin," *Sud Ouest* (daily newspaper), digital edition, July 5, 2011; "Marcel Taillandier," L'Association des Amis du Musée; Colonel Paul Paillole, *Services spéciaux (1935–1945)*, Paris: R. Laffont, 1975; Colonel Rémy (pseudonym of Gilbert Renault-Roulier), *Morhange: les chasseurs de traîtres*, Paris: Éditions Flammarion, 1975; and Pierre Saint-Laurens, *Conte de faits*, *X15*, *Réseau Morhange*, Toulouse: Éditions Signes du Monde, 1995.

1. H. R. Kedward, Refusal and Revolt: Spring 1943, *In Search of the Maquis: Rural Resistance in Southern France*, New York: Oxford University Press, 1993, p. 29.

2. War Department Notice, "Still Missing in Action," to David and Rose Meyerowitz, April 21, 1944.

3. Letter from Max B. Goldman to War Department, April 3, 1944.

CHAPTER 19

The chief sources for Chapter 19: Sergeant Arthur S. Meyerowitz, Debrief and Escape and Evasion Report No. 758, June 17, 1944, marked "Secret," 18 pages; Appendix (B) to Escape and Evasion Report No. 758, Sergeant Arthur Meyerowitz, January 18, 1944, 3 pages; and Service File No. 32000985, 1941–1945, Sergeant Arthur S. Meyerowitz, 137 pages.

"Marcel Taillandier," L'Association des Amis du Musée; Colonel Paul Paillole, *Services spéciaux (1935–1945)*, Paris: R. Laffont, 1975; Colonel Rémy (pseudonym of Gilbert Renault-Roulier), *Morhange: les chasseurs de traîtres*, Paris: Éditions Flammarion, 1975; and Pierre Saint-Laurens, *Conte de faits*, X15, *Réseau Morhange*, Toulouse: Éditions Signes du Monde, 1995.

UK National Archives and Royal Air Force Service Records, RAF DPA SAR Sections, Officers of the RAF, RFC, RNAS, Second World War (1939–1945): Details of Those Who Crashed Overseas: RAF Squadron Combat Reports No. 644 Squadron: LL228 "A" for Able Piloted by Flight Lieutenant Frank Cleaver DSO; Military Record of Lieutenant R.F.W. Cleaver, Service No. 1457098/124411, Royal Air Force (RAF); Flight Lieutenant R.F.W. Cleaver, "(Secret) Evaded Capture in France," WO/208/3320, including Gibraltar Debrief, June 17, 1944, and Appendices B, C, and D.

1. Sergeant Arthur S. Meyerowitz, Debrief and Escape Evasion Report.

2. "Notice of Distinguished Service Order (DSO), Flight Lieutenant R.F.W. Cleaver," *London Gazette*, October 29, 1943, p. 1.

3. UK National Archives and Royal Air Force Service Records, RAF DPA SAR Sections, Officers of the RAF, RFC, RNAS, Second World War (1939–1945): Details of Those Who Crashed Overseas: RAF Squadron Combat Reports No. 644 Squadron: LL228 "A" for Able Piloted by Flight Lieutenant Frank Cleaver DSO.

4. Ibid.

CHAPTER 20

The chief sources for Chapter 20: Sergeant Arthur S. Meyerowitz, Debrief and Escape and Evasion Report No. 758, June 17, 1944, marked "Secret," 18 pages;

Appendix (B) to Escape and Evasion Report No. 758, Sergeant Arthur Meyerowitz, January 18, 1944, 3 pages; and Service File No. 32000985, 1941–1945, Sergeant Arthur S. Meyerowitz, 137 pages.

"Marcel Taillandier," L'Association des Amis du Musée; Colonel Paul Paillole, *Services spéciaux (1935–1945)*, Paris: R. Laffont, 1975; Colonel Rémy (pseudonym of Gilbert Renault-Roulier), *Morhange: les chasseurs de traîtres*, Paris: Éditions Flammarion, 1975; and Pierre Saint-Laurens, *Conte de faits, X15, Réseau Morhange*, Toulouse: Éditions Signes du Monde, 1995.

UK National Archives and Royal Air Force Service Records, RAF DPA SAR Sections, Officers of the RAF, RFC, RNAS, Second World War (1939–1945): Details of Those Who Crashed Overseas: RAF Squadron Combat Reports, No. 644 Squadron: LL228 "A" for Able Piloted by Flight Lieutenant Frank Cleaver DSO; Military Record of Lieutenant R.F.W. Cleaver, Service No. 1457098/124411, Royal Air Force (RAF); Flight Lieutenant R.F.W. Cleaver, "(Secret) Evaded Capture in France," WO/208/3320, including Gibraltar Debrief, June 17, 1944, and Appendices B, C, and D.

1. Michael Grant, "Resistance Groups in Toulouse," *1st Humanities*, Toulouse, 2002, p. 1.

2. UK National Archives and Royal Air Force Service Records, RAF DPA SAR Sections, Officers of the RAF, RFC, RNAS, Second World War (1939–1945): Details of Those Who Crashed Overseas: RAF Squadron Combat Reports No. 644 Squadron: LL228 "A" for Able Piloted by Flight Lieutenant Frank Cleaver DSO. Quote from Flight Sergeant John Franklin.

3. Ibid.

4. Flight Lieutenant R.F.W. Cleaver, "(Secret) Evaded Capture in France," WO/208/3320, including Gibraltar Debrief, June 17, 1944, and Appendices B, C, and D.

5. Ibid.

6. Ibid.

7. Ibid.

8. Sergeant Arthur S. Meyerowitz, Debrief and Escape Evasion Report.

9. All quotations from second half of page 195 through page 199 are from above-cited chief sources from UK National Archives Royal Air Force Service Records RAF (1939–1945). "Details of Those Who Crashed Overseas: Flight Lieutenant R.F.W. Cleaver, (Secret) Evaded Capture in France," WO/208/3320, June 17, 1944, and Appendices B, C, and D.

CHAPTER 21

The chief sources for Chapter 21: Sergeant Arthur S. Meyerowitz, Debrief and Escape and Evasion Report No. 758, June 17, 1944, marked "Secret," 18 pages; Appendix (B) to Escape and Evasion Report No. 758, Sergeant Arthur Meyerowitz, January 18, 1944, 3 pages; and Service File No. 32000985, 1941–1945, Sergeant Arthur S. Meyerowitz, 137 pages.

"Marcel Taillandier," L'Association des Amis du Musée; Colonel Paul Paillole, *Services spéciaux (1935–1945)*, Paris: R. Laffont, 1975; Colonel Rémy (pseudonym of Gilbert Renault-Roulier), *Morhange: les chasseurs de traîtres*, Paris: Éditions Flammarion, 1975; and Pierre Saint-Laurens, *Conte de faits, X15, Réseau Morhange*, Toulouse: Éditions Signes du Monde, 1995.

UK National Archives and Royal Air Force Service Records, RAF DPA SAR Sections, Officers of the RAF, RFC, RNAS, Second World War (1939–1945): Details of Those Who Crashed Overseas: RAF Squadron Combat Reports No. 644 Squadron: LL228 "A" for Able Piloted by Flight Lieutenant Frank Cleaver DSO; Military Record of Lieutenant R.F.W. Cleaver, Service No. 1457098/124411, Royal Air Force (RAF); Flight Lieutenant R.F.W. Cleaver, "(Secret) Evaded Capture in France," WO/208/3320, including Gibraltar Debrief, June 17, 1944, and Appendices B, C, and D.

1. All quotes on pages 200–203 are drawn from Sergeant Arthur S. Meyerowitz, Debrief and Escape and Evasion Report No. 758, June 17, 1944, marked "Secret," 18 pages; Appendix (B) to Escape and Evasion Report No. 758, Sergeant Arthur Meyerowitz, January 18, 1944, 3 pages.

CHAPTER 22

The chief sources for Chapter 22: Sergeant Arthur S. Meyerowitz, Debrief and Escape and Evasion Report No. 758, June 17, 1944, marked "Secret," 18 pages; Appendix (B) to Escape and Evasion Report No. 758, Sergeant Arthur Meyerowitz, January 18, 1944, 3 pages.

Flight Lieutenant R.F.W. Cleaver, "(Secret) Evaded Capture in France," WO/208/3320, including Gibraltar Debrief, June 17, 1944, and Appendices B, C, and D.

CHAPTER 23

The chief sources for Chapter 23: Sergeant Arthur S. Meyerowitz, Debrief and Escape and Evasion Report No. 758, June 17, 1944, marked "Secret," 18 pages;

Appendix (B) to Escape and Evasion Report No. 758, Sergeant Arthur Meyerowitz, January 18, 1944, 3 pages; and interviews with Seymour Meyerowitz.

Flight Lieutenant R.F.W. Cleaver, "(Secret) Evaded Capture in France," WO/208/3320, including Gibraltar Debrief, June 17, 1944, and Appendices B, C, and D.

1. Debrief, June 17, 1944, and Appendices B, C, and D; interviews of Seymour Meyerowitz.
2. Flight Lieutenant R.F.W. Cleaver, "(Secret) Evaded Capture in France," WO/208/3320, including Gibraltar Debrief, June 17, 1944, and Appendices B, C, and D.

CHAPTER 24

The chief sources for Chapter 24: Sergeant Arthur S. Meyerowitz, Debrief and Escape and Evasion Report No. 758, June 17, 1944, marked "Secret," 18 pages; Appendix (B) to Escape and Evasion Report No. 758, Sergeant Arthur Meyerowitz, June 18, 1944, 3 pages.

Flight Lieutenant R.F.W. Cleaver, "(Secret) Evaded Capture in France," WO/208/3320, including Gibraltar Debrief, June 17, 1944, and Appendices B, C, and D.

1. Sergeant Arthur S. Meyerowitz, Debrief and Escape Evasion Report.

CHAPTER 25

The chief sources for Chapter 25: Sergeant Arthur S. Meyerowitz, Debrief and Escape and Evasion Report No. 758, June 17, 1944, marked "Secret," 18 pages; Appendix (B) to Escape and Evasion Report No. 758, Sergeant Arthur Meyerowitz, January 18, 1944, 3 pages.

Flight Lieutenant R.F.W. Cleaver, "(Secret) Evaded Capture in France," WO/208/3320, including Gibraltar Debrief, June 17, 1944, and Appendices B, C, and D.

"Marcel Taillandier," L'Association des Amis du Musée; Colonel Paul Paillole, *Services spéciaux (1935–1945)*, Paris: R. Laffont, 1975; Colonel Rémy (pseudonym of Gilbert Renault-Roulier), *Morhange: les chasseurs de traîtres*, Paris: Éditions Flammarion, 1975; and Pierre Saint-Laurens, *Conte de faits*, X15, *Réseau Morhange*, Toulouse: Éditions Signes du Monde, 1995.

1. Flight Lieutenant R.F.W. Cleaver, "(Secret) Evaded Capture in France," WO/208/3320, including Gibraltar Debrief, June 17, 1944, and Appendices B, C, and D.

2. Ibid.

3. Colonel Paul Paillole, *Services spéciaux (1935–1945)*, p. 426.

CHAPTER 26

The chief sources for Chapter 26: Sergeant Arthur S. Meyerowitz, Debrief and Escape and Evasion Report No. 758, June 17, 1944, marked "Secret," 18 pages; Appendix (B) to Escape and Evasion Report No. 758, Sergeant Arthur Meyerowitz, January 18, 1944, 3 pages.

Flight Lieutenant R.F.W. Cleaver, "(Secret) Evaded Capture in France," WO/208/3320, including Gibraltar Debrief, June 17, 1944, and Appendices B, C, and D.

1. All quotes on page 235 are drawn from Sergeant Arthur S. Meyerowitz, Debrief and Escape and Evasion Report No. 758, June 17, 1944, marked "Secret," 18 pages; Appendix (B) to Escape and Evasion Report No. 758, Sergeant Arthur Meyerowitz, January 18, 1944, 3 pages.

CHAPTER 27

The chief sources for Chapter 27: Sergeant Arthur S. Meyerowitz, Debrief and Escape and Evasion Report No. 758, June 17, 1944, marked "Secret," 18 pages; Appendix (B) to Escape and Evasion Report No. 758, Sergeant Arthur Meyerowitz, January 18, 1944, 3 pages; and Service File No. 32000985, 1941–1945, Sergeant Arthur S. Meyerowitz, 137 pages.

UK National Archives and Royal Air Force Service Records, RAF DPA SAR Sections, Officers of the RAF, RFC, RNAS, Second World War (1939–1945): Details of Those Who Crashed Overseas: RAF Squadron Combat Reports No. 644 Squadron: LL228 "A" for Able Piloted by Flight Lieutenant Frank Cleaver DSO (including statement of Flight Sergeant John Franklin); Service No. 1457098/124411, Royal Air Force (RAF), Flight Lieutenant R.F.W. Cleaver, "(Secret) Evaded Capture in France," WO/208/3320, including Gibraltar Debrief, June 17, 1944, and Appendices B, C, and D.

1. Noemí Ruido, "Joan Garcia Rabascall: Representative of the British Consulate of Barcelona in Lleida during the Second World War," *The Evasion Networks During the Second World War*, p. 1.

2. Alberto Poveda, *Paso Clandestino*, Madrid: *Los otras listas*, 2004, pp. 172–173.

3. Ruido, p. 1.

4. Details of Those Who Crashed Overseas: RAF Squadron Combat Reports No. 644 Squadron: LL228 "A" for Able Piloted by Flight Lieutenant Frank Cleaver DSO (including statement of Flight Sergeant John Franklin).

5. Sergeant Arthur S. Meyerowitz, Debrief and Escape and Evasion Report No. 758, June 17, 1944, marked "Secret," 18 pages; Appendix (B) to Escape and Evasion Report No. 758, Sergeant Arthur Meyerowitz, June 18, 1944, 3 pages.

6. Cleaver, Debrief, Appendices B, C, and D.

CHAPTER 28

The chief sources for Chapter 28: "Marcel Taillandier," L'Association des Amis du Musée; Colonel Paul Paillole, *Services spéciaux (1935–1945)*, Paris: R. Laffont, 1975; Colonel Rémy (pseudonym of Gilbert Renault-Roulier), *Morhange: les chasseurs de traîtres*, Paris: Éditions Flammarion, 1975; and Pierre Saint-Laurens, *Conte de faits*, X15, *Réseau Morhange*, Toulouse: Éditions Signes du Monde, 1995.

1. Pierre Saint-Laurens, *Conte de faits*, X15, *Réseau Morhange*, p. 70.

2. Ibid.

3. Ibid.

4. Ibid.

5. Ibid.

6. Ibid.

CHAPTER 29

The chief sources for Chapter 29: Sergeant Arthur S. Meyerowitz, Debrief and Escape and Evasion Report No. 758, June 17, 1944, marked "Secret," 18 pages; Appendix (B) to Escape and Evasion Report No. 758, Sergeant Arthur Meyerowitz, June 18, 1944, 3 pages; Special Order 31: Arrival of Sergeant Arthur S. Meyerowitz at Gibraltar, Received by Military Liaison Office, American Consulate, Colonel Horace W. Forster, June 16, 1944, and Service File No. 32000985, 1941–1945, Sergeant Arthur S. Meyerowitz, 137 pages.

UK National Archives and Royal Air Force Service Records, RAF DPA SAR Sections, Officers of the RAF, RFC, RNAS, Second World War (1939–1945): Details of Those Who Crashed Overseas: RAF Squadron Combat Reports No. 644 Squadron: LL228 "A" for Able Piloted by Flight Lieutenant Frank Cleaver DSO; Service No. 1457098/124411, Royal Air Force (RAF), Flight Lieutenant R.F.W. Cleaver, "(Secret) Evaded Capture in France,"

WO/208/3320, including Gibraltar Debrief, June 17, 1944, and Appendices B, C, and D.

1. Sergeant Arthur S. Meyerowitz, Debrief and Escape and Evasion Report No. 758, June 17, 1944, marked "Secret," 18 pages; Appendix (B) to Escape and Evasion Report No. 758, Sergeant Arthur Meyerowitz, June 18, 1944, 3 pages.

2. Ibid. (A phrase commonly used by the Allies to greet escaped airmen and pilots of World War II.)

CHAPTER 30

The chief sources for Chapter 30: Sergeant Arthur S. Meyerowitz, Debrief and Escape and Evasion Report No. 758, June 17, 1944, marked "Secret," 18 pages; Appendix (B) to Escape and Evasion Report No. 758, Sergeant Arthur Meyerowitz, June 18, 1944, 3 pages; Special Order 31: Arrival of Sergeant Arthur S. Meyerowitz at Gibraltar, Received by Military Liaison Office, American Consulate, Colonel Horace W. Forster, June 16, 1944, and Service File No. 32000985, 1941–1945, Sergeant Arthur S. Meyerowitz, 137 pages; and Secret American Questionnaire for Service Personnel Evading from Enemy Occupied Countries, Sergeant Arthur S. Meyerowitz, June 18, 1944, 2 pages.

UK National Archives and Royal Air Force Service Records, RAF DPA SAR Sections, Officers of the RAF, RFC, RNAS, Second World War (1939–1945): Details of Those Who Crashed Overseas: RAF Squadron Combat Reports No. 644 Squadron: LL228 "A" for Able Piloted by Flight Lieutenant Frank Cleaver DSO; Service No. 1457098/124411, Royal Air Force (RAF), Flight Lieutenant R.F.W. Cleaver, "(Secret) Evaded Capture in France," WO/208/3320, including Gibraltar Debrief, June 17, 1944, and Appendices B, C, and D.

1. UK National Archives, Gilbrator Record Group (WW2). Excerpt from the Great Siege Tunnels.

2. Service No. 1457098/124411, Royal Air Force (RAF), Flight Lieutenant R.F.W. Cleaver, "(Secret) Evaded Capture in France," WO/208/3320, including Gibraltar Debrief, June 17, 1944, and Appendices B, C, and D.

3. Cable from Colonel Horace W. Forster to London, European Theater of Operations, June 16, 1944.

4. Secret American Questionnaire for Service Personnel Evading from Enemy Occupied Countries, Sergeant Arthur S. Meyerowitz, June 18, 1944, 2 pages.

CHAPTER 31

The chief sources for Chapter 31: Interviews with Seymour Meyerowitz; Western Union Cablegram from Sergeant Arthur S. Meyerowitz to David and Rose Meyerowitz, June 17, 1944.

1. Interviews with Seymour Meyerowitz.
2. Ibid.
3. Ibid.
4. Ibid.
5. Ibid.
6. Western Union Cablegram from Sergeant Arthur S. Meyerowitz to David and Rose Meyerowitz, June 17, 1944.
7. Interviews with Seymour Meyerowitz.
8. Ibid.
9. Ibid.
10. Ibid.
11. Western Union Telegram, War Department to David and Rose Meyerowitz, June 29, 1944.
12. Ibid.
13. Ibid.
14. Ibid.

EPILOGUE

All of the sources and dates of the quotes in the epilogue are cited in the text: Letter from Mademoiselle Thoulouse (in Toulouse, France) to Rose Meyerowitz, March 28, 1944; letter from Madame Rigal (Beaumont-de-Lomagne, France) to Arthur Meyerowitz, December 14, 1945; letter from Rigal family (Beaumont-de-Lomagne) to Rose Meyerowitz, January 21, 1945; letter from Robert A. Ardichen (Bordeaux, France) to Arthur Meyerowitz, April 18, 1945; letter from Charlotte Michel (Lesparre, France) to Arthur Meyerowitz, May 5, 1945; letter from Charlotte Michel (Lesparre) to Arthur Meyerowitz, June 3, 1945; four postcards from Christiane Michel (Bayonne, France) to Arthur Meyerowitz, July 17, 1945; letter from Christiane Michel (Lesparre) to Arthur Meyerowitz, August 27, 1945; letters from Arthur Meyerowitz to Michel family (Lesparre) July 19 and August 8, 1945; and letter from Charlotte Michel to Arthur Meyerowitz, May 8, 1947 (Bordeaux). Letter from Captain Dorothy Smith to Sergeant Arthur S. Meyerowitz, December 14, 1944; letter from Captain Dorothy

Smith to Sergeant Arthur S. Meyerowitz, March 13, 1945; and letter from Sergeant Arthur S. Meyerowitz to Captain Dorothy Smith, January 9, 1945.

1. Interviews with Seymour Meyerowitz.
2. "DSO Notice, Lieutenant R.F.W. Cleaver," *London Gazette*, October 3, 1944, p. 1.

Photograph by Shaun Couture

Seth Meyerowitz, the grandson of U.S. Air Force Staff Sergeant Arthur Meyerowitz, is a web entrepreneur and the president of a global online marketing company. He has traveled the United States speaking on behalf of Google for its Get Your Business Online program, and it was his web and marketing savvy that allowed him to unearth the declassified saga of his grandfather.

Peter F. Stevens is an editor, a journalist, and the author of eleven books.